Fa...
Feelings

Family
Feelings

Daily Meditations
for Healthy Relationships

Martha Vanceburg
and Sylvia W. Silverman

BANTAM BOOKS
NEW YORK · TORONTO · LONDON · SYDNEY · AUCKLAND

FAMILY FEELINGS

A Bantam Book / October 1989

Grateful acknowledgment is made for permission to reprint the following:

Poems by Raquel Jodorowsky and Nancy Morejon from WOMEN BRAVE IN THE FACE OF DANGER (Crossing Press, 1985). Reprinted by permission of author Margaret Randall.

Poems by Debbie Wald from WOMEN BRAVE IN THE FACE OF DANGER (Crossing Press, 1985). Reprinted by permission of author Debbie Wald.

"Rebecca," IKON, Fall 1983. Reprinted by permission of author Fran Baskin.

"Black Mother Woman," by Audre Lorde, The Massachusetts Review, 1972. Reprinted by permission of The Massachusetts Review, Inc.

"The Gloves," THE COMING HOME POEMS (Long River Books, 1986). Reprinted by permission of author Margaret Randall.

"Childhood Is the Kingdom Where Nobody Dies," by Edna St. Vincent Millay from COLLECTED POEMS (Harper & Row, 1934, 1962). Reprinted by permission of the estate of Edna St. Vincent Millay.

Work by Char Madigan and Rose Tillermans, St. Joseph's House News, 1987. Reprinted by permission of St. Joseph's House.

Lyrics from "One Too Many Marriages," by Bob Dylan. © 1964, 1966 Warner Bros., Inc. All rights reserved. Used by permission.

Library of Congress Cataloging-in-Publication Data

Vanceburg, Martha.
    Family feelings : daily meditations for healthy relationships / Martha Vanceburg and Sylvia W. Silverman.
      p.   cm.
    Includes index.
    ISBN 0-553-34705-5
    1. Family—Prayer-books and devotions—English.   2. Devotional calendars. I. Silverman, Sylvia W. II. Title.
BV255.V36 1989
242'.2—dc20   89-6661
                                             CIP

Published simultaneously in the United States and Canada

PRINTED IN THE UNITED STATES OF AMERICA

BM   0 9 8 7 6 5 4 3 2 1

For our families

Continuity implies growth and change and, if dei-fied, it would be two-faced, looking forward as well as backward.

—Charles Rycroft

The Roman god of beginnings and endings, Janus, had two faces, and the New Year was sacred to him. His figure reminds us today that every ending is also a beginning. Any fresh start builds on what went before, as after any conclusion something survives and continues.

When families gather for the great celebrations of beginnings and endings—births, marriages, and funerals—they're also celebrating their continuity. Individuals die, but the family continues, just as human life has survived the cruelest wars, plagues, and massacres. The birth of new life always signals new possibilities, but also the continuity of the family that will shelter the new child. Children ultimately become parents, and they rear children who will be parents in their turn. Families are growing, changing entities, and their cycles of endings and beginnings carry life on in a continuous stream.

Our feelings—anxiety, grief, joy—belong to individuals and to events. The stream of continuity, in our families and in our larger world, is too powerful for anything but awe. We participate in this awesome cycle; each of us is vital to it, yet in its immensity life's continuity gives us a healthy sense of proportion.

THOUGHT FOR TODAY: Because I contain all that I have been and all that I will be, I can bring my best efforts to the present moment—which is the only time I have.

Somehow ... parents ... see children as second chances for themselves.

—Loudon Wainwright

Life keeps presenting us with second chances. The only traps, the only dead ends, are ones we construct for ourselves. My life is tailor-made for me; no one else in the world has my possibilities, and the same is true for you.

One trap we sometimes set for ourselves is thinking we can live our lives through another person— through a child or a lover, or a public figure we admire. I fill my own niche, no one else's, and no one else can fill mine.

Our lives are destined for our own special joys and accomplishments. Every person has her or his special relationship with the world and with sources of spiritual wealth and comfort. When we try to live through others, we cheat ourselves—and them, especially if they're our children.

THOUGHT FOR TODAY: I'll have all the chances I need to succeed in my life, and so will my children in theirs.

*Believe me, child, life is a continual labour, check-
ered with care and pleasure, therefore rejoice in your
position, take the world as you find it and you will I
trust find heaviness may endure for a night but joy
comes in the morning.*

—Rachel, Lady Russell

When we come across words like these, written nearly
four hundred years ago by a mother to her daughter,
we're struck by their aptness: Life is both hard and
good. There's much in Lady Russell's life we wouldn't
recognize. Her speech, her housekeeping, and her
clothing would be archaic and strange; yet her wisdom applies to our lives as surely as it did to her
daughter's. Probably the daughter sighed when she
got this letter; perhaps she rolled her eyes and said
the seventeenth-century equivalent of "Moth-*err*!"
Yet she undoubtedly wrote or spoke similar words
to her own children, when they left home.

Wise counsel may seem to fall on deaf ears, but
it's remembered when the time is right. We can't
control what others do with our wise words; all we
can do is pass them along.

THOUGHT FOR TODAY: Like light and shadow,
joy and sorrow create each other mutually.

Privacy is a big word in our house, now that I have taught it to my children.

—Anna Quindlen

What a shock it is when a child whose bottom you wiped says, "You can't come in!" In our culture children learn early to value privacy, and wise parents understand the importance of respecting it. After all, that's how children learn respect for others. It may be tempting to rummage in our children's drawers, read their letters, or unlock their secret boxes, but it's disrespectful both to them and to ourselves as parents, putting us in the position of guards or spies. Parents need privacy too, and it's easier to convince children of that when their rights are respected.

Everyone needs private space and private possessions, though these are sometimes difficult to ensure in crowded dwellings. Children need to know that parents support their right to privacy. Paradoxically, parents can feel rejected by their children, especially when children treasure secrets; but it helps if we remember that parents' task, from the moment their children are born, is to prepare them for independent lives. The more space they are given to grow at their own pace, the more trust they will feel for their parents.

THOUGHT FOR TODAY: Solitude and calm are precious gifts of privacy. We can exchange them with our parents and our children.

Everything has been thought of before, but the problem is to think of it again.

—Goethe

The powerful ideas have all been thought of already: love, faith, surrender, generosity. That doesn't mean, however, that everyone who knows about them acts upon them. Fear, greed, and anger have all been thought of as well. The point is, we have a choice. We can choose to act out of old patterns, or we can make fresh choices that seem more likely to bring about success.

Surely our parents must have resolved not to make the same mistakes their parents made, just as we've promised not to pass on what we think were their mistakes—and our children vow to correct the mistakes they think we've made. In every generation, each one of us has the power to do so.

Nothing is new under the sun. Yet in our lives, each day is new, precious, unique. We won't do anything that hasn't been done before, many times; but it will be new for us. If we can approach our lives with reverence and freshness, we'll have solved "the problem."

THOUGHT FOR TODAY: Each day is a new beginning, and I can choose what I will do with it.

*Wrath and bitterness speak themselves and go with
their own force; love is shame-faced, looks shyly out
of the window, lingers long at the doorlatch.*
—Harriet Beecher Stowe

Many of us express anger much more easily than
tenderness, even toward those we love—sometimes
especially toward them. Love makes us vulnerable;
we may not want to risk revealing ourselves, for fear
we'll be hurt, even by our closest family members.

Yet when we avoid such risks, we also shut out
great possibilities. Real love doesn't make demands;
it illuminates both lover and beloved. If we love one
another selflessly, without expectations, our spirits
will grow strong and we will have nothing to fear.

There is no greater gift we can give to those we
love than to reveal ourselves fully to them. Growing
up in families, we all sustain bruises on our tender
spirits, and we learn to armor ourselves against them.
Sometimes it's not until we're ready to start families
of our own that we even think about disclosing
ourselves. Softness and vulnerability call forth tenderness from others, making us ready for joy.

THOUGHT FOR TODAY: I'll invite love to estab-
lish itself in my heart. I'll make room for it, as a
preferred tenant.

Unroof any house and you must find there confusion.
—Ralph Waldo Emerson

Would it be fun to look in on families as if they lived in dollhouses, and we could take off their roofs? We'd see dirty dishes, people banging on bathroom doors, tear-stained pillows; we'd see parents hugging children, and beating them; we'd see brothers and sisters fighting and cooperating. The families with the most expensive furnishings wouldn't be the happiest. The happiest wouldn't be the neatest or best organized or the most "successful."

We all have sentimental ideals of family life, sometimes based on memories but sometimes on television shows. We're apt to forget that these are, at best, ideals; at worst, they're oversimplified, cartoon images. What they are *not* is real families made up of women, men, and children with real bodies, minds, and spirits and real needs, who are living in a changing world.

Other families may look better than our own, because we haven't unroofed their houses. Confusion may be another word for fullness. Ideals can lead us, but our real task is to do the very best we can with what we have—our own real-life families. If we do this faithfully, our efforts are sure to succeed.

THOUGHT FOR TODAY: Nothing that is growing and changing can be perfect.

If you have never been hated by your child, you have never been a parent.

—Bette Davis

Some parents are so fearful of negative emotions that they stifle any sign of hatred or anger in their children. How will young people ever learn to manage their feelings, if they're not allowed to have them? *Acting* on hatred should certainly be discouraged, but *feeling* hatred is quite a different matter. All of us need to learn for ourselves that it's possible to have violent and destructive feelings even toward those we love, and to let them go. Feelings in themselves have no power to harm. Children learn self-control by regulating their own behavior.

Of course, children will sometimes feel hatred for their parents; parents have power, and they say "No." If a parent can't accept a child's outburst of anger or hostility—as a temporary state, like a squall at sea—then the child may come to think of anger as a powerful weapon to use against the parent, or else a shameful secret that must be hidden. Such hidden anger leaks out in twisted forms; sometimes it's turned against the self.

Feelings are real, but they don't have power unless we give them power. The most murderous rage, the most blissful ecstasy, last only moments unless we grip them tight. We can make a habit of hatred, as we can of love. But we cannot let hatred go unless we know it for what it is.

THOUGHT FOR TODAY: I'll remember that my feelings are necessary and real, and only my actions need to be controlled.

If a snake can't grow, it will strangle. The tightness of a skin that doesn't fit is a signal that it's time to slough it off in order to grow.
—Eknath Easwaran

Change and growth are laws of life, yet sometimes we don't want to recognize that those we love and live with—our children, our partners, our parents— are changing. Or that we ourselves are.

Young children grow rapidly; we can't deny their changes, for they occur before our eyes. Adolescents undergo deep changes in their bodies and spirits, and we're at least intellectually prepared to accept them. Adults never stop growing and changing, though sometimes we deny this, out of our desire for stability. Part of loving is respecting each other's growth.

I need to grow; you need to change; we may grow and change at different rates, out of phase with one another. But if we remain gentle and open to each other, we can survive these transitions together. I will let my family and friends see that I am open to change, and pray that in turn they will stay open to me. In our journeys, we all slough off many tight skins.

THOUGHT FOR TODAY: I will acknowledge others' right to change, even when their growth seems to interfere with mine. This, too, will change.

She understood that parenting was a series of such small daily deaths, and that learning to let go of your charges was as crucial as learning to take them on.

—Lisa Alther

"Stewardship," mused a friend one night, when we were discussing parents and children. "We shouldn't say 'My kids,' I'm not their owner. My job is stewardship."

We're all deluded at times into thinking of children as "ours." Truly, we're just the caregivers who make it possible for them to thrive. Our task is not to polish them so they'll reflect credit back on us, but rather to let them grow into their own selves, as healthily as they can, whether or not we agree with the choices they make, of diet or dress, jobs or lovers, hair styles or music or religion.

When we accept the stewardship role, we're much better able to relinquish it when the time comes, and to remain in loving contact with those we have cared for. No bitterness need accrue; no resentment need linger. There will always be hard traveling on the road from childhood to maturity, but it's a journey each one must make for herself.

THOUGHT FOR TODAY: Let me look on each day as a new life, and the care of children as a series of births, for them and for me.

The shortest way to do many things is to do only one thing at once.

—Samuel Smiles

A woman who was raised on a farm said, "I don't know how my mother did it. She raised five of us kids, did all our wash in an old wringer washer, grew vegetables and put them up, kept chickens, helped my dad with the cows and pigs, and had a part-time job in town, and at haying time she worked right alongside the men. I've got one kid and I'm exhausted all the time."

Now, her mother was undoubtedly a woman of energy and competence, but her life was also subject to fewer distractions, free from the sensory overload that affects everyone today through the speed and intensity of communications. We're constantly assaulted by print, bombarded with messages, urged, scolded, wheedled, threatened, *talked to* by radio and TV, billboards, phone calls, and the mail. Every one of these messages is an interruption of our work, our personal program.

Of course, this clamor affects our family life. It affects every area of our life. If we are to "do only one thing at once," we need to develop extraordinary powers of concentration. Merely to get from the beginning of an ordinary mass-media-influenced day to the end of it, with some semblance of serenity, is a feat. We should honor ourselves when we achieve it.

THOUGHT FOR TODAY: Before I measure myself against others, I must understand their lives as well as my own. If this isn't possible, maybe I should throw away my measuring tape.

No one ... who has not known that inestimable privilege can possibly realize what good fortune it is to grow up in a house where there are grandparents.
—Suzanne LaFollette

Not every grandfather is wise or handy; not every grandmother is a wonderful cook or a skilled nurse. Some grandparents are bedridden, or chronically ill and cranky. Some require a lot of care and aren't able to give much attention to others. Yet their presence in the home is still a privilege for their grandchildren, for they are living witnesses of human history, a link with the past, an evidence of the continuity of family life.

Children learn history in school, but they learn life in their families. How much more vivid it is to hear about the Depression or the Second World War from someone who was there, who was involved, who can tell you what life was like in a steel mill or a defense plant or in battle, what it was like to shop with ration coupons, and what the popular songs and dances were. In a real sense, grandparents help children believe in the world. And at its best, the relationship between grandparents and grandchildren can be a liberating alliance of old and young against the authority of the parents, showing old people the values of the young, and young people the strengths of the old.

THOUGHT FOR TODAY: Did I have access to my grandparents' hard-won wisdom about the world? I'll make mine available to my grandchildren, if I have any.

The lesson children can learn from play, which is possibly of greatest value, is that when they lose, the world does not come to an end.

—Bruno Bettelheim

When family members play together, they sometimes slip into precast roles: somebody plays winner, somebody plays cheering section, somebody plays loser, somebody plays coach. Over the years we spend together in our original families, children and adults slip into these roles gradually.

Some children show talent for certain roles. My younger daughter invented a clown personality; everything was a joke to her. The happy-sad clown began as a way to lose without humiliation, but she carried it to an extreme; her clown act became a coping mechanism that protected her from losing—but also from winning. Someone who wins all the time, on the other hand, in the safety of the family, may be spoiled for the very different rules of the outside world.

Such preset roles only come to be problems if they never vary. We can make sure, in our families, that we're not teaching one person to become a loser. Healthy play makes sure everyone gets the experience of winning and losing. One way to ensure this is to alternate different games. One can't win every time—but losing doesn't mean one never wins.

THOUGHT FOR TODAY: I'll look at the games my family plays, to see whether we've rigged them.

It might not matter at all what I said or what advice I gave my daughter, what frantic last-minute attempts I made to lay down some motherly counsel (dare I say wisdom?) on her lovely shoulders. I knew her racing motor was already drowning out my effort. She was ready to go. But was I?
                                                —Jane Fonda

Becoming independent is the hardest lesson in life, both for children and for parents. Some of us never learn it; we remain hooked to our parents or our children in ways that threaten our spiritual wholeness and prevent us from growing.

Change is the one constant in life. The baby changes from a creature that is wholly dependent on the care of others to a toddler who can say "No," a child who wants later bedtimes, an adolescent who needs to test parental limits, and finally an adult with parental responsibilities of her or his own. All of these changes involve the parent as much as they do the growing child. And often it seems that when one is ready for the next stage, the other isn't.

It helps to realize that independence doesn't mean loneliness. Healthy growth means separating from our parents, from our children—but we remain connected, just as we're connected, always, to the universal family of humankind. Faith in the rightness of our growth will help us through the changes, help us to stand on our own, autonomous and connected, able to both give and receive.

THOUGHT FOR TODAY: If I can accept the inevitable rightness of change, I will be ready for whatever comes my way.

Everything that lives
Lives not alone, nor for itself.

                      —William Blake

The happiest people are those who dedicate their lives to others. Theirs is real wealth and fulfillment; they have everything they want. Sometimes parents claim to live for their children, when it's clear that they're living *through* them, taking vicarious gratification in their achievements. How much better for parents to savor their own achievements and to give of themselves freely and joyously, so their children will have models worth emulating.

    Happiness lies in developing our connection with all of life, not just our family members, and freeing that connection from our egos so the stream of generous energy can flow through us and back to its ultimate Source. Every move we make sets up a ripple with far-reaching effects. We'll never see the ultimate results of most of our actions; they will flow past us, in space and time. But the more freely we give ourselves, the more will be returned to us.

THOUGHT FOR TODAY: As others enrich me, so I give back richness. And it will come back to me, manyfold.

In the old days
when a person's hands grew stiff and feet swelled up
and they couldn't remember their daughter-in-law's
   name
they died
but today a person should live as long as possible
"I have lived long enough," she said
"Oh No!" They said, "don't say things like that!"
                     —Fran Baskin

"Experts" of all kinds encourage us to give over our power to know what is best for us. Sometimes, it's true, we need expert attention. But sometimes we let our desire for control and controllability interfere with our deep knowledge of life and of our place in the universe.

Painful though it is to loving friends and family, one who is ill and old may simply wish to die. The great cycle of creation includes death as well as rebirth, and we are helped to be whole when we can accept the dying side. Death is the last great transformation of our present consciousness: not enemy, not friend, but simply fellow traveler.

THOUGHT FOR TODAY: Clinging to my wishes for someone else is an attempt to control her or his life. Today I'll remember to love and let go.

We are all sculptors and painters, and our material is our own flesh and blood and bones.
                              —Henry David Thoreau

It's often hard to limit our artistic skills to our own selves. We're constantly tempted to add a color here, or smooth a rough place there, on someone else's portrait, especially when that person is a family member who seems to ask for the attention. Yet perhaps the most important part of loving others is respecting their integrity. Each of us is the sculptor, the painter, of our own work of art only.

Children need care during the long years of their childhood—but they don't need interference. Nobody does. We are all entitled to our own feelings, our own choices, our own palette and carving tools, from the youngest age. All the skill we have is needed for our own portrait and, miraculously, every stroke counts. No attention is wasted; our lives will reward us with a true image for the loving care we give ourselves.

THOUGHT FOR TODAY: Today and every day I will remember: I am my own work of art.

Here on this land I touched the blood
and rattling bones of others
brought here or not, as I was.

—Nancy Morejón

Family backgrounds of many of us hold terrible stories—stories of persecution, slavery, exile, many kinds of violence. And family relations can perpetuate violence. Techniques that people must learn for survival can actually threaten survival if they're continued when no longer needed.

If we were beaten when we were small, we learned to use force against those weaker than ourselves. When we are punished or humiliated for making the inevitable mistakes children make, we learn to lie and sneak, to enjoy the punishment of others, and to feel that innocent mistakes deserve such punishments.

But we can choose to break our connection to this kind of violence, physical and emotional. Abuse within the family is terrorism of the purest kind, and no one deserves to live with it. When we make the decision to end abusive behavior, there are many places we can turn for help. The most important in the long run may be our own spiritual source, which is with us always and provides unfailing guidance.

THOUGHT FOR TODAY: I can begin to reconcile the violence of the past. All that is needed is my own decision.

I am always at a loss to know how much to believe of my own stories.

—Washington Irving

For young people, families are their connection to the past. For older people, families are their connection to the future. Past and future both reach us through the medium of particular experience. We listen to our grandparents' and parents' tales of how they fared through great historical moments, and we realize that any one person sees only a tiny piece of the whole picture. We tell our children and grandchildren of how we fared, and they hear the same lesson. All of these stories are true, but how much of them can we believe?

The sum total of world events at any given time is too immense to contemplate. That's why we tell family stories of how world events affected us—an armistice, an earthquake, a famous wedding, a famous death. These historic moments interweave with our own family moments, births and marriages, divorces and deaths, and let us see our own stories against a larger backdrop.

Children love to keep family stories alive and vivid. "Tell me again how you first met Grandpa, Grandma." "Say again about what happened when I was born." These stories give us a place in the world, roles, names, imaginative substance. We believe them, because in a sense we are made of them.

THOUGHT FOR TODAY: Our stories prove both that we're all different and that we're all the same.

There are four things a child needs—plenty of love, nourishing food, regular sleep, and lots of soap and water—and after those . . . some intelligent neglect.
                                              —Ivy Baker Priest

Intelligent neglect helps us to develop our sense of privacy and the rewards of solitude. Pity the person, child or adult, who is unable to be alone! When we're alone, we're most accompanied, closest to our spiritual guide, the source of our reverence and of our power.

Sometimes it's hard for parents to bestow intelligent neglect. For the best of reasons, they crowd their children, overscheduling their days and managing their lives. Sometimes the neglect is anything but intelligent—when troubled, irresponsible parents shirk the first four needs, children get the message that they're not wanted.

In parenting as in gardening, balance is vital: enough nourishment, judicious pruning, and some intelligent neglect will produce the longed-for result.

THOUGHT FOR TODAY: As my parents did when they were raising me, I'll do the best I can with the tools at hand.

God loves an idle rainbow
No less than labouring seas.

—Ralph Hodgson

Idleness has been given a bad name. Many people consider it kin to the deadly sin of apathy, or sloth. Some people snap, "The devil finds work for idle hands." Children usually understand their own needs for occasional idleness, but too many grown-ups forget about it (or have it ridiculed out of them). So parents may resent their children's hanging out, "doing nothing," and badger them to keep busy, be productive.

Yet it's during "idle rainbow" moments that our spirits refresh themselves. No one is ever literally doing nothing: our nervous systems keep our brains working all the time, secreting, breathing, processing information in our marvelous biological feedback system. A dreamy, abstracted child may need lots of time for spiritual refreshment. When healthy people spend their free time idly, and aren't bored, that's their choice, and their families must learn to accept it.

The laboring seas make a great deal of noise and commotion—but at each ebb tide they lose the ground they gain at the flow. Loving someone means accepting their differences; meditation and prayer can help us detach from them, with humility.

THOUGHT FOR TODAY: The rainbow and the sea are lovable in and for themselves, not for their achievements.

It's very hard to hear my mother's voice coming out of me.

—Whoopi Goldberg

I know a woman who disliked her mother, whom she thought a spiteful old woman, and vowed she would never be like her. Her daughter—who had loved her grandmother—vowed the same about *her* mother. Both grew to be very much alike, and very much like their mothers; of course, they resembled each other most in disliking their mothers. How did they come to travel the same path?

We repeat some things our parents tell us because they prove to be true and useful. Sometimes, however, we feel like hollow microphones that simply transmit the words of our forebears. If we'll pause for a moment to meditate and detach ourselves from our immediate resentments, we need never feel overtaken by someone else's program. The key is letting go of what we dislike, for the more energy we devote to hatred, the more hatred controls us.

Some families hand resentments down from one generation to another. In trying to reject the teachings of their parents, children may harden into resentful miniatures of them. We aim to be flexible, to achieve our own resolutions. If we don't learn how in our families, we have to teach it to ourselves, first through acceptance of our family legacy and then through detachment from it.

THOUGHT FOR TODAY: When I have my own words to speak, I'll say them in my own voice.

There is more to life than increasing its speed.
                    —Mohandas K. Gandhi

Any time is a good time to take stock of values and to see whether our behavior is congruent with our beliefs. In such stock taking it's useful to write down some qualities we value: honesty, generosity, accountability, effectiveness. Then we can ask ourselves, do we value honesty at the expense of generosity or efficiency? Does accountability excuse cruelty? What quality do we admire most? If it turns out that we value effectiveness and promptness—in a word, speed—over kindness, we may need to reorient our thinking entirely.

Efficiency eases work, but it can curtail or eliminate other values in life. Unquestionably, airplanes are faster than bicycles; but travel by bicycle allows you to smell wildflowers along the roadside; to feel the movement of air, the sun, and the rain; to speak with people along the way; to stop for refreshment.

A small child going for a walk is interested in everything: dead leaves, old cigarette butts, cellophane wrappers. As we grow up, we learn to filter out a lot of what we see, classifying much of it as waste. Only some of it merits our interest; but if we come to value efficiency and speed above all else, we will filter out too much. We'll deprive ourselves of the human responses that nourish our spirits.

THOUGHT FOR TODAY: Warm human relationships are more valuable than efficient ones. Speed can't breach my solitude; love can.

A mother is not a person to lean on but a person to make leaning unnecessary.
—Dorothy Canfield Fisher

After a few weeks or months, most baby animals are ready for independence. Humans spend nearly a quarter of their lives just getting ready. If we're lucky, our families help us to grow straight, so we can stand alone.

Growing up means learning to make decisions that are right for us, in tune with the larger design of our life as it's woven into the pattern. We'll always need other people for companionship, love, and cooperative work, but by the time we're ready to choose how we want to live we should be able to stand by ourselves.

Even when our families aren't able to give us the best start in life, we have the power to remake choices, rechoose activities and companions that will grow along with us. Our human mothers may be precious loved ones or they may be strangers; the aim of our search for self-knowledge is the power to mother ourselves. We need steady nurture all our lives, and no other person can supply it. Opening ourselves to contact with a power greater than ourselves lets spiritual nourishment flow as needed.

THOUGHT FOR TODAY: Leaning weakens the backbone. I'll learn to walk with others, hand in hand.

The greatest pleasure I know, is to do a good action by stealth, and to have it found out by accident.
—Charles Lamb

We all want to have our good deeds discovered; that's human. It's human, too, to do good deeds in secret—not because we want to eat our cake and have it, too, but because humans have needs for both privacy and publicity. We need privacy or even secrecy to give our imaginations room to grow. And we need publicity, or at least recognition from those we care about, to let us know that others applaud our growth. "How'm I doing?" is an important question for us all.

All adults and all children have both these needs, everyone in different proportions. In a large, noisy, public family, a private person can feel invaded; in quiet, private families, an extrovert can feel stifled. Balancing our needs can be difficult—for doing good by stealth, and for having it found out; but love and trust can help us discover what is right for our families. Others' needs are as important to them as mine are to me. Respect for their expression ensures my peace of mind.

THOUGHT FOR TODAY: Other people's actions can't embarrass me; they and only they are responsible.

Because I have loved life, I shall have no sorrow to die.

—Amelia Burr

Any death is a loss, but deaths of family members affect us most deeply, because their lives held most meaning for our own. It will help us to mourn well if we remember that full lives are the happiest, and living fully means giving of oneself to others. Insofar as our loved ones gave of their care and compassion, to that extent they were fulfilled in their lives.

We need never be ashamed of mourning fully; grief is as integral to our lives as laughter. And we need never be ashamed to let go of sorrow after a death we have mourned and accepted. We loved them in life; we grieved their death; and we can remember them joyfully.

THOUGHT FOR TODAY: Let me live so that when I die no one will mourn my lost possibilities.

It wasn't raining when Noah built the ark.
> —Howard Ruff

Noah believed in his independent vision enough to go ahead with his project, even though his family and neighbors doubted his sanity. According to the story, it was his strength of conviction that saved life in the world. Sometimes, pursuing a vision of what is right for us will bring us into conflict with those who love us, our parents, our grandparents, our siblings, our children. Yet we owe it to ourselves to be true to our beliefs.

We can't save ethics for a rainy day. That's like saying we can lie all week and tell the truth on Sunday. Ethics are like shoes: if we save our good ones for special occasions, we won't ever be comfortable with them. But if we wear poor shoes all the time, our feet will give us trouble. Honesty and integrity should be worn every day, and if honesty compels us to heed a different drummer, then that's the rhythm we march to.

Even if we're marching to another drum, we can still stay in the same parade as our loved ones. If they trust us, because we have disclosed ourselves to them, they're more likely to respect our independent vision.

THOUGHT FOR TODAY: Virtues of character are good all the time—in emergencies as in tranquil times. I'll practice honesty and respect whenever I can.

No one hasn't failed. . . . One could say that failure is an essential ingredient of success.
                                        —Judith R. Rossmiller

Every healthy person understands what it is to fail, and to succeed, for we all have failed many times and then finally succeeded at such tremendous tasks as walking, talking, toilet training, and reading. The process of becoming civilized is a difficult one; supportive caregivers praise children lavishly for successes and don't rub in the fact of failure. But sometimes adults or siblings do punish children for their inevitable failures, or ridicule them, without reinforcing their successes. It's possible for people to grow up feeling like failures, even though growing up is little short of a miraculous success in itself.

Sometimes family members keep these feelings of failure alive in a teasing or bullying way. Even though the speaker can swear it was meant as a joke, a barbed remark often stings because it lands on that naked place in our spirit where we feel that we have failed.

To claim credit for our successes, we must change the message we send ourselves. Every outcome that is less than we desire is not a failure; it's a partial success. Our lives are made up of mixed experiences, all of them partially successful.

THOUGHT FOR TODAY: No one is a failure; failure is a label we stick on our disappointments.

Which is harder, to be a good winner or a good loser?
—Bertie Denham

Brothers and sisters are natural rivals. If one shows clear superiority in a certain sport or art, the other(s) may choose not to compete. Sometimes a whole family is gifted in a single area, producing family string quartets or volleyball teams or building contractors. When brothers and sisters and parents and children learn to cooperate on joint projects, all members get the opportunity to learn to be both winners and losers.

Families need shared work or play, even if it's not so serious. Some families structure all their activities as competition; others approach them more cooperatively, with each member having a task. Under cooperative rules, everyone can win. Competitive families can teach each other the humility necessary to be good winners and good losers, but only if the patterns of winning and losing change from time to time. If the same family member is always the champion, others learn inequality, and resentment.

Except for games, life doesn't present us with many situations in which winning or losing is clear-cut. That's the appeal of a game, I suppose: It creates a temporary situation in which no one has any doubt about what she or he is supposed to do. Most of life is more uncertain. If we grow up thinking of every encounter as a competitive one, we may be robbing ourselves of life's highest prize—serenity.

THOUGHT FOR TODAY: Competition alone is not healthy for growing things. The fulfilled life is one of doing one's best and accepting the outcome.

At every step the child should be allowed to meet the real experiences of life; the thorns should never be plucked from the roses.

—Ellen Key

It used to puzzle me that my children preferred workaday household objects, adult tools and equipment, to toys. The most attractive, expertly designed toy clocks and games and blocks would be neglected while they fumbled the batteries out of flashlights or stacked cans from the kitchen cupboards. It puzzled me until I figured out that children learn by imitation, and they were imitating us. We didn't play with those scientifically designed toys, either. (Small cans of tomato paste made perfect building materials.)

We found that letting them use "real" things didn't hamper their imaginations at all. As long as we took reasonable care, we could let them play with many household objects. And the same held true for other experiences. We never concealed illness or death from them, or pregnancy and birth. Childhood is preparation for life, not a substitute for it.

THOUGHT FOR TODAY: The thorniest flowers have the sweetest scent.

Play the part of a whetstone, which can make steel sharp, though it has no power itself of cutting.
                                            —Horace

Is there any way we can be sure of helping others to achieve their own best desires? How can we be like the whetstone, enabling our loved ones to hone their edges but not cutting ourselves?

Unconditional love is the most supportive gift we can offer another, love that doesn't depend on talent or success. Of course, we admire accomplishments, but the love that nourishes the spirit doesn't measure itself by them. Our children need to know they are loved regardless of grades or scores, athletic prowess or musical talent, or any other attributes— loved for themselves alone. And so do our other intimate family members.

Beauty, brains, and talent are all precious gifts, but love is more precious than any of these. To develop their full potential, human beings need to know that love cannot be withdrawn. Unconditional love illuminates our lives, as sunlight sustains flowers.

THOUGHT FOR TODAY: Today I will show, by my actions and responses, that I love unconditionally those dear to me.

I have no sympathy with the old idea that children owe such immense gratitude to their parents that they can never fulfill their obligations to them.
—Elizabeth Cady Stanton

Once in a while, every parent must feel as though nothing could ever repay her or him for the emotional effort, the sheer grind, of rearing children. But a moment's pause for reflection will allow us to see that just because the obligations of parenting can never be returned, the effort must be freely given. If we let go of any expectations, we will find ourselves rewarded beyond measure.

To put it another way, if parents insist on gratitude from their children, in words or deeds, they'll merely be disappointed. Truly nothing can repay parental labor. But if the bearing and rearing of children are gifts, gifts we receive and then pass on, then the rewards of parenting are guaranteed.

Each of us can be a medium or channel for transmitting the gift that comes to us through our parents. We give it as we received it, joyfully.

THOUGHT FOR TODAY: Any resentment I feel as a parent can be turned into a blessing if I remember that I freely gave what can never be repaid.

*In the modern world there has been a great divorce
between work and prayer, and we have tended to
feel we were holy only when we were serious.*
                              —William Irwin Thompson

In the oldest systems of worship, events of daily life
were touched with spiritual meaning. Many families
nowadays set spiritual observance off to one side, in
brackets, and label it "For the Sabbath." One brief
exposure every week, in one set place, is expected to
nourish our spirits adequately.

Some of us are more fortunate. Church or temple
is a central part of our lives, where we regularly
share music, food, study, companionship. Or we
may focus our spirituality on prayer and meditation
rather than on an observance led by clergy; these we
can practice as often as we like. Some of us make a
little shrine in our home, a place to be peacefully in
touch with our spiritual source, where our family
can worship as we see fit. Some of us make periodic
retreats, in solitude or in communities, where we
renew our spiritual commitments.

Still, we may not realize that work and play can
both be forms of worship. Anything can, so long as
it calls forth our wholehearted dedication. Work
and play are made holy if we remember to invoke a
power greater than ourselves to bless us, and dedicate our effort, our enjoyment, to that source.

THOUGHT FOR TODAY: Prayer may not always
be easy, but it never needs to be boring.

Pregnant women, during the time they are with child, must tell the child they're carrying everything they see when they're walking through the woods.
—Rigoberta Menchú

No one knows exactly what can influence a human child in its mother's womb. Western medicine used to believe that few substances passed from mother to infant; now we know that many do. Other belief systems hold that even the mother's speech and thoughts can influence her child.

We all know that emotions have physical effects, and physical events reflect in our emotions. Feelings are facts. Few of us could say with certainty that there is a clear distinction between our bodies, minds, and spirits. When we are happy, we feel well. Isn't it interesting to think that this feeling of happiness might be communicated to a child within?

Happiness depends largely on our own decision to be happy, to let go of any shame, resentment, or guilt shadowing our lives. We can choose a positive outlook, an acceptance of those things we cannot change and a challenge to change the things we can. Whatever our state—of wealth, of health—this day is all we have, and what we do with it is all we can do.

THOUGHT FOR TODAY: My best chance for true happiness is attunement with my world.

Only by doing what we ourselves consider to be right and good can we travel the road of self-respect.
—Garth Wood

Small children have a keen instinctive sense of justice. They know when they're being treated fairly, and they know when they're being cheated or bribed. All of us can tell the difference between fairness and injustice, but it's in our families that we learn to label these bad or good.

For the very poor in many cultures, lying and thieving are necessary for survival, and parents teach this to children as carefully as middle-class parents teach fair play and politer manners.

It's when we leave our families that we discover for ourselves what feels right and good. We may have learned survival techniques from our parents that are harmful and destructive to the lives we lead now. Our parents may have suffered from various kinds of addictive or deluded states that can be harmful—as harmful as thieving or lying—such as stifling angry feelings; distrusting the opposite sex; or blaming their defects on others.

All of these habits may have had their uses once, when we were children in a sick family. But once we are living independently, taking responsibility for our own lives, we also take responsibility for our moral beliefs. We can't be fully moral beings alone; but in this project, help is always at hand.

THOUGHT FOR TODAY: If I don't trust myself, I can't trust anyone. When my behavior is congruent with my values, I can trust and respect myself.

Grown-ups have to act as if they know. That's how they show they love you, by knowing more stuff; it makes you feel secure.

—Jill Robinson

Children are shrewd observers, and it's by observing their parents that they learn how grown-ups behave. In the preteen and teen years they start putting their observations into action, trying out different behaviors. Parents are sometimes aghast at the behavior their children reflect, and sometimes we forget they're still children, who need firm limits and a lot of love.

Children and parents can wound each other so easily that in some families the generations put up barriers to protect themselves from one another—but these barriers keep out love and understanding as well as hurt. Young people must try out different behaviors before they know what feels right to them. What they dish out to us, we have earned.

THOUGHT FOR TODAY: Love and prayer will get me through adolescence, my own or my children's.

Life goes around in circles.
—Robert Westbrook

The behavior we learn in our original families forms the basis of the way we act with our own partners and children, for better or worse. It was in our families that we learned the patterns we believe are adult or childish, parental or filial, masculine or feminine.

Many of us believe our families taught us some bad lessons, useless or destructive behaviors, and we vow never to repeat them in our new families or relationships. Yet we may find we echo our upbringing without wanting to. We can't help it; that's who and how we are. Are we doomed to go around in circles forever, programming our children to teach their children the mistakes our parents learned from our grandparents?

Let us transform the image of a circle to that of a spiral. We can't change everything about ourselves, but we do have the power to let go of the anger, fear, and self-doubt that undergirds such old behaviors as prejudice and violence. We'll always have strong feelings, but by spiraling upward we can transform fear into nurture, and violence into the energy needed for change.

THOUGHT FOR TODAY: The spiral dance can help me reach as high as I want to go.

*I have the feeling that I
have lost things
abstract but important
and am waiting for them to find me.*
                                    —Helen Harrington

Inside every person is an ideal of a perfect, loving family—parents whose authority is wise, and welcomed; sisters and brothers who share one another's sorrows and deepen each other's pleasures; children whose brilliance and cheerful obedience gladden our hearts. Some of us mourn this ideal as a lost one; this is how things used to be, we feel. We look for explanations or blame when reality falls short—as it must.

Expecting others, who are all at least as imperfect as we are, to conform to such an ideal is a sure way to set ourselves up for disappointment. How much more content we would be if we remembered that ideals by their nature are abstract. An ideal is important because it is an image of our highest desire; it can never be fully realized. We have not lost the gift of family love; families are no more fragmented, chaotic, or estranged than they ever were. Our whole life can be a journey toward our ideal for our families.

THOUGHT FOR TODAY: My ideals can guide me, but I'll achieve happiness in accepting my loved ones as they are.

Adolescence is a kind of emotional seasickness. Both are funny, but only in retrospect.

—Arthur Koestler

Motion sickness comes from unfamiliar rhythms—the roll of the sea, the pitch of a car or plane. The traveler is off solid ground; usual habits of movement are of no use. In much the same way the emotional storms of the teen years are produced by changed rhythms and changing relationships. We undergo rapid changes in size and temperament; we're no longer children who need and expect constant concern from our parents or caregivers, but we're not yet fully able to look after ourselves.

Parents of adolescents may find these years of broadening shoulders, deepening voices, and sprouting hair particularly stressful, though if they allow memory to speak clearly they'll often recall how difficult their own teen years were. There's nothing really funny about anguish, though we may laugh with relief after it's past.

Both parents and children will weather the teen years better if they can be generous with themselves and with one another. The adolescent's changes are as shocking to him or her as they are to parents. *Everything* changes. From the vantage point of years, adolescence may look funny, but every adult can recall the pain of change.

THOUGHT FOR TODAY: I'll try to be wise enough to be sympathetic to others' troubles, having remembered my own.

Bringing up children was uphill work most of the way ... mundane things like food, clothes, toys, and TV programmes became inextricably bound up with ethics and morality, so that you were constantly struggling to justify your behavior in an attempt to communicate your values to your children.
—Dorothy Simpson

Everything our caregivers did when we were babies and children communicated to us. If we were beaten, we learned to use violence. If we were held and read to, we learned to associate books with pleasure. Adults may not always intend exactly the meanings they pass on, but every iota of experience has meaning and value for children.

It is a lifelong task to sort out the values we received in our families. Some we'll want to pass on to our own children, if we have them, and others we won't. We must remember to tap our spiritual source for guidance when we try to understand these; it's too heavy a burden to shoulder alone.

THOUGHT FOR TODAY: My behavior communicates my values, and help is always at hand; I need never struggle alone with moral or ethical questions.

The reverse side also has a reverse side.
> —Anonymous (Japanese proverb)

We tend to think of good and bad as absolutes: things are totally wonderful, will make us happy ever after, or else they're utterly dismal and their consequences will be disastrous. What we ignore in this scheme is that we can't see the larger reality of which our small personal reality is a part.

It's tempting to think of our families in this unreal, absolute mode as well. Mother is wonderful, Uncle Bob is a shambles; Dad can do no wrong but Step-Mom is a witch. People and events are richer and more complicated than this, and the ripple effects they have on our lives extend far beyond what we can see. Even family tragedies—death, divorce, bankruptcy, imprisonment—may have far-reaching benefits. The thickly textured fabric of our destiny may transform apparent failure or success into something quite unexpected.

And the other side has its other side. Life isn't a coin, flat and double-sided; life is full of curves and dips, sudden angles, gradual changes, none of which can be predicted on the basis of what has gone before. The best we can do, on our winding path, is to dedicate ourselves to the journey.

Success means letting go of outcomes, recognizing our relative ignorance, and trusting in a source of power greater than ourselves. My family is never all good or all bad; I'll respect our human variety and remember that.

THOUGHT FOR TODAY: The side I see is not the only side. Fortunately, ultimate outcomes are out of my hands.

. . . I have peeled away your anger
down to its core of love
and look mother
I am
a dark temple where your spirit rises
                                        —Audre Lorde

Family relations aren't easy, but they're simple—in
the sense that all people share the same few powerful motivations. Anger can cover over some other
feeling, often fear or vulnerability. If we can peel
away the outside feeling, we will come upon a tender core that can be touched, gently, to reveal a
loving spirit.

But family members can harden themselves against
each other; often, in fact, we feel we need the most
armor against those closest to us. Because we know
the same moves, the same evasions, we are the most
powerful enemies.

Real harmony with our families will come when
we can open ourselves to them, removing the defen-
sive shells and letting our true spirits rise and speak.
We'll do this when we learn to trust them, and we'll
only do that when we can trust ourselves.

THOUGHT FOR TODAY: I won't expect the impossible from my family or myself, nor will I harden
myself unnecessarily.

Take short views, hope for the best, and trust in God.

—Sydney Smith

Since the only moment that truly belongs to us is the present moment, it makes sense to take short views. The longer our view, the less we can participate. Of course, it's possible to take a long view and renew it constantly; this is how we bring our present behavior into line with our long-range goals. If we seriously want to excel at a sport, or law school, or marriage, we need to act in such a way, in the present moment, as to increase the probability that we'll reach our goal. This means practicing, studying, faithfully working at the relationship. If we keep both our short-term and our long-term goals firmly in mind, we'll always know what to do.

Yet we can't control the outcome of our present actions. "You're responsible for the effort, not the outcome," a wise friend told me, so I know that when I do the best I can, I've given myself the best chance for happiness. After the effort, all I can do is hope and trust.

To live without hope would be to deprive ourselves of sunshine; to live without trust in a power greater than ourselves would be to choose loneliness. We need never be uncertain. If we do our best, our future is assured. We are all members of one family; love and nurture are ours for the asking.

THOUGHT FOR TODAY: Today I'll remember that my life is full of partners. When I do my part to make it successful, I've done the best I can.

Change is the one human constant.
>   —Carroll Smith-Rosenberg

No matter what we think, family patterns that are
normal in our culture haven't been ordained by anything but custom. Carroll Smith-Rosenberg, a histo-
rian of the family, has seen in her work how families
survive change. Healthy, happy families can exist
when both parents work outside the home or within
it; when either father or mother is responsible for
housekeeping or child care, or when both share in it.
Families have always fostered others' children, and
parents of all sorts send their children to be fostered
by relatives or friends.

Single-parent families have always existed, and
different patterns of support for them have emerged
at different times. Each society has norms for the
evolution of families, from the care of young children to the care of aged parents, and each has appropriate rituals for the cardinal points of change:
birth, maturity, marriage, divorce, death.

The point is, families change and the institution of
the family survives change. Much trouble among
family members is due to the fact that people, even
close and loving relations, grow and change at different rates. We need to accept others' changes and
attend to our own: they bring us to the threshold of
joy.

THOUGHT FOR TODAY: I'll remember that everyone in my world has a personal timetable for
change, and I'll try to respect the timetables of others as I want them to honor mine.

The essence of romance is the promise of being cared for, being special, being loved for who you really are, and being granted a future of absolute security.

—Liz Heron

Enjoyable as romantic fictions are, we cannot confuse them with life. The books, movies, and TV shows that cater to our romantic illusions need to be understood as expressions of deep, infantile wishes. At some time, everyone wants a partner who never says "No," or who will make all our decisions for us.

But real life presents us with partners who have more or less the same unconscious wishes as we do. They too cherish fantasies of endless love or total security or thrilling adventure—and they need to make the same adjustments as we do to cope with jobs, homes, schools, children, and parents.

Romance can be fun if we understand clearly that it's an escape from reality and not another, more desirable reality. The only reality is in this beautiful, fragile, uncertain world, where imperfect creatures love and struggle with each other. Our best energies are needed to make our own spirits loving.

THOUGHT FOR TODAY: Once I've acknowledged my own needs for approval and security, I can respond to others'.

In the world there are different and still more different people. Sit and mix with everyone, the way a boat joins the river.

—Tulsidas

Boats join the river from different launches. They come in many varieties—canoes, ketches, trimarans, dinghies, speedboats, barges—and a river pilot learns to steer among them. People need the chance to meet diverse others. Parents do their children no favor by shielding them from experience, making sure they meet only people like themselves. The world may sometimes be cruel and difficult, but no one achieves wisdom or compassion while retreating from it.

People of different colors, people with different abilities, people from Buddhist, Christian, Jewish, and Muslim faiths; rich people, poor people, people speaking different languages, eating different foods— these are all people we want our children to feel comfortable with. And more—we'd like our children to have open hearts, so they can learn from all, for all have something to teach.

Fear puts up walls between people that love and understanding can breach. Let us take pride in our own culture, but never at the expense of another's; ours is only one of many. Differences can only enrich our experience, and the absence of difference impoverishes us.

THOUGHT FOR TODAY: Today I will seek out difference, so my family will come to value a world that is like a rich chord, where differences harmonize.

The details of other people's lives are intriguing because, after all, everyone's life is a variation on the same theme.

—Penelope Franklin

Living in houses or apartments, going our separate ways, it's easy for us to forget that we're part of a great human choir, all singing pretty much the same music. Love, anxiety, and spiritual hunger are common to us all. Our problems are very like all human problems, and our contentment has similar roots: faith and acceptance lead us to serenity, whoever and wherever we are.

Families sing the same chords over and over again—loves and losses, joys and humiliations, fears for our children, conflicts over independence, rivalry between siblings and sometimes between generations. Although separate, we're all connected to one another, all related in the human family, and we're deeply interested in other people's doings. How are they surviving the strains that we too are suffering? How did they deal with the problem that's threatening to tear us apart?

Our world is home to a huge family that has endless possibilities for creativity and nurture. How nice to think there are no strangers; just sisters and brothers we haven't met yet.

THOUGHT FOR TODAY: Our common experience is a cause for rejoicing. Like everyone else, I'm a necessary part of the human family.

A deep distress hath humanized my soul.
                    —William Wordsworth

Most of us experience sorrow long before we have a word for it—the sorrow of losing our infant comfort, of weaning away from a mother or other loving caregiver, or of having a sibling usurp our place. Such early grief is compensated by growth. Other deep distress—death, injury, or illness—is not compensated, and the only way to redeem such sorrow is to grieve fully. This then becomes a humanizing process, a softening of the spirit.

Adults sometimes try to shield children from distress, from the knowledge that a parent is sick, or dying; or from full acceptance of the child's own limitations. When sorrow is disguised or smothered in this way, half admitted but half denied, it squeezes out of shape. The work of grieving is incomplete.

Knowledge; grief; acceptance; this is the healing sequence. Adults cannot let go of sorrow if they never were allowed to feel it, as children. Rage is a part of grieving, and we cannot let go of rage until we admit it to the light of consciousness. Every one of us has been wounded, some more deeply than others, and every one of us has the power to heal ourselves. The deep well of compassion opens as a result of this healing.

THOUGHT FOR TODAY: My total humanity depends on my acknowledgment of grief. Only after I accept it can I let go.

If you want to know how important you are to the world, stick your finger in a pond and pull it out. Will the hole remain?

—Maya Angelou

We are individual units of one grand design, each of us unique. We all need to know how important we are—not to water, nor to rock, but to one another. Our fingers, our lives, our strivings and successes, may not leave a visible mark on the world, but each of us imprints on the lives of countless others. If one of us is pulled out, a hole remains, to be filled with love, grieving, and remembrance.

For we are all woven into the same fabric, parents and children, friends and strangers. The most precious legacy that we can hand on to our families, and to all who enter our lives, is the knowledge that we are part of one another. We share an origin and a destiny; our real family is all of humanity.

THOUGHT FOR TODAY: I will remember to treat all who cross my path with the same respect and care I'd like to receive. My spirit can be a gift to them, as theirs are to me.

Children can find other children to be pals. Children need fathers to be fathers.

—Garrison Keillor

Pals are our equals, but parents have authority over us. We learn healthy habits of discipline and control over ourselves when our parents use their authority wisely. But nobody's perfect; all parents make mistakes, while doing the best they can under the circumstances. Often the mistakes are in the area of authority—it's exercised either too harshly, so that we come to resent any controls placed on us, or too laxly, so that we feel fearful about our ability to control ourselves.

But fathers are more than authority figures. They're a child's first example of what a man is, what he does in the world. No pal can cut this pattern for a child. Children who don't live with their fathers find fathering figures in other places, uncles or teachers, grandfathers, clergy, or counselors. It's a precious position to hold. Unfortunately, some fathers are uneasy in their responsibility; they try to dissolve fatherhood into "palship." It may feel too heavy to be a father to one's child, but time for prayer and meditation can help one over the hard parts.

THOUGHT FOR TODAY: The hard part is finding within myself the knowledge of what to do. I'll pray for confidence in my own best judgment.

I was a child who clutched the amulet
of childhood in a terror of time. I saw
archangels, worshipped trees, expected God.
                                        —Dilys Laing

Children have a great capacity for wonder and terror. The simple awe of a child before the universe is
so great, many spiritual teachings aim to recapture
it. When we become parents we can recapture our
own sense of wonder in our children—and if we
become grandparents, we get to repeat it again.

As parents we hurry to calm our children's fears—
but as children, those fears were part of the magical
relationship we felt with the world. How can we feel
again the sense of the miraculous? Perhaps through
our senses—through music or sculpture or wilder-
ness experience—or perhaps through meditation—
going inside ourselves and emptying our minds of all
the facts, dates, and explanations we've acquired—we
can approach a child's purity of response.

It's true, the world is terrifying when we can't
explain it—but it's also rich with many possibilities
that our human explanations ignore. I can recapture
a sense of holiness, of mystery, when I surrender to
the child within me.

THOUGHT FOR TODAY: I will set aside some
time today to empty my mind and open myself to
wonder.

The worst sin toward our fellow creatures is not to hate them, but to be indifferent to them: that's the essence of inhumanity.

—George Bernard Shaw

Indifference isn't a natural state for human beings; as a species we are insatiably curious, with strong needs for contact and bonding with others. People who lack these traits are ill; "the essence of inhumanity" is an unhealthy withdrawal from our natural state of lively involvement.

Children pretend to be indifferent when they've been punished; they play at hardening themselves against pain or anger, protecting their vulnerable feelings of sadness and shame. We all must harden ourselves to some degree, or we'd be constantly outraged and in pain over the cruelty and injustice of the world. But indifference mustn't become a habit. Parents who neglect their children do as much harm as those parents who abuse them.

Children who have been treated with indifference grow up lacking in essential human sympathies. They've had to harden themselves against pain far worse than blows. On a grand scale, indifference to our fellow humans results in the mass slaughter of war. Our best hope for a peaceful future is a loving present.

THOUGHT FOR TODAY: Indifference always begins as a shield against pain. Today I'll begin to disarm myself.

"You got to leave room for the fool in everybody . . ."
—Ntozake Shange

Everybody's personality wears different faces—angel, urchin, drill sergeant, or perhaps a royal personage. Some of us are cast as fools by our families. We're the ones who amuse the others; we can make mistakes and joke about them. Sometimes we complain that no one takes us seriously.

Some of us, on the other hand, are cast as serious people, competent, thorough, maybe a bit dull but trustworthy. Our brothers and sisters put us in their wills as guardians to their children. We arrange powers of attorney. We sometimes feel that no one has left room for the fool in us.

No matter how responsible we appear to the rest of the adult world, inside each of us is a fool in cap and bells, who longs to play practical jokes and sing nonsense songs. We may feel constrained by other people's expectations—especially our families'—to hide this foolish face and pretend that the grown-up is our only identity.

Both faces can exist within the same person. But most families don't allow such a wide latitude of behavior; our families expect us to be all one thing or all another. It's up to each of us to give expression to all our different selves, all our different faces. If we want the right to be fools, we must assert it, as well as our right to be taken seriously.

THOUGHT FOR TODAY: Why should I be afraid of looking foolish or too serious? The only way to avoid mistakes is not to do anything at all.

What we spent, we had;
What we gave, we have;
What we kept, we lost.

—Anonymous

Fear drives some of us to hold tightly to the important things in our lives—some to our lovers, spouses,
or children; some to ideas; some to money or possessions. Yet the tighter we clutch them, the less
good they are to us. People resent tight bonds; children rebel, spouses and partners feel suffocated. Ideas
that we cling to have a way of hardening us, distort-
ing our perceptions; we need to be able to detach
from our beliefs and test them against real life if
we're to be congruent in our thoughts and actions.

It's easiest to see the truth of this in the case of
money. When we hoard it, it loses all power. Misers
die poor. Attachment to possessions makes us poor
as well, if we come to value real estate, boats, or
jewels more than harmony and love. Happiness comes
when we learn to give freely what is precious to us.
Then we are rich indeed.

THOUGHT FOR TODAY: People and things that
we truly love, we're willing to let go. They will
return to us.

Being young is beautiful, but being old is comfortable.
—Marie von Ebner-Eschenbach

The history of fashion is full of examples of suffering for the sake of beauty, from the ritual scars of tribal societies to the cosmetic surgery of our own tribe. We see and hear references to celebrities who have their noses trimmed or their tummies tucked, as though flesh were as malleable and unfeeling as cloth, as though every mark on our bodies didn't also mark our minds and spirits.

Where do we get the idea that "we" are somehow separate from our bodies? For the sake of civilization, all young children must learn to mute or deafen their flesh. Did we learn also that a neat appearance could front for a disordered spirit? We can't scream or speak when we want to; we must learn to speak language instead of squeals and groans; we're taught not to hit those younger or weaker than ourselves, or to take things from them. We're taught, in fact, to disregard most of the desires of our bodies, and we have great difficulty sorting these out.

But as we age, we grow more comfortable. Desire loses some of its urgency and most of its novelty. We have the confidence of years of successful cooperation with the demands society places on our physical being; we can relax. A great deal of anxiety accompanies youth's quest for beauty. One dividend of aging is that we find beauty in comfort.

THOUGHT FOR TODAY: I can see in the old and young of my own family how our flesh is tamed and then released. Old age, I see, has its advantages.

All my children are prodigies.
                              —Anonymous (Yiddish proverb)

Within each one of us is the spark of a unique
human spirit. Parents see this gleam of brilliance in
their children and nurture it as best they can, though
schooling, culture, and the world exert their influence to make us all the same.

Each of us is gifted in a special way, yet we are
the same: creatures of the same creation. Each of us
is essential to the pattern of the whole. So parents
watch their precious children learn to speak the
common language and behave like every other child,
walking in line and singing in chorus. Sometimes we
grieve secretly for that lost spark of uniqueness.

Parents may search for the two-year-old elf inside
the grown-up engineer or schoolteacher, but it's still
there, contributing warmth and color to the new
patterns, the new connections we make. We're still
geniuses at being ourselves.

THOUGHT FOR TODAY: My special qualities are
precious—and not just to me. I'm an essential part
of the universal mosaic.

*I have to start at the beginning, and the beginning
was me.*

—Henry E. McGuckin

The world is born fresh in every infant, it's said, and
we each create reality for ourselves. Our families
provide us with a sense of rootedness in that reality.
When we trace our family connections even one or
two generations back, we get a sense of how widely
human families stretch across the earth.

Tragically, some family trees are broken by war
or exile. The wars of this century have lopped
branches off many family trees; the beginning starts
again, with us.

Others may feel large old families like a weight
upon their shoulders, with family secrets, triumphs,
shames, property, and cousins branching out to
darken the sky. In such a family it may be difficult
to think of oneself as the beginning of anything.

Yet we are always both—a link in the timeless
chain of human connections and the source of a new
world, a true beginning. We are a living legacy of
our families' history, whether our family is a genetic
or an adopted one, and we're also the creators of
our own fresh lives. We can choose, each moment,
how to continue the story that begins with us.

THOUGHT FOR TODAY: At every moment, I am
both continuing my life and beginning it again.

The world is older and I in it
  am older,
burning, slower, with the same passions.
                              —Margaret Randall

Clothes we grow out of; childhood illnesses we grow
out of; our characters we don't grow out of. People
become more like themselves as they age—more passionate, or perhaps more serene, more obstinate or
more easygoing. The tracks that were laid down for
us early are the tracks in which we run, our whole
lives.

What does change—and what we can choose to
change—is our behavior, the directions those tracks
take us. A parent who was strict and obstinate about
child-rearing may turn that strictness in another direction, like conservation of natural resources. The
obstinacy is still there, but its object now is whales
or redwoods rather than children. The same passions can serve different ends, with different effects.

Truly, we create our own worlds. As we age, our
world grows older; we have more of a sense of
history, having lived through many turns of events.
And as our families age, we feel the same feelings
toward them but we can choose, increasingly, how
we express those feelings. One of the great rewards
of getting older in our world is mastering our passions.

THOUGHT FOR TODAY: Nothing is lost as the
world grows older; everything is transformed into
something else, even our passions.

The broken cord may yet be joined again
But in the midst a knot will yet remain.
> —Anwari-i Suheill

Just as a surgeon can tell from an x-ray that a bone has been broken, however smoothly it has healed, so intimate relationships that have been broken and reconciled are never exactly the same. Often, like healed bones, they are stronger for the break. But sometimes healing is fragile; forgiveness has been incomplete, and the relationship is constantly at risk of being broken off again.

Couples who get together again after separation or divorce can sometimes make the new coupling fresher, stronger, better in every way, if they open themselves entirely to one another, letting go of old responses and relating to each other strictly in the present. All relationships benefit from staying in the present.

So the knot that remains after estrangement and reconciliation can be a tangle of old, half-buried fears and angers, or it can be a stronger bonding, based on fearless self-disclosure and love. It takes courage, always, to reconcile a family feud, whether between spouses or siblings or more distant relations. Such a healing always includes acknowledgment of wrongs, sincere apology, and forgiveness—and self-forgiveness. The newly mended cord, if all parties to the breach are brave and generous, will reward them with its strength and beauty.

THOUGHT FOR TODAY: There are at least two parties to every separation. My own part is all I can ever claim responsibility for.

This death was to those left behind a remediable death, that is, one they fancied might have been avoided, like death from starvation. They felt they knew the circumstances that had done this girl to death and guilt was always with them.
                                    —Josephine Herbst

The sense that any death is remediable is a tragic and dangerous one to harbor. The dead cannot be brought back; all that this feeling keeps alive is guilt. And guilt, though it may be sanctioned by religious and social custom, often is a punishment for those who have done no wrong.

Families can be little laboratories where guilt is preserved through the generations—guilt for death or abandonment, blame for real or imagined snubs. Many of us inherit such guilt: "Your mother stole all our grandmother's jewelry," or "Your grandfather just left those kids." It has nothing to do with us or our lives, yet we accept it, so that guilt is always with us.

Forgiving ourselves is a first step in any program of family healing. To recover from guilt we must first give up the need for it, admitting we alone are responsible for our own acts. We can make mistakes and learn from them. We can apologize and even atone, but guilt we haven't earned and don't need. We can do nothing about the past. Let's live in the present.

THOUGHT FOR TODAY: I'm grateful for mistakes, because from them I can learn how to live better, but I'll accept no guilt.

*One never knows how much a family may grow;
and when a hive is too full, and it is necessary to
form a new swarm, each one thinks of carrying
away his own honey.*

—George Sand

Millions of people watch families fight over their honey
on *Dallas* and *Dynasty*, and we love to see how hate-
fully they treat one another. Have you seen it in your
own family? Money and property can poison family
relations; even the most mature among us can completely lose our senses over questions of inheritance.

Families needn't be rich for this to happen, and it
doesn't always center around bequests. When grown
children leave home, they may want to take a favorite lamp or tablecloth, golf clubs or jewelry. Everyone in the family may feel she or he has a right to
Grandpa's bridge trophies. The value of the property seldom has anything to do with its importance.

The resulting fights are never wholly about property, or even about money; they're about family feelings. We all crave love and recognition, and few of us
ever feel we get as much as we deserve. It's hard to
ask for what we want; and so we displace our
craving onto bonds, silver, or Mama's old fox fur.

Once we understand our desires, we can begin to
reach for our real feelings, what we really need and
want from our family members. We may not get what
we ask for; but if we don't ask, we'll get nothing at all.

THOUGHT FOR TODAY: Straightening out family
feelings means there can be enough honey for
everyone.

I appeal to parents: Never, never say, "Hurry up," to a child.

—Vladimir Nabokov

Children, who are learning so much about the world so fast, need time to daydream. Daydreams let the systematic parts of the brain rest, and give exercise to the visionary ones. Inside every adult is a child with the same needs. Too often, adults hustle children along as though they were slightly defective machines that need constant cleaning, feeding, and reprimanding in order to function. If we've been treated this way, we may have learned to be ashamed of our daydreaming selves. We hide them, and soon they retreat far beyond our conscious power to enjoy them.

The power to dream and to imagine is precious; it can enrich our lives and widen our possibilities. We want to nourish it, not stifle it, in our children and in ourselves. We needn't be afraid that the dreamers will forget to brush their teeth, to flush, or to get up on time. Those who have had ample time for dreaming have well-nourished spirits; they will be generous and considerate with others as well as with themselves.

THOUGHT FOR TODAY: Schedules are for convenience, so that I will have enough time to do everything I want to do—including daydreaming.

Tomorrow is not another day.
It is today. Begin.

—Raquel Jodorowsky

Two days I can do nothing about, goes the old saying, are yesterday and tomorrow. And yet we know the past prepares the future: if we haven't planted bulbs in the fall, we won't have tulips in the spring; if we haven't trained for it, we're not likely to finish a marathon. How can we live in each precious moment, especially in growing, changing families, yet keep a sane and healthy perspective on the future—and the past?

Today is all we have. By living fully, moment by moment, according to our best knowledge of how to conduct our lives, we can assure ourselves a high quality of experience. Faith in our personal connection to a source of spiritual strength will help us through the pain that is an inevitable part of life. We need never repress or deny our reality; it is part of us. By embracing all of life, we guarantee that our present is as good as we can make it.

Although we can't predict or control the future, by living fully and well we ensure that we'll be able to look back on a wonderful past, and we prepare for ourselves a future in which we'll reap a rich harvest. Time is an unbroken chain, and each link is inscribed with our name.

THOUGHT FOR TODAY: Help me to surrender the past. Living in the present is my hope for the future.

Be ye angry and sin not; let not the sun go down upon your wrath.

—St. Paul

Anger can be a healthy response. But humans are such flexible creatures that we sometimes channel other feelings into our anger: fears, for example, or sadness. Instead of discouraging expressions of anger, especially in our families, we might try to find out about it. What feeds our anger? Are we using it to cover up something else?

Some of us were encouraged, one way or another, to feel our anger and express it. Our parents may have punished us for directing angry behavior at them, but still approved of our anger at cruelty or injustice. Anger may have been more acceptable in our families than fear or grief. Anger, after all, makes us feel strong, while fear lets us know we are vulnerable. Yet how wrong it is to strike out angrily at something that frightens us! Fear means that we need reassurance, comfort, and understanding, not the combat anger seeks.

There will always be some anger on which the sun must set, including our righteous wrath at injustice. If we reconcile ourselves to injustice, we'll never succeed in changing it. But righteous wrath is different from holding a grudge. We can resolve or detach from our anger directed at one another, for we can learn to tell the difference.

THOUGHT FOR TODAY: Strong feelings are gifts. I will unwrap mine carefully.

Loneliness is never more cruel than when it is felt in close propinquity with someone who has ceased to communicate.

—Germaine Greer

Although we're all connected on this beautiful blue sphere, at times we deliberately shut ourselves off from one another. Our intimates may feel this as anger or punishment, and it may cause them great anguish. It harms the one who shuts off communication as well, for it violates our organic unity with loved ones and with our greater human family.

Perhaps the one who ceases to communicate has been hurt; perhaps isolation feels safe. That is a delusion. It's never safe to cut one's lifeline. Keeping an open channel of communication with our higher power will help us learn how to redress our injury, how to forgive, how to heal.

Isolation can actually be lethal, unlike solitude, which is necessary for our spiritual renewal. Life itself directs us to stay in touch, to keep our feelings flowing, to experience anger, love, fear, or tenderness as they come to us and through us—to feel our feelings and then let them go. Solitude can help a wounded spirit to heal. Isolation hardens a scar.

THOUGHT FOR TODAY: I will pray for the strength to keep my guard down. If my spirit is strong, I won't need defenses.

There was a child went forth
And the first object he look'd upon, that object he
became.

—Walt Whitman

Children are impressionable, we say, as though they
were little fiber mats that we could inscribe with
feelings and information—like printing a newspaper.
Children come into the world with quite a lot of
splendid equipment for testing and proving things;
they are not empty space waiting to be filled.

What children don't have is the ability to detach
themselves from what they see. So they're distressed
when they see pain, and pleased when they see pleasure. They take what they see very personally, iden-
tifying with heroes and against villains. As we grow
up, we learn to put some distance between ourselves
and outside objects—though at the movies or watching TV we let ourselves become what we look upon,
as wholeheartedly as children.

We're in no danger, as children are, of confusing
stories with reality. But perhaps we're getting things
backward, when we can walk calmly past a homeless person and then be moved or excited by a
football game or a book. Perhaps we need to soften
our spirits until they are impressionable again, for
only if we fully believe in the suffering of others will
we be moved to change it.

THOUGHT FOR TODAY: I can choose how I respond to the world and how I act in it.

*No entertainment is so cheap as reading, nor any
pleasure so lasting.*
                    —Lady Mary Wortley Montagu

More than entertainment, reading opens the world to
us, making the past accessible and the foreign familiar. Parents are often surprised, especially if they
come from backgrounds where reading was not valued, at how much their children love being read to.
Almost everyone enjoys it, and any family or circle
of friends can start a reading group at any time.

Reading can also be a precious gift to others—to
friends or strangers in the hospital, to blind listeners,
to schoolchildren. When we visit old people in nurs-
ing homes, we can pass a pleasant visit reading to
them. The shelves of any library hold such a wealth
of pleasure, information, and challenge that the ded-
icated reader need never fear boredom.

This gift of a lifelong pleasure should be every
child's birthright. If the habit of reading has lapsed,
it can always be revived—although be warned: Reading has no calories and won't impair your ability to
operate a motor vehicle, but it may be addictive and
is definitely mood-altering.

THOUGHT FOR TODAY: Reading can direct us
outward, toward the world, and also inward, toward
the enrichment of our spirits.

Money will buy a pretty good dog but it won't buy the wag of its tail.

—Josh Billings

Other people's feelings are as uncontrollable as the wag of a dog's tail, and when we find ourselves counting on certain responses from people in order to feel good about ourselves, we're in trouble. Of course, we don't want our loved ones to respond negatively to us; we want them to be happy. But there's a deep and necessary distinction between wanting those we love to be happy in their lives and *needing* them to be happy *for our sake*.

Those of us who give a great deal of time and energy to others sometimes risk our emotions in this way. Especially when we deal with small children—or anybody who's irrational and demanding—we may find ourselves staking our well-being on someone else's feelings. At best, this is manipulation. At worst, it's madness: we may utterly lose touch with our own feelings and desires.

Mothers, fathers, nurses, doctors, therapists, social workers—all are prone to this form of distorted thinking and feeling. To recover from it, we need to reassure ourselves that we are lovable, and loved, in and for ourselves. We must strengthen our spiritual connection and through it, our respect for the autonomy of others—spouses, lovers, parents, children, dogs.

THOUGHT FOR TODAY: My feelings are my own; they come from my life. They are not dependent upon others.

Being constantly with the children was like wearing a pair of shoes that were expensive and too small. She couldn't bear to throw them out, but they gave her blisters.

—Beryl Bainbridge

There's a special kind of claustrophobic despair that a parent can experience, "being constantly with" young children, especially single parents. No matter how much you love your children, how delightful or imaginative or what good company they are, they still demand more emotional sustenance than they provide. Even parents with partners, in households with enough money, feel this strain, this blistering of the spirit.

It's from such strain that much abuse of children comes, perhaps from parents who were abused when they were children. Since the only real preparation for parenting most of us ever get is our own upbringing, we tend to pass on the bad with the good— the sick, destructive actions of our parents as well as their loving care. To break this chain of transmission, we must first recognize what we're doing: acting out a script we didn't write.

Then we need to forgive ourselves, for our rage and resentment at our children, for our behavior toward them, and for the violence that we've done to ourselves in expecting the impossible. Forgiveness comes readily when we surrender our spirits to the universal power of love and acceptance.

THOUGHT FOR TODAY: The power to change is within my grasp. All it takes is patience, surrender, and the will to love myself.

We must seek god in error and forgetfulness and foolishness.

—Meister Eckhart

We look for things where they're likely to be found: we dig for oil or gold where the earth resembles places they've been found before. We look for trilliums and morels in the spring woods and Canada geese in the autumn sky. For miracles, we look to the gaps in ordinary life—to errors and nonsense and lapses in memory, places where our conscious control gives over and *something else* peeps through, something nourishing and timeless that many people call god.

So much of life is controlled and programmed that we have to seek deliberately for this miracle of life that is everywhere and all-sustaining. It's covered over with habit, duty, custom, automatic response. We find god in our families, in the unmotivated, unconditional love between family members, especially parents and children, and in the serious, joyous explorations of an infant.

These gaps in the fabric show us that our little plans and disappointments, our comings and goings, our schemes and defeats, are utterly incidental to the universe. We can't see the totality of creation; we occupy only one corner of it. But when we glimpse the miraculous, we can take comfort from knowing we are where we need to be; errors aren't wrong, they're opportunities for growth. Forgetfulness and foolishness aren't lapses; they are demonstrations that even if our little human clockwork stopped, the great mechanism would go on turning.

THOUGHT FOR TODAY: In my family and in the rest of my life, I'll cherish opportunities for seeking god.

A husband and wife build their home for many things, but particularly for quarrels. A home is where you quarrel in.

—Buchi Emecheta

Family quarrels often spill out of the home. A quarrel between wife and husband may carry on through their children for generations, especially if the quarrel has to do with deep divisions in the self. Extreme social pressures like racism and poverty can enter into these intimate quarrels, poisoning the home and becoming part of the family legacy.

Such poisonous quarrels need to be brought out of the home, for if confined there they erupt in violence. We sometimes give the name of "family quarrel" to troubles that a skilled third person could help to resolve—a counselor trusted by both parties.

Some quarrels should be kept private; they are nobody's business but the quarrelers', and they can be resolved peacefully. But some need intervention, and appealing to privacy in such a case is really a mask for shame. If we're troubled about the difference between the two kinds, then laying the quarrel out in imagination before a spiritual guide can help to straighten us out, so that our home can be more than the place of quarrels.

THOUGHT FOR TODAY: I choose to resolve my quarrels, even when that means asking for outside help.

Fate chooses our parents. We choose our friends.
                                        —Jacques Delille

Some adolescents seem to choose friends who will
offend their families—crewcut conservatives when
the families are liberal, or leather-bearing toughs
when families are conventional; young people who
appear snobbish or crude or lawless or spineless, or
whatever quality parents particularly want to discourage. These perverse choices can be extra hard
on parents when the children are chosen, adopted,
or foster family members.

But choice is a sophisticated concept. Many young
people approach maturity slowly and cautiously,
trying out different social meanings for themselves.
It's healthy for them to seek out friends who challenge their parents' ways of dealing with the world—
though parents may have difficulty seeing it.

Often we choose friends our parents do like, after
our adolescent years. We find we're comfortable
with the same kinds of people. And we learn this by
trying out different friendships.

THOUGHT FOR TODAY: What is fate, and what
determines choice? If I've resolved most of my family conflicts, my choices and fate's may be the same.

Gauge a country's prosperity by its treatment of the aged.

—Nahman Bratzlav

All human societies make rules for the care of the ill and frail, including the very young and very old. In societies of scarcity, when feeding an unproductive body places great hardship on the providers, sick people, old people, and infants needing special care may be allowed to die. We command great wealth in our society, and our sophisticated medical technology can provide miracles of rescue. Yet our social policies don't always allow for the care of aged people and infants.

It isn't the gross wealth in a society that counts, nor even public accumulations of it, in weaponry or museums. It's equality of distribution that determines real prosperity, which has a spiritual as well as a material dimension. Those who seek the accumulation of things, and starve the young and deprive the old, will find that their spirits don't prosper. They are shutting themselves off from life's true richness, the vision of harmonious abundance.

THOUGHT FOR TODAY: Spiritual wealth is always within my reach; I have only to accept it.

Take rest; a field that has rested gives a bountiful crop.

—Ovid

Working parents of young children, and working children of old and invalid parents, have more than full-time jobs; they work in the labor market and then come home to the unpaid job of caring for family members and the home.

Single parents and other full-time caregivers need plenty of rest. Not just sleep but actual vacations: time away from home, a strong, pleasant contrast to our usual lives. We love our charges enough to want the best care for them; that's why we give it ourselves. But we need to care for the caregivers, too; we can't keep up a high quality of care if we neglect ourselves. Our physical, spiritual, and emotional health depend on resting our spirits as well as our bodies.

THOUGHT FOR TODAY: Whatever other roles I may play in life, I'm always my own full-time caregiver, and I owe myself a high quality of care.

And the eyes of them that see shall not be dim, and the ears of them that hear shall hearken.
                                    —The Vision of Isaiah

The warnings of prophets from thousands of years ago sound remarkably like the thundering of doom-sayers today. Good and evil, fear and desire, seem to be pretty constant notions in human society, and so does the tendency to predict that our present wickedness will bring about its end.

Some prophets of doom look at the world narrowly, dividing it up into "us" and "them"; often "they" are young people, a new generation whose music and manners are different from ours and offensive to us. The true prophet points out that "them that see" are any of us who are willing to open our eyes to the world and its wonders and dangers. The young are our children. We're all connected in our earthly family, and we all have the same capacity for seeing and hearing, for these eyes and ears belong to the spirit.

The vision we perceive is of the frail, precious unity of life on earth, and the message to our spirit's ears is that we must protect it. The young are our allies in our work for peace and harmony, no matter how they cut their hair, or dress, or what music they listen to. Their stake in this world is even greater than ours. We can accomplish more together than alone.

THOUGHT FOR TODAY: Today I'll remember to share the vision and the message with everyone.

"I'm afraid I take myself very seriously."
"No one else will, if you don't. It's necessary to believe in your own importance."

—Nina Bawden

When we're growing up, our belief in our own importance is often fragile. Our parents, brothers, or sisters can crush us with their words or their hands; we can be made to feel puny, paltry, unimportant. Life, in families and out, can threaten our good feelings about ourselves. When we have children of our own, it's important for us to remember just how painful those snubs can be.

True selflessness, self-forgetfulness, is only possible to those who have a good solid sense of worth. We can give away only what we already have; if we feel we are worthless, then the gift of ourselves doesn't mean very much.

If we haven't received a strong sense of self-worth in our families, we'll have to construct it for ourselves. Our opinions matter. Let us not belittle ourselves; a healthy sense of our own importance—not a grandiose inflation, which comes from deep insecurity—is good for us. Then, when we turn our energies outward, our gift has deeper meaning and more value.

THOUGHT FOR TODAY: Never let me forget: I am my favorite person, the most important in my life.

The art of being wise is the art of knowing what to overlook.

—William James

When we played hopscotch, our rules called for blindfolding the most successful player and making her hop and jump the course by touch alone. I remember that when I was poised on one leg, blindfolded, I felt off balance, and almost any little distraction, any pebble on the sidewalk, would make me falter. The same is true now of my spiritual equilibrium. If I'm truly centered I know what is important, whereas if I'm out of kilter somehow, trifles loom large.

But balance depends on my using all my perceptions. When I blindfold myself, I willfully cut off an important source of information—whereas if I were truly sight-impaired, or truly had one leg, I would learn to get that information from my other senses. So wisdom also has to do with making the most of my powers.

In family life we sometimes treat pebbles as though they were roadblocks. We give up too easily, especially if we're tired or frustrated, and we may act like blindfolded hopscotch players, wobbling on one leg, reacting disproportionately to very small disturbances, neglecting to summon our considerable powers of memory, humor, gratitude, and faith to help us judge what really looms large and what can be overlooked.

THOUGHT FOR TODAY: Balanced judgment calls for me to be fully present, using all my skills for the daily tasks of family life.

Children use the fist
Until they are of age to use the brain.
                              —Elizabeth Barrett Browning

Every child begins by using violence, and most children soon learn violence isn't a good way to resolve disputes. So why aren't we all pacifists? Nations still design foreign policies that depend on threats of violence—to enforce decisions that are mainly about economic planning and markets.

Think about our families. How are decisions made? Does the threat of violence back up every statement parents make? Do siblings have to fight over privileges? Not all violence in families is physical. Verbal violence, although devastating to children's self-respect, can even be quiet. If our families aren't violent, how do we reach decisions and get things done?

The world desperately needs techniques for waging peace—not just the absence of active fighting but the ability to resolve conflicts peaceably, without the threat of bloodshed. All of us, in every aspect of our lives, can use what we know about living in peace. Peace must begin in our families, or it cannot begin.

THOUGHT FOR TODAY: There is a saying: "Let it begin with me." Today in my life I can begin love, truthtelling, and peace.

Love is an act of courage, not of fear; love is commitment to others.

—Paulo Freire

Infants who are loved with an unconditional love that nourishes their bodies and spirits learn to love and accept themselves. As they grow older, they're able to love others, courageously and wholeheartedly. They develop both a firm sense of their own individuality and the capacity to merge with others, to transcend themselves and to set their egos aside.

Only those who feel securely cared for are capable of selfless devotion and courage. The world needs people who are able to struggle for justice, to wage peace. Global issues enter all our lives, as poisoned rain falls everywhere. The place where we can influence world affairs is in our own families, where the people who will make tomorrow's decisions are raised. We hope to have children who will make brave and compassionate choices in their lives, and we prepare them best by showing them our courage and compassion. Love is the most powerful force for change, for it is the creative power of the universe.

THOUGHT FOR TODAY: Today I renew my pledges of love, knowing I'll have the courage to back them up.

Ten dervishes may sleep under one blanket
But one country cannot contain two kings.
                    —Anonymous (Gulistani proverb)

Some of our personal resources seem to stretch infinitely—love has that capacity. In families where love is unconditional and freely given, no one need worry that love for one child is taken away from another. There's always room for one more under the blanket.

Authority is a limited resource. If everyone— parents, children, the dog—asserts authority, then no one really has very much. Families can be dead-locked over the question of authority. Who has power to make decisions for others? Who has a right to share that power?

The exercise of power over others changes with time. In the life cycle of any family, power tends to shrink, from a blanket that covers several people to a number of individual cloaks. When family author-ity has been successfully wielded, family members are able to acquire it for themselves, in the form of self-discipline, self-control. Wise and flexible author-ity combined with unconditional love will keep us warm and well cared for.

THOUGHT FOR TODAY: I will contemplate my resources, and I'll learn to separate those I can tap infinitely from those that are sufficient for me alone.

All opened in the spring. The prairies, like a great fan, opened.

—Meridel Le Sueur

The arrival of spring stirs ancient feelings in us—blossoms, birds, the smell of turned earth—reminding us that no matter how we have hardened our exterior shells, beneath them we are loving, vulnerable children. If we have children of our own, we see them repeat the magnificent journey from birth to personhood, and they remind us of our own childhoods —the joy and the pain. We may wish for them to restrain and harden their spirits, so they won't be hurt as we were.

Yet only by softening and opening ourselves do we stay fully human and receptive to love. When we close ourselves to pain, we also shut out joy. Spring causes pangs because its fragrance evokes birth, and it's painful to be born, to give birth to ourselves anew, afresh, soft and full of hope.

The good things in life come to us when we're ready to receive them. Even the most open heart has its blind spots, but if we are willing to risk love, we can open ourselves ever more fully. We can show our children, by our willingness to give birth to ourselves, that vulnerability is preferable to hardness.

THOUGHT FOR TODAY: Even the tightest shell can soften and open. By opening the splendor of my spirit, I receive richness.

Is it so small a thing
To have enjoy'd the sun,
To have loved light in the spring,
To have loved, to have thought, to have done?
                                        —Matthew Arnold

Ordinary life is full of beauty, pleasure, suffering, and struggle. On our path lie pebbles that are really diamonds, as well as potholes that are deceptively deep. To deal with these ups and downs we train our senses to block out some information—so we don't smell air pollution and we don't hear the noise of traffic—but on our journey we also need to keep ourselves open, to let in what is precious.

To smell the changing seasons in the air, to feel our bodies' rhythms of sleep, hunger, and digestion, is to know our deep connection to all living creatures. We travel singly, yet we are always accompanied, and the same sights, sounds, scents, and needs are felt by our sisters and brothers.

When I feel the miracle of my presence among so many, I feel connected at my spiritual center, and this sense of connectedness gives me the strength to squeeze the juice from life. When we feel our oneness with all life on the planet, then the small events of daily life are enhanced for us.

THOUGHT FOR TODAY: Without spiritual sustenance, a half-full cup appears half empty. To the fulfilled spirit, each day is a blessing.

I dedicate to these imprisoned flowers a little of the pity that goes out to caged animals.

—Colette

Human intervention changes the history of rocks, rivers, oceans, and mountains, as well as animals and plants. We are the species that manipulates the world, now that we've discovered how to do more than survive in it. Like caged animals, "imprisoned flowers" have their life cycles interrupted by humans, though they all rejoin the great cycle of death, decay, and rebirth.

Belatedly, human beings are learning some of the consequences of our larger interventions: by irrigating some deserts and making them flower, we've created others. By producing goods, we've also produced scarcities. The by-products of manufacturing are now poisoning the earth. Decisions to make deadly weapons have created a tyranny in which nuclear weapons themselves hold us hostage to their lethal power.

It would be well for us to begin to tread lightly, viewing the vulnerable world with compassion and concern, and teaching this to our children. We can tell them that all living things, from flowers to fellow humans, are part of the same family, bound by love and responsibility, and the smallest creatures deserve our care. If our beautiful world is to continue to nurture us, we must spread the message of our interconnectedness to all branches of the human family.

THOUGHT FOR TODAY: Today I'll approach everything I do with thoughtful concern. My stewardship extends to all living things, for they too are a part of my family.

*Even though your kids may not be paying attention,
you have to pay attention to them all the way.*
                                        —Bill Cosby

The highest honor we can give one another is our
undivided attention. When young children turn their
attention to something their whole bodies quiver;
their toes curl, even their hair seems to concentrate.
Too often grown-ups let habits and assumptions
fracture our attention, especially hardworking parents who customarily listen with half an ear, watching with one eye. We need to pack so much activity
and caring into our days that we tell ourselves we
simply can't find time for the attention we know our
children deserve. Or else we set aside fifteen minutes
a day, slap the label "Quality time" on it, and
expect our family relationships to deepen.
    Parents can develop a kind of sixth or seventh
sense—a constant hum of awareness so that when a
subtle signal lets us know our undivided attention is
required, we can be there. Children don't perform
on schedule, but parents need to be flexible enough
to give attention when it *is* needed.
    And not just children—friends and family, other
adults, sometimes acquaintances or even strangers
call on us for the gift of our attention. In bestowing
it, in meeting their human need, we're enriched.

THOUGHT FOR TODAY: In attending to others,
as in all things, I need flexibility and balance. I
know what *I* want, in terms of attention, and this is
what I give.

Quarrels would not last long if only one party were in the wrong.

—Duc de La Rochefoucauld

When a quarrel lasts a long time, especially between family members, it's almost always because both sides are getting something from it—something dramatic, like a sense of honor violated or upheld. People don't keep resentments alive without some reward.

For family quarrels to resolve, at least one person has to let go of the reward—self-righteousness or pride or envious resentment. When one part of a system changes, the system changes; this is especially true of the closed system of a quarrel. It takes two to have a tug-of-war.

If I am a party to a long-standing quarrel, I have the power to let my end of it go. I can't control how other people behave; and if others choose to cling to their resentments, I'll regret their choice. But at least I can clean up my part of the act, by owning my wrongs and ceasing to quarrel. A tranquil conscience will be only the beginning of my reward.

THOUGHT FOR TODAY: I may not have the power to bring peace to my whole family, but it's a gift I can give myself.

*Real happiness is cheap enough, yet how dearly we
pay for its counterfeit.*

—Hosea Ballou

Looking at a family that has suffered with alcoholism or other chemical dependency, one sees a para-
dox: the abused substance is costly, and its constant
consumption adds to every family member's unhappiness. Sobriety or getting straight costs nothing,
and no happiness is possible without it. How is it
that well-intentioned people trap themselves in misery?

Substance abuse is an illness, a habit, a way of
life. Its roots are not well understood, but its effects
are. In an addictive family, every member suffers.
Most families suffer financially, but even the rich are
impoverished by the emotional deprivation that goes
with the illness.

To grow up in such a family means adapting to a
damaging, distorted way of life where values are
turned upside down. Often it means living in secrecy
and isolation, ashamed of one's parent(s) and angry
at one's own powerlessness. Help is at hand for all
who suffer from the effects of substance abuse. Many
groups follow a Twelve Steps program based on
Alcoholics Anonymous; they're as close as the yellow pages. Substance abuse interferes with spiritual
growth, and we all deserve to grow unimpeded. The
Twelve Steps speak directly to spiritual malaise, and
they help us find solutions that lead to serenity.

THOUGHT FOR TODAY: Recovery from addic-
tion is priceless and, like the other best things in life,
it's free.

If you are honest you have, in fact, no idea where childhood ends and maturity begins.
—P. L. Travers

"Act your age!" we snap, but mostly we have no idea what—aside from table manners or toilet training—we mean by that. Maturity has something to do, we think, with controlling our impulses; but most of us grow up unevenly, learning to master some of our drives and struggling with others throughout our lives. We know that our childhood remains a part of us; it revisits us in our dreams. When we're with the members of our original nuclear family, no matter how old we are, the family feelings often remain the same. The years vanish; we are as loving or envious, as admiring or impatient, as we ever were.

The seed contains the plant within it. Young children are born with the potential to be everything they'll ever be. Our bodies' cells contain information about our growth, and about possible future directions we'll take. But the line between child and adult can never be firmly drawn. Our hearts, if we're lucky, remain young forever, even when we achieve the longed-for liberation from impulsive desires.

THOUGHT FOR TODAY: The child within me has a thoughtful side, just as the adult I am knows how to play. I'll strive to maintain them in harmony.

Even when a bird is walking, we sense that it has wings.

—Antoine-Marin Lemierre

Some children are frankly exceptional, their special qualities evident almost at birth. Some may have unusual spiritual attunement; some show signs of remarkable intelligence; some have extraordinary physical gifts. All of us are born gifted, though not all our gifts are perceived in our immediate families. We may have to leave the nest before we can spread our wings.

Some of us are gifted with deep understanding of others, and our gift is that we evoke the best qualities in those we meet. Each of us can be attentive to others' special attributes, and our family is the best place to start, because we know its members so well. Bonds between family members can always be strengthened, particularly if we tend to take one another for granted. If we let go of our assumptions about each other, we begin to sense the extraordinary powers, the wings, that are invisible in ordinary day-to-day existence. We'll then reap the rewards of others' special gifts.

THOUGHT FOR TODAY: Of all my gifts, the most precious connect me to those I love.

Sticks in a bundle are unbreakable.
> —Anonymous (Kenyan proverb)

Our culture is individualistic. We extol the power of single human beings to achieve success in any endeavor, and when things go wrong we look for reasons in individual behavior or psychology. This approach has enabled us to create a society in which unprecedented numbers of people believe in realizing their potential, but we are a lonely people. We sorely lack community.

In collective endeavors, we surrender our individual wills for the common good. Most of us get our earliest experience of community in our families; we're asked to give up our pleasure or convenience in return for some undefined value like "togetherness," and sometimes we resent it. If our family community taught us rivalry, sulking, or domination, these can poison our later attempts at collective action.

One stick is easily snapped; a bundle is unbreakable. Labor unions and political parties have used this truth successfully. Collectivity is too valuable for us to let family hangovers spoil it. Even a world of self-actualizing individuals needs to learn communal techniques for tackling the big issues that affect our lives: peace, prosperity, and freedom. Letting go of childish resentment, we know how to work together.

THOUGHT FOR TODAY: I can join with others for collective action without giving up anything I value. Community can be nurturing, not suffocating.

Love is like the measles; we all have to go through it.

—Jerome K. Jerome

One of the characteristics of romantic love is that it doesn't last. We don't know that, however, while we're in its grip. Romantic love most often affects young people, but middle-aged and old people can contract this infection too, especially if there's an emptiness in their emotional lives.

When teenage children are "going through it," glum or hysterical, talking for hours on the phone, short-tempered, distracted, and impatient or else totally absent, parents need all their resources of mature understanding. But when a parent falls in love, children may feel emotionally abandoned. Even quite grown children may be frightened of losing the parent's love and attention; they may resent a new prospective partner and treat him or her badly. Young children don't have the experience that can see them through such a trying time; a single parent who falls in love needs to make extra efforts to be close to small children, to help them understand that love is expansive, not exclusive.

THOUGHT FOR TODAY: Romantic love can, at first, appear to have more to do with selfish needs than shared ones; but real love makes room for other loved ones.

"The rain may fall on us," my mother said, *"but we do not melt."*

—Edith Johnson Mucke

After a spring rainstorm, some children once found a dead baby starling that had been swept out of its nest. Solemnly they buried the scrawny little body, singing all the sad songs they knew and making a grave marker out of an old roof shingle. They picked flowers for Tweety's grave and wept over it. Their parents smiled at these ceremonies, but they didn't make fun of them; they understood that this was a practice run of grief and mourning for the many losses their children would know and, they hoped, survive.

Even in privileged lives there are losses and reverses, and the most valuable lesson children learn in their families is that they can survive grief and loss. Life goes on, even after devastating sorrow like the death of a parent or spouse, but full grieving and mourning are essential to survival. The river of life carries pain as well as satisfactions, and we can't dam up our tears any more than we can bank our joy. We flow with the river, weeping as we need to and ceasing to weep when our pain subsides.

We don't forget. Those children will remember Tweety always, with fondness and a distant ache for all creatures that die young. But loss need not vanquish them; they will grieve for a time, and they will survive.

THOUGHT FOR TODAY: Our deepest grief is always for ourselves. If I am free of fear, I can survive the pain of loss.

*Since I have begun to imagine god as feminine
I have felt birthed into a new way of being.*
                                    —Rose Tillermans

When our bible was translated into English, the
deity was established as a father god, ruling over a
large family of mainly wayward children, with a few
dutiful sons and daughters. Thinking about religion
in this familial way is a bit confining, especially for
those men and women among us who have been
patiently rethinking gender roles in recent years.

The notion of a family where the father is a supreme authority belongs to fiction rather than fact.
In families with two parents, both are likely to share
the tasks of earning money, caring for children, and
maintaining a home. When a family has a single
parent, it's far more likely to be a mother than a
father, perhaps sharing authority with other family
members.

We each invoke the spiritual authority that re-
flects our own personal needs for transcendence,
whether it corresponds to our human family structure or not. However we envision our source of
guidance, serenity, and unconditional love, it is always available.

THOUGHT FOR TODAY: For my spiritual rebirth
I can envision my spiritual authority in whatever
form works best for me.

The first step in liquidating a people is to erase its memory.

　　　　　　　　　　—Milan Kundera

All families are the scenes of battles, defeats and victories, rage and joy. We are who we are because of our histories. We have survived heroic personal achievements, every one of us: we have all learned to control our bodies, to talk, and to walk; we have learned to read; we have gone to school; we have fallen in love, and learned to live independently. Every one of these triumphs was achieved at some cost; some pain has accompanied every stage of our growth.

It's important for us to keep these memories alive, as far as we can—to remember that we have accomplished difficult things, very well. When we feel sad and despairing about our abilities, when we doubt ourselves—and everyone has moments of doubt or despair—we can call up pride in what we've already done. If we remember our pains and our changes, our defeats as well as our triumphs, we will be gentler and more generous with our families, our friends, and ourselves.

THOUGHT FOR TODAY: Let me hold the memory of the blend of joy and pain that makes me who I am.

It is so hard to melt away the influences of an early life, to counteract all the lessons of the first ten years, to tear up the weeds that are early planted.
                              —Lucretia Peabody Hale

Essential lessons are learned in our early years—how to read and write and keep ourselves clean, the immense lessons about the world that fill our infancy and childhood. But we also learn a lot of lessons that aren't useful, and these we must later unlearn.

Just about everybody receives some false legacies from his or her family—resentments, prejudices, snap judgments based on people's color or gender or religion. We need to uproot such weeds, to return our minds to a state of openness. When we were young we were powerless to keep out errors, but now that we have some knowledge of the world and can evaluate information, we can distinguish the good things that were planted in our early years from the not-so-good.

It may feel like disloyalty to purge ourselves of false assumptions, especially if we learned them from our loved ones. But it's not disloyalty, it's good spiritual gardening. Only by clearing away prejudices can we live each moment as it comes, experiencing the world in all its abundance and accepting every day as a special gift.

THOUGHT FOR TODAY: I deserve to harvest my own experience, so I will weed out the false assumptions I may have been given.

If nobody makes the rules then it turns into a game without any rules, and nobody wins that kind of game.

—John MacDonald

Sometimes in families, the unspoken rules are the strongest: "Don't upset your father," or "Make Mommy feel better." No one ever states them, yet everyone understands them. Such unspoken, even unconscious, rules can make us deeply uneasy.

The process of growing up and separating ourselves from our families may depend on our articulating these unspoken rules. This can also stir anxiety, because what's unspoken is a secret, and secrets mustn't be articulated. Secrets have no place in healthy families. They are only powerful if we give them power, and if we want to maintain and transmit old family shames and family angers.

Secrets may bind family members together, but they are an obstacle to growth. To free ourselves from secrets we need to name the game and state the rules in clear language. In this way we gain perspective on our family system, so we can choose freely how to participate in it. Everything we do has some kind of rules. When they're unclear, we strive to understand them. When they're unfair, we try to change them.

THOUGHT FOR TODAY: No one has a fair play in a game with secret rules. I'll do my part to clarify my unspoken rules.

Miss not the discourse of the elders.

—Ecclesiasticus

The world moves so fast, it is easy to convince ourselves that old people just don't understand it. This is true for preteens mastering computer software, young adults working at jobs that didn't exist a few years ago, parents coping with children who grow up too fast and grandparents who seem to live forever. If we are old, we can see through the microcircuitry, condominiums, nuclear missiles, and all the other flashing signs of our postmodern times to the human reality. Greed, bigotry, love, and forgiveness: these characterized the world of our childhood and they still shape current events.

The "discourse of the elders" can help us to understand this: though we wear different clothes and move from place to place in different ways, we are the same human beings who have always loved, fought, longed for peace, and sought the divine presence. Without this discourse it's easy to forget our long heritage and to think we are somehow new.

THOUGHT FOR TODAY: Wisdom, like the day, is always fresh.

The most elusive knowledge of all is self-knowledge.
—Mirra Komarovsky

As we travel our path to self-knowledge, in the context of our families or alone, we discover that the journey lasts a whole lifetime. Knowing oneself is a matter of acceptance as much as understanding. Especially when we are young, we can make endless puzzles out of the twists and turns of consciousness and motivation. But by resolving to accept ourselves as we are and to live fully in each moment, neither regretting the past nor trying to control the future, we'll gain some of that elusive knowledge.

Keeping things in the moment, we can't go far wrong. About yesterday we can do nothing. Tomorrow will present itself regardless. All we really have is today in which to act, to love, to let go, and to know ourselves.

Letting go of the anxious mental track that sends us messages of doubt and complication, we may learn to know ourselves better. Family members may have prerecorded that track; we may have a family tradition of anxiety and futile attempts to control the future or remake the past. But we can choose to change this in our lives. Everyone is imperfect; we all strive to be better. The flawed, but growing, seeking creature that I am is the best possible me.

THOUGHT FOR TODAY: Today I will look at life with eyes that see only the present. That way, nothing of importance can elude me.

*When I was a boy of fourteen, my father was so
ignorant I could hardly stand to have the old man
around. But when I got to be twenty-one, I was
astonished at how much he had learned in seven
years.*

—Mark Twain

Many of us idealize our parents when we're very
young. Then when we get old enough to see that
maybe they're not the smartest, wisest, most truthful
and heroic people in history, as well as the best
cooks, we feel disillusioned. They made mistakes;
they got drunk, got divorced, went bankrupt, burned
the toast. If we can't rely on them for perfection,
whom can we trust?

Accepting imperfection is a difficult part of growing up because even if we're able to accept our
parents', we may expect the impossible of ourselves.
It's well to remind ourselves that perfection is an
idea, an intellectual toy. Even in geometry, nothing
is truly perfect. Beating myself up for my imperfections is as silly as punishing the irregularity of a
circle.

Once we can accept that all qualities are mixed,
we may be surprised at how much wisdom and
goodness our imperfect parents have to share with
us. And—as a corollary—we might know more than
we think we do.

THOUGHT FOR TODAY: If human beings could
be perfect, life might have the qualities of geometry—
neater than it is, but a lot less interesting.

Because each had discovered years before that they were neither white nor male, and that all freedom and triumph was forbidden to them, they had set about creating something else to be. Their meeting was fortunate, for it let them use each other to grow on.

—Toni Morrison

Brothers and sisters can get typecast in families: the quiet one, the noisy one. "You were always so cooperative." Even when we're grown, we may lapse back into our familiar roles and become totally quiet, noisy, or cooperative with our family members. And if we don't behave this way, we feel our families treat us *as if* we did. At an early age, children need relationships outside the family to help them practice different behaviors, try out other ways of being.

The best friends are those we can use to grow on, like a trellis. They help us to spread, and we do the same for them. Bossy kids need to learn to submit; quiet kids need a chance to make noise. Constructive friendships let us try out different roles.

Sometimes we're able to bring the new behavior back to our families, at the risk of teasing or denial. Aside from the personal rewards of such growth, it can be immensely pleasing to hear a parent or sibling say, "You've really changed. You used to be so _____!"

THOUGHT FOR TODAY: Today I'll give special thanks to the people in my life who foster my growth.

The child says nothing but what it heard by the fire.
—George Herbert

Small children are a reliable test for sincerity—like a litmus test. They won't turn blue when confronted with hypocrisy but they'll reveal it nonetheless, by their eager questions and desire to understand. From the mildest social lies to the most severe incongruity between what we say and what we do, children perceive hypocrisy and question it. They have a single standard for behavior; if they feel something, they express it. And they're eager to learn the rules that govern grown-up behavior, since obviously we have different standards from theirs.

The tricky part of growing up is learning to restrain our actions without betraying our feelings. Children depend on their adult caregivers to teach this by example. Honest speech and behavior are simple, and when children are puzzled by adults, it's often because something is being hidden or disguised.

Of course, children soon learn to lie, especially if their families encourage lies or secrets. They bring into the world what they hear by the fire (even if the fire is an incandescent bulb), and parents can be shocked to hear their words return on the boomerang of a child's tongue.

THOUGHT FOR TODAY: My style of expressing myself developed in my family. Have I learned to say what I mean?

Before planting we have to ask permission from the
earth to do it this injury; we have the right to injure
it only for food.

—Rigoberta Menchú

In native American tradition, hunters ask permission
of the animals they kill for food. Native American
Indians believe in living lightly on the earth, taking
only what they need for their lives and respecting
animals, plants, and rocks as partners in the world.
Jewish, Christian, Buddhist, and Muslim traditions
all include prayers that consecrate the simple acts of
daily life: taking food, washing the body, sleep, love,
meditation. All of these traditions regard life as holy
and include blessings for ordinary daily events. As
our lives become complicated by technical systems
and machines, we can lose touch with the elemental
holiness of life.

This holiness is closest to us in our families, where
we see the miracles of growth and change, the cycles
of dying and being born. This rhythm is the same
for us as for all living things.

THOUGHT FOR TODAY: Our web of life covers
the planet. We need to treat every element in it as
necessary, and holy.

If I love you and not a reflection of myself, I must want you to be what you are.

—Judson Jerome

Remember the story of Narcissus? This beautiful young man fell in love with his own reflection in a still pool. Leaning forward to embrace it, he fell in and was drowned.

Less dramatically, we all find ourselves drawn to others who give us back a becoming reflection of ourselves. I'm much more likely to want to get to know you if you signal that you're interested in me, too. But when our aquaintance deepens into friendship, and friendship becomes love, we owe each other much more than a handsome reflection. We owe each other honesty in our responses and the gradual revelation of our most intimate selves.

Between lovers, the love that sustains long-term commitment is based on acceptance. Many of us give this more easily to our friends than to our love partners. Does the daily grind of family responsibility dull our appreciation? Our partners deserve our total acceptance; they deserve our applause. We want them to be who they are. Not provisional acceptance; not grudging acceptance in the hope of change; but full and unconditional welcome.

THOUGHT FOR TODAY: I deserve the highest quality in all my relationships, and I'll make sure I can provide the same loving honesty I need to receive.

We stop loving ourselves when no one loves us.
                                    —Germaine de Staël

Our capacity for love is nourished or stifled by our earliest experiences. Infants who are held tenderly, stroked, and spoken to grow into affectionate, responsive people. As adults, they can express varieties of love, from charitable generosity to warm friendship to passionate sexual love. But infants whose caregivers are emotionally withholding or neglectful grow up with deformities worse than twisted limbs: when they mature, they don't love themselves as fully as they deserve, and they often have trouble loving others. They confuse need or greed with love.

Yet love is available to us all, from the most damaged and needy to the most secure. It may be hard to open our hearts to it. If we've never known unconditional love, we may not know how to love ourselves, which is the first step toward undoing this early damage.

I know a woman—not young and not particularly beautiful—who stands naked in front of her mirror every night and says, "I love you." This is her way of affirming her right to be who she is, her right to be loved for herself alone. We all need love, and many of us need this affirmation. Love is a natural resource, necessary as sunlight. And when we love ourselves well, we become lovable.

THOUGHT FOR TODAY: Today I will begin to untie all the strings I put on my love, for myself and for others.

One of the world's contemporary shortages is patience.

—Howard Simons

If patience were a natural resource, would it be traded on an open market? Would it be subject to government regulation? Would it be renewable? Fortunately, patience costs nothing, though at times it's priceless, and everyone has an inexhaustible supply.

What we call impatience is really our wish to control others. Think of a five-year-old child tying shoelaces: the child isn't impatient, she's frustrated because her fingers won't obey her. We feel impatient in a restaurant, when we can't control the timing of our meal; we fume in traffic, because we don't control the road. We can tap into our infinite store of patience if we'll surrender control. My food will arrive; I'll reach my destination; eventually children learn to tie their shoes.

The desire to control is an aspect of life on this planet that seems, at times, itself out of control. Humans control the fertility of the land, the life cycles of animals, the levels of our rivers and lakes. We talk of controlling the weather. Surely our lives would be more harmonious if we could persuade ourselves to surrender control.

THOUGHT FOR TODAY: Patience is a form of respect for others; I won't try to control people with my wants.

When I have listened to my mistakes, I have grown.
—Hugh Prather

Life holds rich possibilities for everybody; if my life isn't a satisfying one, I'm making choices that are wrong for me. I may feel at the mercy of forces outside my control, especially economic forces, but I can change aspects of my life that will bring me joy and contribute to my spiritual growth. Acceptance isn't resignation; I can accept the reality of my condition and still surrender to change, knowing that I don't see the larger pattern my life fits into, and knowing too that I can't change the family in which I learned my coping behavior.

Over months and years, I experience both failures and successes. At times, my successes look trivial and my failures loom large; can I examine my part in these failures, and learn to change? Unless I'm willing to change, I'm stunting my growth.

I must ask myself whether I'm getting some stingy rewards from refusing to grow—like self-pity or resentment. These are the rewards of failure. When I'm willing to exchange them for the risk of success, then I'm ready for growth. I can listen to my mistakes and learn from them.

THOUGHT FOR TODAY: What do I want from my life? It's within my grasp if I'm willing to change.

Bookkeeping rather than music may be the universal language of Western man.

—Naomi Bliven

Money is a medium of exchange. But to some of us it becomes a thing we worship for itself. Especially in our family relations, this can be a very destructive attitude. Money is neither good nor bad in itself, but it has good and bad uses. Too often parents and children use money to reward or to punish one another; this is a bad use, because money in such cases substitutes for feelings of love, approval, anger, or concern.

To feel our feelings and express them is to make ourselves vulnerable to one another. Sometimes this seems risky, so we express ourselves in terms of accounting: "I need a bigger allowance"; "You'll have to pay the deductible"; "I'm cutting you out of the will."

When we back off from our immediate situation and look at ourselves as part of the intricate web of life on the planet, we can see that most of us are quite rich in material things. In our culture, we tend to acquire possessions as a substitute for nurturing our spirits. But material things can't provide spiritual nourishment. The more we hanker after them, the poorer we become. True wealth comes with indifference to money.

THOUGHT FOR TODAY: I'll resolve to settle my accounts with those I love by remembering that money is a means and not an end; a process and not a goal; a medium and not a message.

The place for endlessness is not in heaven but on earth, and the spiritual abundance that is bound to be brought forth by new generations is not to be feared or merely tolerated. It is welcomed and affirmed.
—Jonathan Kozol

"There's no limit to human stupidity." How often have you said that—or thought it? When a parent, child, or sibling goes back to an abusive relationship for the *n*th time—or Uncle Bill loses a bundle at the track—we can feel that the only really limitless quantity is the measure of human beings' ability to obstruct their own growth.

Yet we know better. It's true that the potential for repeated failure is within us, but our good qualities are infinite, too—our capacity for love; our need for faith; our righteous anger. What we call stupidity in others must evoke our infinite reservoirs of love and tolerance, no matter how often they're called forth.

If my rage feels limitless, that's all right. I don't have to act on my anger, just feel it and let it go. Am I angry because I'm directing other feelings into a channel called rage, because I'd rather feel angry than afraid? My fear is limitless, too; but I can let it go.

All I can do in my family is understand that others have the same capacities for feeling as I do. My task isn't to correct them but to love them. I can work on transforming my infinite spiritual resources into the unconditional acceptance and love I hope to find in others.

THOUGHT FOR TODAY: My strength is in my feelings. I can choose how I express them.

Then give to the world the best you have,
And the best will come back to you.
—Madeline Bridges

No more precious gift can be given to children than a sense of their own worth. In order to merit the best that life can give, we must love ourselves enough to tackle the task before us wholeheartedly. Knowing we are well loved gives us boundless energy, as much as we need for what we have to do. And we'll get back from life, pretty much, what we put in.

Each precious child has unique attributes that will flower abundantly under the warm sun of approval. The approval of loved adults is vital to a child's happiness and growth, though this may be hard for us to remember when one of these infinitely precious beings throws a temper tantrum after we've had a grueling day. We can teach our children to live successfully by loving them for what they are and encouraging them to develop their own special contributions to our shared universe.

THOUGHT FOR TODAY: If I give my best to others, they will learn to treat me in kind.

Age helps one to acquire some of the perspectives necessary to create harmony among the apparent contradictions.

—Roberto Assagioli

I used to think we don't grow any wiser as we grow older, it's just that life presents us with simpler choices. Never again, for example, will I have to do anything as hard as standing on the school playground, waiting to be chosen for softball.

We choose and are chosen, nonetheless, throughout our lives, although our perspective keeps changing. The enormous contradictions of our early years—between freedom and discipline, love and loyalty—resolve themselves in time. As an old person, I'll look back on times in my life when I either did or didn't choose a certain partner, take a certain job, make a certain move. And because I won't particularly care about those things any longer, I'll be able to understand why I made those choices, and what that says about the kind of person I am.

Contradictions can paralyze us, because we believe we want to do opposite things, equally strongly —to take a job promotion *and* to accept an outside offer; to adopt a child *and* to go to graduate school; to protect our privacy *and* to reveal ourselves to our loved ones.

THOUGHT FOR TODAY: There is greater harmony in life than we can perceive at any given moment, and time will disclose it to our inner ear.

Silence is also speech.
>—Anonymous (Fulfulde proverb)

Whole books can be written about family styles of silence. In some families, people punish one another with silence. Children in these families learn that withholding speech is a safe weapon, an acceptable way to show anger, and they learn to hold onto resentments, to sulk and to grudge. This kind of silence needs to be broken, gradually, for it is a tyranny.

Then there are families in which silence is forbidden. Loud, cheerful, perhaps argumentative, these families talk about everything and everyone. Sometimes family members intrude on each other's privacy. Lack of silence can invade my boundaries. I need some quiet—not to sulk or to hide, but to rest.

There are other kinds of silence, with other meanings—peaceful, exhausted, loving. As we strive for clarity in our expressions, we also need to understand what we choose not to say.

THOUGHT FOR TODAY: Let my silence be a tranquil pool, in which I can see the bottom.

*Even as small children we are trained not to listen to
our bodies or trust our sensations.*
                                    —Gay Gaer Luce

Human beings are so flexible, so teachable, we can
be trained to ignore or suppress most of the responses of intelligent animals. We don't sniff one
another when we meet, or run away from cars or
buses, and we actively seek out music that deafens
us and food that doesn't nourish us. We do this in
the interests of civilization, because long ago as a
species we came to value abstract things like language, comfort, safety, and beauty over the hard
natural lives of our hominid ancestors.

Do we give up too much? We're so good at denying our gut responses that sometimes we come to be
quite out of touch with our real feelings. We abuse
substances, stay in exploitative relationships, work
at destructive jobs, at least partly because we've
numbed ourselves to the pain these things cause—
and we raise our children to do as we do.

We also develop diseases—asthma, heart disease,
migraine, ulcers—that express our bodies' anguish
at being ignored. Getting back in touch with our
feelings may mean changing the way we live, the
way we relate to one another. No one can do it for
us; each one of us must strike our own balance
between the truth of the body and the demands of
civilization.

THOUGHT FOR TODAY: If I've learned the wrong
lessons, today is a good time to begin teaching myself some right ones.

It is more important to be aware of the grounds for your own behavior than to understand the motives of another.

—Dag Hammarskjöld

Happy people seldom look for motives. If you're spending time and energy trying to figure out why the important people in your life behave as they do, it's a signal that something's wrong. In alcoholic families, for example, people devote a lot of time to understanding *why* mom or dad acts inappropriately. The important thing isn't *why* someone drinks, or abuses drugs; the important thing is *that* they do. *Why* is a question to ask about our own behavior. Why do I stay in an unpleasant situation? Why do I defeat myself?

We can never fully know other people's motives or intentions. We may speculate about them, as a way of avoiding our own questions. Especially if a spouse, a parent, or a child is treating us badly, manipulating us, we may want to avoid facing the facts. We comfort ourselves by asking *why* they defaulted on that bank loan or missed that appointment. Why these things happened isn't relevant; *that* they happened is.

So if I catch myself playing psychiatrist, murmuring, "Hmmm, I wonder why they did that?" I'll know I'm neglecting myself. I'm not paying attention to my own feelings; I'm not letting myself feel angry, frightened, or sad about what happened. Instead, I'm trying to control the situation with my understanding, forgetting that all I can control is myself.

THOUGHT FOR TODAY: One person is rich and complex enough for me to spend a lifetime understanding—myself.

Be brave enough to accept the help of others.
                                    —Melba Cosgrove

What keeps me from asking for help when I need it?
Usually it's shame. I feel ashamed to admit that I
can't handle everything: kids, job, household, money,
travel, taking out the garbage, going to the dentist.
If I stop to think calmly, I realize that my thinking is
distorted.

Life is hard; we need all the help we can get.
When someone asks for my help, do I feel contemp-
tuous of them? Not at all; usually I feel proud to be
asked. So why can't I give someone else the gift of
asking for their help?

Many of us walk around feeling we should be
Superpeople, totally competent. We probably acquired
this delusion in our families; perhaps in a family
characterized by perfectionism—or by the chaos of
alcoholism or other substance abuse. Children who
grow up in alcoholic families often have a great fear
of being out of control; asking for help is an admis-
sion of helplessness that terrifies them.

Most of us need varying degrees of courage to
surrender and ask for help, especially when we're
troubled or sad. Acknowledging that we can't do
everything ourselves feels like just one more anxiety
to add to our burden. But we were never meant to
struggle alone. As readily as we pray for spiritual
guidance, we can ask for help from appropriate
sources.

THOUGHT FOR TODAY: Today I'll give someone
close to me the gift of asking for help.

The narrowest hinge in my hand puts to scorn all machinery.

—Walt Whitman

Every new mother examines her baby from head to toe, crease by wrinkle, counting fingers and hairs and marveling at the delicate accuracy of the body. Parents care for that marvelous small body constantly for months and years, wiping up, changing, coaxing, scolding, pushing, and pulling, and that early sense of wonder may be forgotten. Bodies of five- and ten- and fifteen-year-olds are no less wonderful, but parents' reactions to them change. Older, bigger bodies can talk and walk and hit, disobey, slam doors, use the telephone, drive cars, get pregnant. They're not examples of the miracle of life as much as they're sources of anger, worry, and anxious pride.

Our attitudes toward our bodies, like our deeply held, unconscious image of ourselves, is largely formed in our families. Sometimes fear and shame crowd out love and wonder. We may learn to think of our bodies as dirty, ugly, or shameful rather than as the exquisite organisms they are. Teaching our children reverence for their bodies is the best way we can help them to value health, vigor, and freedom from drugs and other harmful substances.

THOUGHT FOR TODAY: Every human body is a miracle, and our beauty passes understanding.

They kept more and more trying to get nearer to something that seemed what they called real. Nothing around them seemed very real.
—Josephine Herbst

Some people tell myths or half-truths about their families that contradict other people's memory or experience. "Your father was never drunk a day in his life." "Poor Aunt Sarah never had any children." You may know perfectly well that father was an alcoholic, whose illness deeply affected all family members, and that Aunt Sarah had two children who had to be cared for by someone else, but the family story doesn't include these inconvenient facts, so you're discouraged from talking about them.

When we live with official untruths, our sense of reality becomes thin and slippery. We may even come to doubt our own sanity when our truth is buried or contradicted by someone else's. "Mama never hit any of us kids"; "Nobody in our family ever got divorced." When the circumstances of our lives are lied about by our relations, we need a strong faith in our own identity to keep from feeling at least slightly crazy.

Strong faith is our only shield against this feeling of unreality. Confronting our relatives won't change them; besides, our need is not to change them but to heal ourselves. Belief in our own truth, trust in our own feelings, and connection to our source of spiritual enlightenment—these are the healing tools that will keep us safe and sane.

THOUGHT FOR TODAY: Untruth is catching; I need to vaccinate myself against it by meditation and regular prayer to my own spiritual source.

Criticism, like rain, should be gentle enough to nourish a man's growth without destroying his roots.
—Frank A. Clark

Not all violence draws blood; some kinds of criticism can warp personalities but leave no visible marks. Harsh words, bullying, and ridicule are violent tactics that are totally inappropriate between family members, especially parents and children. Sticks and stones may break our bones, but words can break our spirits. They may be insubstantial as breath, but cruel words can cause lifelong pain.

When we reflect on our motives for criticizing harshly and abusively, we find they always have to do with us, not with the person on the receiving end: "I was feeling lousy"; "I was trying to concentrate"; "*My* father always made fun of *me*." Verbal violence is a form of aggression, and we do it most often when we feel most vulnerable.

All endeavors need encouragement, including constructive criticism. One key to positive criticism is paying attention to others. Even if we have no good words to say, our rapt attention is a gift, precious to our families. Helpful criticism always includes praise for what was done well and recognition of the doer. Words are deeply important. Hard words hurt, and soft words can heal and protect.

THOUGHT FOR TODAY: I'll be careful not to pass on verbal violence, but to transform it into constructive criticism.

Communication is having a clear idea about the other person's joy or pain.

—Mort Katz

We usually have a fairly clear idea of our brothers' and sisters' feelings, because we know how to read their codes or translate their body language. We communicate with one another indirectly.

Communication, of course, is a two-way process. But in many families the emphasis is placed on receiving at the expense of transmitting: children are trained to ignore their own feelings and to take care of others'—those of their immature or neurotic or sick parents. When such children grow up and move away from home, they may get a bad case of the "nobody-understands-me" blues; only their brothers or sisters can crack the code.

We all suffer from this feeling at times. Outsiders have to be told things our family members understand wordlessly. We need to take responsibility for our end of the communication process and become as skillful at sending clear messages as we are at receiving. Then we can communicate with all members of our larger human family.

THOUGHT FOR TODAY: I deserve clear perception of my feelings from the people in my life, and I'm responsible for clear transmission.

Your children are not your children
They are the sons and daughters of
Life's longing for itself.

—Kahlil Gibran

All living things strive for their own fullest expression. Children deeply want to be themselves, the best selves they can be. Learning is a joy, if adults don't turn it into a chore. We all desperately want to be loved, to be good.

There is no mystery about how to help children develop moral goodness: we must model it for them, as vividly and as often as we model toothbrushing or the importance of reading. We must let children see that parents believe it's *important* to be good.

Children are precious beings in our custody, entrusted to our stewardship. They aren't possessions; they belong to themselves. Much trouble in the world would be resolved if we all really believed that we don't own other people. Lovers and spouses entrust themselves to one another's care, not ownership. Children aren't able to choose—they just appear in our lives, needy, demanding, infinitely rewarding. In our care, they bloom.

THOUGHT FOR TODAY: We all need to be loved without domination.

*All our final resolutions are made in a state of mind
that is not going to last.*

—Marcel Proust

We all seek to live in the moment, but if we don't
plan for the future, we won't have one. On the other
hand, if we plan for a future that isn't firmly based
in our present reality, we're not likely to get from
here to there.

The key to successful planning lies in realistic
flexibility. A high school dropout with three children under five who dreams of being a trial lawyer
must make plans that begin with a realistic evalua-
tion of her present situation. What choices are open
to help her reach her goal? What can she do right
now for herself and her family that will further her
chances of going to law school? At least she will
want to make sure she isn't getting in her own
way, and that she gives herself as many constructive
options as possible.

A forty-year-old single person who dreams of having a family needs to look at factors in his life that
are preventing this outcome. Perhaps he no longer
really wants it; perhaps he needs another goal. Or
perhaps it still is the future he wants more than any
other. Any successful plan begins with steps we can
take now, one at a time. Realizing our dreams means
understanding our real choices. Then we can decide.

THOUGHT FOR TODAY: My resolutions should
inspire me, not hem me in. If I've grown out of sync
with my goals, it's time to reevaluate them.

The delights of self-discovery are always available.
                                        —Gail Sheehy

Children's early moments of self-discovery often co-incide with brief separations from their parents. In some families children get plenty of practice: divorced parents may share custody, and children adjust to different households and new step-parents; or extended families may provide long visits with cousins or grandparents. Summer camp can give practice, or staying for a while with a friend's family. But even for young people with lots of experience in different family settings, moving out on your own is a major moment of self-discovery.

It isn't always delightful. You suddenly need to do many things for yourself. How will you get up in the morning without the familiar sounds of running water and banging drawers? No one else will do your laundry or cooking, and no one will rely on you for your familiar chores. You're on your own.

But you are equal to the task of self-discovery, and you'll encounter its delights. Your inner resources of patience, discipline, strength, and creativity are greater than you ever imagined, and your spiritual connection to a higher power guarantees you'll never be alone. As you explore the shape of your own personality, you'll find that the important things are at hand—you have all the love and support you need, for the asking.

THOUGHT FOR TODAY: One of my most delightful discoveries is how capable I am.

The tree whose fruit thou constantly enjoyest,
At the time when thou sufferest its thorn, be patient.
           —Bostan of S'adi

There comes a time when those who were nurtured become the caregivers. Grown children experience the dependency of their parents, who were once strong and giving. This reversal of roles can be difficult and painful, especially when we feel needy ourselves. Every one of us has sore spots, hungers, from our childhood; demands for nurture from others can reawaken them.

This stage of family evolution, when parents need their children's care, asks for great patience and compassion on everybody's part. We need to call regularly on our source of spiritual strength so that we can detach from our immediate situation where need, frustration, and self-pity meet.

To give to another doesn't take away from oneself. In fact, if we can use our spiritual practice to tap the source of all-embracing love, we can make giving an occasion not just for patience and endurance but for joy. All change is an opportunity for growth.

THOUGHT FOR TODAY: Thorns are useful in their season. A thorn is a hazard, but also a necessary protection to the fruit.

*Between the time a gift comes to us and the time we
pass it along, we suffer gratitude.*

—Lewis Hyde

A true gift, according to many systems of belief,
cannot be held or possessed; it must be passed along.
The gratitude we suffer for a gift we can't pass on
may be humiliating; it may keep the recipient stuck
in a passive position that impedes growth. By giving
the gift away, we liberate ourselves.

Suppose parents scrimp and save to give music
lessons to a talented child—the music that child
plays is a gift that passes on the parents' original
gift, and they are richly repaid. Everything parents
give their children resembles this kind of gift, because children will pass along to the world everything they receive. If parents give nurture, humor,
and balance, these will become the child's gifts also.
If the gifts are violence and despair, these too will be
passed along.

Even when "gifts" are destructive, they can be
transformed. If I have been given a violent temper, I
can learn to redirect the violent energy creatively,
through much prayer and meditation. Strong faith
and spiritual surrender can perform this alchemy;
the most lethal gift can be turned to love by human
powers of acceptance and compassion.

THOUGHT FOR TODAY: I cannot choose all my
gifts, but I can decide *how* to pass them on.

It is old age, rather than death, that is to be contrasted with life. Old age is life's parody, whereas death transforms life into a destiny.
—Simone de Beauvoir

Most of us first meet old age in the context of family life. When we're children, relatives are the only old people we know. As we age, we observe the changes of aging in ourselves and in our brothers, sisters, parents. When we grow old, we embody old age for our younger relations. What a sad commentary on the way we live that old age should be not an honored part of life, but "life's parody"!

Most people wish for long life, though the way old people are treated by society makes me wonder why. Old people face discrimination in every area of life; they are disproportionately poor, ill, and disadvantaged. Yet the only faculties that inevitably decline as we age are the physical ones. Old people's mental, emotional, and spiritual resources are equal or superior to younger people's.

We need a new concept of the life cycle, and the place to begin is in our own families. If we honor old people when we are young, viewing them realistically and appreciating the difficulties that a sometimes uncaring society places in their path, then as we age we will grow into people who will work to bring about change, to help society adjust to meet the needs of its growing numbers of older citizens.

THOUGHT FOR TODAY: A good life deserves a good old age.

One can never teach the important things; one can teach maths but not how to love, or how to be charitable and tolerant.

—A. S. Neill

How do we learn to love? From our earliest experience of being loved. We learn generosity from those who are generous with us. And we learn discipline, self-regulation, and the pleasure of work not from being humiliated or punished but from sharing the experience of disciplined adults who enjoy their work.

Children are as quick to imitate as monkeys. Parents don't always realize that children imitate emotional behavior as well as gestures. Parents who are self-centered, resentful, withholding, or fearful pass these traits on to their children as surely as long bones or long eyelashes.

We all learn useful as well as destructive behaviors in our families, because all of us were raised by imperfect people who did the best they could with what they had. Did we learn "the important things"? If not, who can help us to learn them? We have constant support in our lifelong journey toward self-acceptance and serenity if we remember to tap our source of spiritual strength. All our prayers are heard.

THOUGHT FOR TODAY: Learning how to live is my life's work. Today I'll concentrate on gratitude and acceptance.

Let the manners arise from the mind, and let there be no disguise for the genuine emotions of the heart.
—Mary Wollstonecraft

What we call manners are really the practical application of the golden rule: they "arise from the mind" because we always need to think first before we treat others as we'd like them to treat us. The nicest manners are the simplest and least artificial. They allow us to have our genuine feelings, including anger and disappointment, without always acting on them.

While we're teaching our children acceptable behavior, we also have the difficult task of showing them it's all right to have their genuine emotions without masking, suppression, or shame. Living well means having congruence between our heads and our hearts. If we rear our children with love and acceptance, we can help them cope positively with their problems, including their feelings of fear and anger.

Everyone feels angry or fearful at times. It's important to be in touch with these feelings, so we can let them go. If we're ashamed of our feelings, we'll never feel them through; then we won't be able to let them go. They'll crop up inappropriately, a stock response in our behavioral repertoire. Good manners should free us, not constrain us, and they never ask us to lie about our feelings.

THOUGHT FOR TODAY: Starting today, good manners will help me to be more honest in my behavior.

Words that do not match deeds are unimportant.
                              —Ernesto "Ché" Guevara

We all deserve intimate relationships of the highest quality with significant others who keep their promises. Especially between lovers, words may seem weighty as deeds: "I love you" should not be said lightly.

Love performed is more than shared pleasure and tenderness, however. The deeds of love require the daily stamina and courage to support and pay attention to our loved one, to place another's happiness alongside our own. The lover who cannot do these things doesn't deserve an important place in our feelings.

Intimacy means risk—the risk of self-disclosure, of becoming and remaining vulnerable to another person. Without this willingness to risk, the tenderest words lack significance. Especially if we're considering establishing a family with our loved one, we need to be sure we're willing to accept such risks.

Our power to love is part of everything we are, and it calls upon our very deepest responses. Every loving relationship echoes our first blind, dependent love, when we were helpless infants, and we deserve to have our love received with strength and delicacy.

THOUGHT FOR TODAY: My words and deeds must match in order to truly mean the words "I love you."

Appreciation is a wonderful thing; it makes what is excellent in others belong to us as well.

—Voltaire

Appreciate has two linked meanings in our language —it means both to value and to increase in value. When we truly appreciate others, either their actions or their qualities, we do add to their value. First, we give gratitude and pleasure by our praise, and second, we enhance ourselves by welcoming another's grace, intelligence, beauty, or courage.

Generous appreciation makes us more receptive to goodness of all kinds; thus, it actually attracts goodness to us. Like all our practices, appreciation should begin at home, in our families. How delightful it can be to brighten family life with expressions of appreciation, letting those closest to us know they give us joy.

Deep appreciation costs nothing, and it's beyond price. We teach our children the secret of appreciation when we express it to them. The finest tokens of appreciation are the most heartfelt—a song or poem from your child, a piece of work you've done, a hug from your spouse. Other people's gifts enhance our lives, if we open ourselves to them; appreciation is our thanks.

THOUGHT FOR TODAY: My deepest satisfactions come where I'm most appreciated, and I owe it to myself to seek them out.

Facts do not cease to exist because they are ignored.
—Aldous Huxley

The most important facts in our daily lives are our feelings. We don't need to keep most facts in mind—the atomic weight of copper or the principal exports of Brazil—but we do need to pay attention to whether we're feeling angry, fearful, or depressed. If we ignore our feelings, they won't cease to exist; they'll leak into our behavior—especially our family behavior—in sneaky ways.

We've all dealt with people whose shoulders seem to wear an infinite supply of chips. Maybe we've even been such people once in a while. Most likely, this behavior comes from feeling resentful but ignoring the feeling, so resentment seeps out like a toxic fog and poisons all our dealings.

If we're sad or angry, we have a right to be. Just saying "I'm really furious!" can get rid of a lot of anger and can keep us from expressing it inappropriately, to our family members or to strangers.

"Get over it!" we hear from others. But we can never really let a feeling go until we've felt it. Resentment or grief may come back; but we'll have the knowledge that we can let it go.

THOUGHT FOR TODAY: I'll keep my emotional channels as open as I can so my anger and sadness can flow instead of backing up on me.

*Whether women are better than men I cannot say—
but I can say they are certainly no worse.*
—Golda Meir

We'll never know what women and men are "really" like, because boys and girls all grow up in
societies where men's and women's roles have been
constructed for them; prefabricated, we might say,
or ready-to-wear, like uniforms. We can guess at
differences; we can play games like, "If men had
babies, they'd give medals for labor." But in fact
women have babies, and the vital work of caring for
them has never been given a market value. We think
of *work* as paid employment and we devalue tasks
that center around the home and family.

For our social policies to change from antifamily
to profamily, supporting child care, parental leave,
shared jobs, tax restructuring, and investment in
children's health, housing, nutrition, and education,
we need more decision makers—women and men—
who believe in the importance of the family. Perhaps
if women were a majority of our elected representa-
tives and government bureaucrats, they'd make these
decisions faster. But for women to hold these jobs,
we'd need to have the very policies we now lack.

No one has a right to blame either sex, for neither
is better or worse. But all of us have a vested interest
in transforming social policies, for all of us are members of the human family.

THOUGHT FOR TODAY: My role is to be the best
woman or man I can, which means working toward
my common interests with all my sisters and brothers.

You cannot meet the crisis of today tomorrow.
　　　　　　　　　　　　　—Saul Alinsky

Successful parenting includes developing crisis responses. Children need help, information, reassurance, care, at times we do not choose. Most parents have experienced something like the loud question "How do you get a baby?" in a crowded public place. If we respond with embarrassment or anger, then that becomes part of our answer, and the child will always associate human biology with shame or anger.

"What happened to that man's legs?" is another crisis question. Children are worried and fascinated by people in wheelchairs. They're anxious about their own bodies, and they want to know the likelihood of some accident befalling them. If we hesitate to answer, then hesitation becomes part of the answer, and children believe there's some secret we aren't telling.

Parenting involves bigger and more dramatic crises than these, to be sure, but they're examples of questions that can't be put off. If one doesn't respond at the moment, delay becomes part of the answer. The child feels shunted aside or, conversely, may attach greater importance to the question than it merits. Quick as we would be to snatch silver polish or drain cleaner from a two-year-old, we need similar reflexes when our children ask those crisis questions, prompted by their own developing inner lives, and calling on ours.

THOUGHT FOR TODAY: I will pray for the ability to meet today's crises, and for strength to meet tomorrow's.

But the young, young children, O my brothers,
  They are weeping bitterly!
They are weeping in the playtime of the others,
  In the country of the free.
                              —Elizabeth Barrett Browning

Every one of of us knows what it is to be a frightened child, even though we may have come from warm, nurturing families. To be a human infant is to experience cold, hunger, rage, and the terror of abandonment.

Most of us live with this painful knowledge, because we can balance it with the love and support we've received. Some of us dedicate ourselves to the struggle for social justice, vowing to rescue children less fortunate than we were; but for some of us the anguish is too great. We bury our deepest memories and deny our knowledge of suffering.

In some families, spiritual impoverishment produces violence. Violent families have always existed, yet because so many people deny their own connection to suffering there is a conspiracy of silence surrounding families where terror is ordinary—ranging from violent abuse to subtler forms of psychological humiliation that may warp personalities but leave bodies unscarred.

Whether or not we were ever starved or beaten, we can understand the suffering of the abused. Compassion lets us know that most violent adults were abused as children. How can they be healed of their rage and suffering? And how can their children be protected? Those are the only questions that are fruitful.

THOUGHT FOR TODAY: Nothing in life is really alien to me; I have the power to understand, to accept, and to help bring about healing.

Lyricism and tragedy express themselves as best they may in ordinary life; a predestined child will employ new methods to distress her family, that is, to try to be grown up.

—Colette

Most children want to hurry the process of growth, so they can make their own decisions about bedtimes, money, friends, clothes, food, and jobs. So what is distressing to parents about a child's trying to be grown up?

First, it threatens parental authority; second, parents know that a child really isn't equipped to deal with the world on her own, and we fear for her. But it's important for parents not to confuse these two kinds of distress, the threat to authority and the realistic fear. The first comes from our own anxiety that we'll lose control; only the second is really about the child and his or her well-being.

Sometimes parents allow their wishes for control over children to masquerade as healthy caution about their safety. Of course, we must help young people to see that certain acts may have undesirable consequences. By discussion and example, we want to help them distinguish constructive experience from risky experimentation. But let's not kid ourselves about what we're doing.

THOUGHT FOR TODAY: It's difficult to let go of those I love. Yet I know I can't make anyone else's mistakes; my own are quite enough.

When the generous promise,
  they perform.

—Anonymous (Gulistani proverb)

Once I knew a charming man who seemed to be very generous with his time and his possessions. He always volunteered for group tasks, he often offered to lend money, and he hospitably invited people to drop in at his home "any time."

He was less impressive on the follow-through. He seldom showed up when tasks had to be carried out; after grabbing a check, he would have to borrow money to cover it; and if you did visit his home he was often out, or just about to leave. He deeply wanted to be generous, but he just wasn't able to perform generously.

He learned this behavior in his family, where lavish declarations rested on a very flimsy base. His original family was scarred by alcohol abuse and mental illness; his adult caregivers had been well-intentioned people who weren't able to perform according to their good intentions. He learned the importance of appearing generous, but he inspired profound mistrust in others.

Real generosity comes from abundance, not of material wealth but of love. Only those who love themselves can love others effectively. Of all the people who were let down by my friend, he treated himself worst; every time he made a hollow gesture, he suffered. The most important promises are the ones we make to ourselves. If we can't deliver, we shouldn't offer.

THOUGHT FOR TODAY: I will keep my promises so I can be true to myself as well as to others.

The price of hating other human beings is loving oneself less.

—Eldridge Cleaver

Love and hate are simple emotions, and we learn them early. Love starts with the wish to merge our identity with another's, and hate is the opposite, the wish to separate or cut off. Because we are part of one human family, we have a basic love for our fellow creatures. When we learn to hate some of them, our negative feelings clash with this basic love, and the clash consumes energy we could use for better things.

Hatred is energy-intensive. At first it seems to liberate energy, but keeping negative feelings going soon exhausts our emotional reserves. We love everything less—our spouses, children, parents, ourselves, life itself. Hatred is like a vacuum, sucking up the forces that should power our creativity.

If we trace hatred to its root, the anger of an infant whose wishes are denied, we can see how close it is to love. Why should we consume ourselves in negative feelings? We deserve better from our lives than the bitter taste of hatred. Humility and acceptance can help us to let go of hate; if we call on our spiritual guide, we'll be flooded with its love.

THOUGHT FOR TODAY: I deserve my own love and approval. They're more precious than any rewards of hatred.

A miscarriage is only a momentary sadness for others. Then it drifts into forgetfulness as other things crowd in. I knew that. But I resented it. I wanted to have someone to share my sorrow with throughout the very normal stages of grief.
—Linda Little Frederick

No one can measure the size of another's grief. Healing the pain of loss is often slow, when it's thorough, and each one of us must do it for ourselves. We go through similar stages of denial, anger, and acceptance, regardless of whether the loss is a death, a miscarriage, a job, a love affair, or something that others can't appreciate, like the death of an animal companion.

Someone who reacts negatively to other people's grief may have some unresolved grieving of their own to do. "You're just wallowing in it" can be disguised anger that should have been expressed about one's own personal loss.

Families may be a safe place to grieve, or they may be full of these negative barbs, little zingers that come from unexpressed feelings. Someone who has fully grieved a loss doesn't need to put down someone else who's in the middle of the process. Suppressing feeling preserves it, like a fossil leaf caught in a lava flow. Tolerance and compassion are the language of the fulfilled heart.

THOUGHT FOR TODAY: I can offer support for others' grief and respect for their solitude. I know that healing is as individual as pain.

*You've got to do your own growing, no matter how
tall your grandfather was.*
　　　　　　　　　　　—Sir Thomas Overbury

Family can be like a firm structure supporting us, or
it can be like a menacing pile of rock that threatens
to topple and bury us. Some of us have no particular
sense of a long family history. Others may have to
deal with a legacy of guilt or shame.

When our family boasts of its history, the courage
or wealth or brilliance of its members, we may be
tempted to bask in this warmth, though we've done
nothing to earn it. Similarly, in a family that has
suffered from violence, illness, or crime, we may be
tempted to romanticize calamity. We think of ourselves as somehow doomed by virtue of our relatives
or ancestors.

The plain fact is that we have our own decisions to
make, our own path to follow, no matter what
myths our family may recount. You are not guilty of
your uncle's crime, nor can you take credit for your
sister's graduate fellowship. Your family may trace
ancestors back for centuries—but everybody has ancestors, though we may not know their names.

Letting the cloak of ancestry slip off our shoulders, whether it weighs heavily or lightly, frees us to
accomplish our own tasks. Carrying out a family
legacy can separate us from our real feelings; we
need our whole selves to fulfill our personal destiny.

THOUGHT FOR TODAY: I shall think of myself
as an ancestor of great potential, not an heir of my
family's history. The action begins with me.

God comes by daily, hungry, lonesome, homeless, cold.

—Char Madigan

Charity begins at home, we're told. Why is it easier sometimes to feel pity and generosity for those we don't know? Homeless people, starving children; they give us images of great need, with none of the personal baggage our families carry. We all know people like Dickens's Mrs. Jellyby, who devoted her life to "rescuing" African babies while her own children were dirty and neglected.

Our families need the same disinterested love as strangers, though we may not feel able to give ourselves as readily to those who know us intimately. There may be unspoken demands, hidden resentments, from our past. Or we may fear that family members' claims on us will have no limit, and we will be swallowed up by their needs.

It's for us to decide what we can and can't do. Rare people are able to feel both sympathy and detachment for all their fellow creatures, from their own crying infants to check-bouncing sisters-in-law to earthquake sufferers. Most of us aren't so well balanced, but we do what we can. We respond to our family's needs without losing our autonomy, and we can give to others without neglecting our loved ones.

THOUGHT FOR TODAY: I will nurture the sacred in myself so I can respond appropriately to the needs of others.

People generally quarrel because they cannot argue.
—G. K. Chesterton

We seldom get to the bottom of family quarrels even if we *can* argue with our family members. The resentments that cause family squabbles aren't reasonable, and reasoned argument generally won't soothe them. They're old stuff, old jealousies and angers deep in our family structures; they're about punishments and divorces and rivalries that have remained open wounds over the years.

We may call it argument, but it's more likely to be dredged-up memories, attributed motives, and generalizations about the past, present, and future. Statements like "You always . . ." and "You never . . ." have no place in an argument, which should deal strictly with the facts. Family quarrels are almost never about facts; they're about how *we feel* about the facts, and we'd do better to talk about our feelings.

Once we understand that we're not quarreling about our spouse's fifth fishing expedition this month but about abuse and neglect, not about Mother's trip to Europe but about terror of abandonment, then we can choose to cleanse our wounds, feel the feelings, and let them go.

THOUGHT FOR TODAY: Let me learn the right language for healing family quarrels: the honest speech of my heart.

Filling a bookcase is like gathering a social circle.
—May Lamberton Becker

When you were a child, did you ever dream of escaping into the pages of a favorite illustrated book? I can remember gazing at the pictures in a book of Raggedy Ann and Andy stories—one was a forest scene with sinuous creepers and round, improbable flowers that looked good enough to eat—then the Oz books, then fairy tales. My fantasies graduated to stories without pictures; I tried out being Becky Thatcher or one of the March girls. Whenever I needed an escape from frazzled parents, a troublesome younger brother, or a fight at school, I could find one in my books.

Even my schoolchild's library gathered around me friends, adventure, and children whose troubles were as bad as mine, or worse, and who survived them and learned from them. Books can be a vital resource for people of any age—cheap, user friendly, and safe. The growing number of books recorded on audio cassettes makes this expanded world available to even more of us.

Stories of danger and survival, whether fiction, nonfiction, poetry, or drama, have enduring fascination. They also help us to detach from our family difficulties. Few of us have family situations as bleak as Huckleberry Finn's, or *The Color Purple*'s Miss Celie, and they managed to do all right. Books feed the imagination and the spirit; we need them to release our full creative response to life.

THOUGHT FOR TODAY: Books cannot quarrel or betray me, and I'll always find in them something I need.

I don't know about the key to success, but the key to failure is trying to please everybody.
                                        —Bill Cosby

Family gatherings should be times for rejoicing, yet many of us approach them with dread. We feel pulled in contradictory directions, especially if our family, like many, is complicated by divorce, remarriage, or adoption. We don't know where our loyalty lies; because we're loyal to some members, we may feel others disapprove of us.

We care deeply about them, but our parents, brothers, sisters, cousins, and in-laws are just folks, after all, imperfect like us. If they have the power to wound us or to comfort us, it's because we've given them that power. And what we've given, we can take back.

We deserve to behave honestly with our family members, and they deserve honesty from us. It isn't easy to release ourselves from the need to please everybody, the need for approval from every family member. But it's vital if we're going to have cordial adult relationships with them. My own approval should suffice; if I'm in balance, I can enjoy my family without hooking in to them.

THOUGHT FOR TODAY: I can't please everybody, so I might as well please myself.

Wisdom never kicks at the iron walls it can't bring down.

—Olive Schreiner

Acceptance of limits doesn't always mean frustration; it can mean inner change, reconciliation, adjustment of our desires and ambitions to the things we can realistically achieve. We are asked not to give up but to surrender to a larger plan— in which we play a unique part.

Creative response to frustration is an enormously valuable lesson for parents to pass on to their children. One can't do it by preaching; children learn best by example. Children who see their parents meeting life's inevitable setbacks with imagination and the courage to change will have a better model for their own lives than children who see their parents responding with violence or abuse—of people or substances.

Some yelling and screaming may be appropriate, but when the echoes die down, creative imagination comes into play. The lived meaning of wisdom is in our small daily responses. If we can surrender, with humor and courage, the whole family will be stronger.

THOUGHT FOR TODAY: Kicking hurts my feet. Today I'll remember that not all paths end at a wall.

Anger in a house is like a worm in a plant.
                                              —Talmud

Like the worm, anger spoils. If it's held and nourished, anger can poison relations between spouses and between parents and children. The way to restore health in a family is to get rid of the worm—let go of the anger. But anger is an old and powerful feeling. Some of us come to depend on it for energy. How can we get rid of it—and what can we use in its place?

At the root of anger are always deep resentments, deep feelings of threat or injury. The first step in getting rid of them is knowing what they are. These feelings may be deep, but they're not secret; we can find, if we meditate and pray, the origin of the anger that corrodes our family relationships. Is it a cluster—words, actions, a history of pain and resentment? Seldom is there a single cause.

It may be that early resentments have drawn later feelings into the path of anger, so that we come to feel anger instead of fear or sadness. This kind of anger becomes a habit, a way of coping with the world. If we can find the worm that gnaws us, we can change our anger habit.

We may respond with anger because it makes us feel strong, and our worm gnaws at our feelings of self-worth. By strengthening our connection to our spiritual source, we can rid ourselves of poison; the source of love and wisdom lets us know we are uniquely valuable.

THOUGHT FOR TODAY: Perhaps I learned anger from others. I deserve to teach myself a better response.

One comes as a novice to each age of one's life.
—Sébastien-Roch-Nicolas Chamfort

Life's major transitions are rough; no one knows how to be married, or orphaned, or widowed, or adolescent, before the fact. We go through our early changes in a family setting, and we may have the image of others' experience to guide us; but that's like saying we know how to run a mile from watching a race. Until we experience each new stage of life for ourselves, feel it in our brains and hearts, inhabit it with our bodies and spirits, we really don't know it.

Many of us set unrealistic goals for ourselves: winning a place on the swim team by June; making a million before we're thirty. Or else—less obvious, but just as unrealistic—we expect ourselves to know how to behave in a totally new phase of life. *I should know better*, we tell ourselves, and so we compound the anguish of uncertainty by punishing ourselves for being uncertain.

Life is a gift. Even apparent losses are gifts: they can deepen our tenderness and understanding, so that we treat ourselves and others more gently. We're learning throughout our lives, learning to be where we are. Admitting our powerlessness and surrendering our control, we can face each day freshly and authentically.

THOUGHT FOR TODAY: Today is my gift to myself. I'll enjoy the novelty of being exactly where I am.

I have never been hurt by something I didn't say.
                                        —Calvin Coolidge

No one else is hurt by our unsaid words, either. Each of us must judge when to speak what we feel. Ordinarily we balance our needs for clarity and honesty against our sense of what's appropriate. If we think we might spill some inappropriate anger—or anxiety, or affection—we may choose to keep silent.

But this ordinary balance is tilted when we speak to young children. They don't know what's appropriate; for them, everything is new. They take what we say very literally, and they use grown-up talk to piece together an image of the world.

Parents are often surprised at what children hear and remember. For years I thought someone was a fancy cardplayer because I'd heard my father talk about his double-dealing. What's important to adults becomes important to children, and when they hear parents speak with the force of anger, children understand that the words are meant to hurt.

Our children deserve respect when we speak to them. Choosing when to speak and when to keep still is an expression of this respect, as well as of our self-restraint. Hasty speech is often disrespectful, and silence may be preferable.

THOUGHT FOR TODAY: I'll take seriously what I say, because those who hear me will.

*It is more important to know where you are going
than to get there quickly. Do not mistake action for
achievement.*

—Mabel Newcomer

Two sisters live a thousand miles apart. They write
occasional letters and talk often on the phone. Their
lives are quite similar, filled with work, children,
committed relationships, houses, and pets. Yet when
they ask each other "How's your life?" one always
says, "Oh, things are pretty much the same," and
her sister says, "Oh, things are crazy!" and recites a
long list of details: lost data files, chicken pox in
second grade, skiing accident, the cat's kidney stones.

What a difference in perspective! One sister feels
tossed around by her life, pulled in different directions. When she makes a successful presentation at
work, she feels euphoric, but if work goes badly she
plunges into depression. When her kids get chicken
pox, she itches. The other sister swims serenely in
her life, doing the best she can moment by moment.

One's life seems full of excitement, the other's a
tranquil pond. Which is better? No one can say. But
each of us can choose how we live—immersed in
trivia, buffeted by details, or more serenely, taking a
long view and trusting in a power greater than ourselves. When we stop spinning our wheels, we start
to get somewhere.

THOUGHT FOR TODAY: Jumping up and down
may wear me out, but it doesn't make progress on
my journey.

A baby is always born with a loaf of bread under its arm.

—Dorothy Day

A new soul should be entitled to the best the world can offer—peace, music, laughter, love, nourishment physical and spiritual. We feel this deeply for our children, conceived in love and born in hope, taking their places in a world torn by strife and hunger. So many of their entitlements are beyond our power to bestow. How can we give them what they deserve?

Our sense of justice, the clean outrage we feel at injustice, is our spiritual loaf of bread. It's inborn; young children know what's fair. And if they're treated unfairly, they quickly learn what they need to survive. We can give them the entitlement that *is* in our gift: justice in our smallest dealings. Honesty, clarity, and fairness in family relations will teach children moral integrity.

In an often unjust world, let justice begin with each one of us. We who can feed our children, we who are rich in the things of the world, can flourish also in our spirits. Let us give our children justice with their bread, so they will pass on both to their children. Each of us has this power to begin to transform our world.

THOUGHT FOR TODAY: What have I done with my own entitlement? And what stands in my way?

If all the year were playing holidays
To sport would be as tedious as to work.
—William Shakespeare

Life isn't fun for many adults, and we communicate this to our children. We work at jobs we don't really care about, live among people who are slightly un-real to us, and play at tepid amusements. Nothing we do engages our strong feelings; nothing matters deeply enough to tap our passions. We're mildly depressed much of the time, and our pleasures don't refresh us.

The good life is a satisfying life. For our children to learn this, they must have models of satisfaction. Why do we work at boring jobs when there's so much to be done? Or do we just blame our boredom on our jobs, our partners, our families? Tedium we create for ourselves; satisfaction is also within our grasp.

Whatever we do in life, whether it's keeping house or sorting mail, teaching, selling, data processing, lawyering, or carpentry, if we do it with zest we'll be rewarded with satisfaction. When we work hard, we can play creatively, refreshingly.

Some of us may be seriously depressed, and in need of professional help to break through our dull preoccupations to the vibrant pulse of life. We're all in place, in a pattern larger than any of us can appreciate, and its beauty and rightness lets us join in harmony with the universe.

THOUGHT FOR TODAY: If I'm feeling flat, I'll look to the mountains. There are no peaks without valleys.

*My spirit is a clear window, although most of the
time others expect me to be a mirror.*
                                        —Deanna Foster

Why should I smile when someone else is happy, or
fret when someone else is worried, or weep when
someone else is sad? These aren't my feelings. Did
my parents let me know they wanted to see themselves mirrored in my eyes? Subtly, many children
learn to block out their authentic feelings and observations and to show adults only reflections of
themselves.

Children are clear windows, and adults who are
uneasy with feelings may discourage their expression, until the clear windows become silvered over
with pretense and exaggerated concern. And so we
learn to cloud ourselves, and we teach our children.

How can I recover the clarity of my spirit? It's
there, waiting to be revealed. All I need do is trust
myself. This may be hard at first, if I've made myself
into such a successful mirror that I don't even perceive my own feelings. But little by little, as I let go
of other people's expectations, I will own my real
feelings and responses.

THOUGHT FOR TODAY: I have the power to be
authentically myself; the universal source of strength
nourishes me.

We glance with suspicion at those who swim against the tide.

—Eugene McCarthy

The tide of conformity is powerful, especially for young people, who are desperately anxious to learn how to succeed in this puzzling world. Each one of us has interests and needs that don't fit with those of the mass, however, and at some time everyone swims against it. When we stop to think about it, each individual who makes up the mass we call society has some interests and desires that impel him or her against the tide. When we're lucky enough to find others with those interests, we form crosscurrents.

Understanding that many currents can coexist, we don't feel threatened by other crosscurrents. We can encourage young family members who may be feeling forced to swim in directions that are wrong for them to set up their own crosscurrents. We learn the satisfaction of increased intimacy with them as well as the knowledge that we're helping to strengthen self-determination.

Whether the issue is personal appearance or taste, intellectual interests or sexuality, it takes energy to swim across the tide. By extending love and trust, family members can liberate the energy for independence.

THOUGHT FOR TODAY: Those who can help us swim against the tide are sometimes lifesavers.

Children don't have to be raised. They'll grow.
—Buffy Sainte-Marie

As a simple seed contains a flower's splendor, so every child has within it the potential for superb maturity. Children are more complex than flowers, and the path to adulthood is a long and winding one, with some alternate routes, covered bridges, and a few detours. But it's not uphill all the way; everything in their nature seeks its fullest expression.

When adults find themselves struggling with young children around issues like feeding or bedtime, it's always because adults seek to impose a pattern of behavior that's convenient for them rather than for the child. All children want to be fed, rested, and independent, just as all seeds want to be plants. They'll come to these things in their own time.

Older children have more complicated problems than these, but the principle is similar: each child has her or his own internal plan for growth, her own choices, her own potential. When developmental issues become a struggle, it can be because adults are interfering with this plan.

THOUGHT FOR TODAY: Have all my petals unfolded, or was my growth impeded? I'll pray for the patience to become my fullest self.

If death betrays us and we die badly, everyone laments the fact, because we should die as we have lived.

—Octavio Paz

Until this century, most people died at home. When an old person died, the family would gather. After the death, family members washed the body and dressed it for burial. Funeral ceremonies included some sort of wake or gathering when friends would come and condole with the bereaved. Because so many people died young, death was a familiar presence in most families.

Nowadays, most children survive childhood. The dangerous years are young adulthood, especially for men: from the ages of eighteen to twenty-four, the main causes of death are violent ones, car accidents and assaults. Family members mourn these deaths with special bitterness, for they appear preventable.

Mixed with our sorrow is disappointment; we feel young people should have the chance to grow up, to learn about life. And yet young lives complete themselves, however abrupt or violent the ending may seem to us. Nothing in our power can bring them back. If we accept such deaths, our grief will be helped. They belong to the universal pattern, only a part of which we see. Who are we to say whether our loved ones die well or badly?

THOUGHT FOR TODAY: Accepting the inevitable will soften my grief.

All change is not growth, as all movement is not forward.

—Ellen Glasgow

Even people who welcome change may come to dread some of the changes of old age. As bodies seem to lose grace and competence, and minds seem to dull, we long to stave off changes, to stop the inevitable progress of our human flesh in time. Our grown children may be disturbed by these changes in us; they may treat us with impatience or even cruelty. Our contemporaries sicken and die. We feel we are slipping backward, losing much of what we held dear.

Yet what we perceive is not the whole of life. What may appear to be backward movement is really part of a spiral progression. We are participants in a vast dance of birth, life, and death. Our changes were meant for us; as we lose some things, we stand to gain others.

The precious opportunity of old age is the prize sought by all the holy sages of every faith: detachment. Instead of bemoaning our distance from youth, let us rejoice at our opportunities for serenity. The world may be dimmer and more remote to our aging senses, but the jewel of detachment comes ever nearer to our grasp.

THOUGHT FOR TODAY: Our part in the larger story is unfolding as it should. Wherever we are, we're right on schedule.

What does a society owe to its members in trouble, and how is that debt to be paid?

—Peter Marin

Most families have some experience of trouble—illness, injury, violence, crime. A family deals with trouble like a tiny society, offering help to victims and seeking justice. Some families keep secrets; when a member of such a family is in trouble, other family members build a wall of silence around the problem, whether it's cancer, divorce, a drug bust, bankruptcy, or AIDS. The trouble becomes a family secret, protected from outsiders and surrounded by shame.

So much energy goes into building and maintaining these walls of secrecy that people have very little left for pursuing happiness in their own lives. Do you know anyone whose whole life has become a martyrdom to some family secret? There are many people who dedicate themselves to shame and silence. How freeing it would be for such living statues to express their feelings, own their anger and fear, and then let go of these feelings and get on with their lives.

What families owe to their members in trouble is an honest response; support if we can give it, but no guilt or shame. Secrets are always partly dishonest, and dishonesty distorts our perceptions. We owe clarity both to those in trouble and to ourselves.

THOUGHT FOR TODAY: Secrets bind pain. Why should we devote our lives to pain? As far as I can, I'll use my energy to deal with problems, not hide from them.

There is no reason to believe that Isaac Newton was actually thinking of anything much before he was hit on the head by an apple.

—Virginia Graham

Great discoveries, most people believe, come from years of intelligent speculation and tinkering. No one can produce brilliant concepts on demand; the best way to prepare for success is to forget about the outcome and concentrate one's efforts on the process. Well-nourished spirits are the best speculators and tinkerers, and love and acceptance are the best nourishment.

When we lay high expectations on our children or ourselves, are we getting in their way—or our own? It seems that high expectations are a sure recipe for disappointment; love and acceptance guarantee success for any project, whereas expectations thwart it.

We can't predict or control what will happen, once we start to tinker, or how other people will behave—even our children. Once we realize this, we'll be helped to let go of our expectations. And we'll be rewarded many times over. Our true power is the power to surrender our will; to let what will happen, happen.

THOUGHT FOR TODAY: Today I'll practice letting go of what I could never hold.

*All women become like their mothers. That is their
tragedy. No man does. That is his.*
>   —Oscar Wilde

Gender is whatever we decide it will be. Short of
reproductive biology, there is nothing *male* or *female*
about any specific activity. But if adults insist that
male and female are opposites, then young boys
and girls have to do some mental gymnastics to
square that notion with what they see around them.

A girl may see her mother lifting heavy groceries
or heavy furniture or heavy babies, whereas her
father works at a desk. If she is then taught that men
are strong and women are weak, is she going to
disbelieve her eyes? If a boy is discouraged from
cooking or cleaning because these are women's things,
what is he going to think about tenderness and
nurture?

Most of us understand that women and men are
far more alike than different. But our cultural images present the differences as more important than
the similarities, and children have a hard time seeing
past these images. Instead of stereotypes or TV and
billboards and in ads in magazines, children need to
see models of responsible behavior from adults of
both genders, women and men who can be both
strong and tender, cooks and doctors.

THOUGHT FOR TODAY: Growing up is hard
enough on children without learning gender stereotypes they'll have to unlearn later on.

I live with a friend
A friend
   whose life is hopelessly intertwined with mine
with whom I have long since crossed the boundaries
of friendship
a   *friend*   *a comrade*   *a family*   *&*
a lover.

—Debbie Wald

We are seekers, and our journeys take us along winding paths. Some of the other travelers we meet will become companions, friends, lovers, even chosen family. In their company we will find our spirits quickened, our horizons broadened. They will evoke deep feelings, both positive and negative.

We deserve to love and trust others, and we deserve to be loved and trusted by them in turn. No book or map exists to help us on this part of our journey, but we need to listen to our own spirits for guidance. The most damaged among us know how to be healthy and whole, how to nurture ourselves so that we may offer nurture to another.

If we are gentle with ourselves, accepting of our own rhythms, we will soon speak fluently the language of the heart. Once I love myself, I can truly love others.

THOUGHT FOR TODAY: Love and friendship can grace my life; they begin with me, as lover, as friend.

The fundamental defect of fathers is that they want their children to be a credit to them.
                                        —Bertrand Russell

Father and mother alike may suffer from this defect. Unfortunately, it may be hereditary; parents whose own parents depended on them for pride and satisfaction are likely to lay these same expectations on their children. The sad thing about this defect is that it's a symptom of insecurity and dissatisfaction in one's own life. A woman or man who feels fulfilled in work and love won't look to children for credit.

Credit shares a root meaning with *credible*, and it means "belief." "Credit" cards are only as good as the company's belief that cardholders will pay their debts. "You're a credit to us" means "People will believe that we are good people because we produced you."

What a hollow satisfaction! We all know of children whose achievements have been the result of anxious prodding by their parents. The only credit in such accomplishments rests with the child, who often risks personal misery to carry out the parental agenda.

Success in living can't be measured, least of all by someone else's criteria. There's no objective scale for happiness, love, or serenity—just the glow of satisfaction. Let's remember to be humble; our children's best will be different from our own.

THOUGHT FOR TODAY: I am the only person whose actions I'm responsible for. It takes all my energy and moral strength to be a credit to myself.

Of course motherhood is the wild card, however neatly you stack the pack.

—Liz Heron

Parenting is the most important thing most of us will do in our lives, and it's also our effort that will have the farthest reaching effects. How odd and tragic that it's often left to chance! We get no preparation for motherhood or fatherhood, except for the way our own parents behaved—and most of us thought at one time or another they could have used some training.

Whatever our value system, we need to take seriously our ability to have children, and teach them to take theirs seriously, too. Rearing children is our connection to the future; how we act as parents should reflect our faith in the ultimate worth of humanity.

We're all links in a continuous chain, and what we communicate to others will come back to us. Do we want to pass on the contempt for life that's implied by irresponsible parenting, or do we want to strengthen the love and reverence that children deserve?

THOUGHT FOR TODAY: I need to play my cards as wisely as I can, with partners who'll agree with me about the aim of the game.

Wherever people worked, and also wherever they amused themselves, children were mingled with adults. In this way they learnt the art of living from everyday conduct.

—Philippe Ariès

Children still learn from everyday conduct, though adults may not realize that they're always teaching "the art of living." When children see adults using alcohol, drugs, or food to manage their feelings—"I'm so nervous I just have to have a doughnut"—they learn to do the same. If children see adults break off a discussion or an argument and storm out of the house, or turn on the tube, they will learn to do that, too. How can we educate our children to listen, discuss, reason, or persuade?

It's very hard to teach good living if we're not doing as well as we want to. The good life isn't a matter of commodities, as we know, but rather of well-directed energies, satisfying work and relationships, and serenity. How we work and amuse ourselves is really how we live. We may have learned some unproductive lessons from the adults who reared us. Let's take care not to pass them on to our children.

THOUGHT FOR TODAY: If I want my life to change, all I need do is attune to my spiritual source, and I will be answered.

You're right from your side,
I'm right from mine.

—Bob Dylan

Between family members, especially parents and children, most disputes are settled in terms of power, not intrinsic right and wrong. From "I don't want to go to bed" to "Can I have the car tonight?" parent-child conflicts tend to be controlled by whoever owns the bed or the car.

Because parents hold most of the cards in these games, it's only polite for them to acknowledge the rightness of the child's position. Yes, it's understandable that you want to stay up and play/read/watch TV, but you have to go to school in the morning and you won't be as bright as you should be if you don't get a full night's sleep. I understand that you want to use my car tonight, but I have plans that I can't cancel. Next time tell me in advance, and we'll work something out.

Acknowledging the merit of another person's position can only strengthen one's own position. If we truly believe there is rightness on the other side, then humility compels us to find stronger reasons for our own. And if we show our children we can be generous opponents, we earn their respect for the next conflict. Once in a while, we may even be convinced by them.

THOUGHT FOR TODAY: Conflict can be creative. When I'm part of an argument, what have I to learn from it?

Even God cannot change the past.

—Agathon

Remember the movie *Superman*, in which the hero saved the heroine by reversing the earth's rotation, thus rolling back time—in fact, changing the past? It's a favorite fantasy. Many of us savor old shames or injuries, brooding over how we might have behaved. I wish I had a nickel for every time I've said, "If only I hadn't done that."

Regret is purely useless, however, unless we can learn from it. Are mistakes of any use to us? All parents make mistakes, because family life is such a complex process, and it goes on for so long that we can learn from them. No one can change the past, but we can enrich its texture in our memories and perhaps learn new behaviors from thinking about it.

In another moment, reading this page will be part of your past experience. If we can learn to act differently the next time—avoiding mistakes we've made, or learned from our parents—we'll gain some wisdom from the past to use in the future.

THOUGHT FOR TODAY: The past has only the power we give it. Through prayer and meditation, I'll learn to use my power in the present moment, the only time I have.

*Once you discover you are black, then you have to
be black.*

—Charles W. Thomas

To discover one is black, in a white society, means
to discover racism. In Black Africa there's no such
recognition, for a child. To be a Black American
means to struggle constantly against racism. White
Americans believe they can choose whether or not to
join this struggle, but they delude themselves. If
we're not part of the solution, we're part of the
problem.

Once you discover you are Arabic, Asian, Hispanic,
or Jewish, the conclusion may be the same. These
discoveries come early. Black and mixed-race families can see clearly how race stratifies our society
and how racist assumptions poison our communications just as sexist assumptions do. For many of us,
these prejudices feel "natural"; yet they're as much a
matter of our own choice and decision as any other
attitudes. We can remake our attitudes toward race
and gender, if we choose.

We owe it to the future to live so that all our
children can perceive the terrible costs of racism, for
people of all colors. Racial injustice cripples our
society. Until we help to heal ourselves, we cheat
our children of the chance to be fully human.

THOUGHT FOR TODAY: I will do what I can to
honor our multiracial society and to work for a
world in which all colors are honored equally.

We've had bad luck with our kids—they've all grown up.

—Christopher Morley

Every parent at times mourns the disappearance of the younger child—the roly-poly infant vanished inside the serious adolescent; the skinny kid inside the cool young adult. Yet we know from looking within ourselves that those earlier phases survive. The diapered infant is there, with enormous appetites and fears, and the kid who felt picked on, the anxious adolescent, and the young adult desperate to appear cool.

We all have the capacity to feel as infants, to play as children. For some of us, tapping the child within feels dangerous. We're frightened or ashamed; we block out the good memories—the taste of raindrops on the tongue, sliding on the ice, the soft smells of spring —and keep alive only our humiliations and our losses.

There's some pain in every life, and we deny our past if we remember only happiness. But it's equally false to shut out the good times and hold on only to suffering.

Would it be wonderful to have all the past at hand, within easy reach? I think it would be confusing. But it comforts me to know that earlier selves are folded into what I am now, showing me my progress. Years from now, the self that reads these words today will have joined them, for my life is a continuing journey and I change continually to meet it.

THOUGHT FOR TODAY: Growth is never bad luck; I'll demonstrate this to my parents and my children.

With love we can triumph over illness, ignorance,
misery, and even the catastrophes of nature.
                                        —Ernesto Cardenal

Some parents see the birth of a child who is obviously different—one with Down's syndrome or spina bifida, for example—as tragedy. Parents for whom children are a direct mirror of their own success may see such a child as a failure, rather than as a special opportunity for love.

Children aren't investments or possessions; they are beings as unique and precious as we are, entrusted to our care for a few short years. A child with special needs challenges us to realize our human potential fully: our generosity, our creativity, our ability to transcend our own egos. We can't see the whole intricate pattern of the universe, but we can trust in the rightness of our placement within it.

Whatever their shapes or their capacities, our children belong to themselves. They may never share our tastes or our values. All we're promised is that if we love unconditionally, we'll be loved in return.

THOUGHT FOR TODAY: Birth is never a catastrophe; every child is a joy.

It seems to me that it's as easy to teach a human being to say thank you as it is to program a computer to print it out.

—Dorothy Storck

Electronic processes ease many aspects of our lives—scales, calculators, and monitors measure and accompany our actions, whether we're buying food or paying a computerized water bill or riding in a bus or train or plane with microprocessor guidance and dispatch systems. Chips don't get bored or distracted; their efficiency can be safeguarded by other chips.

Just because a thing can be done electronically, however, isn't a good reason for human beings to stop doing it. In *Modern Times,* Charlie Chaplin satirized job efficiency with an eating machine that fed a worker automatically, whether he was hungry or not. If there were computer-operated devices that could feed, bathe, change, and rock our babies, would we want them? Every tired parent has moments when the answer would be "Yes"—but we know human touch is essential for babies' growth.

In family life, we may sometimes feel we get too much human contact. When we grow up and go to work as systems engineers, for example, or programmers, we might jump at the chance to teach computers to take over some human functions. Perhaps some day we will live in a world where human beings and robots have important social interactions, but we're not there yet. People still need other people.

THOUGHT FOR TODAY: I'll strive to be as real as I can, and to say what I mean, not what someone has programmed me to say.

We ask advice, but we mean approbation.
—C. C. Colton

What do we want to hear from our families? From our parents we want cherishing, at any age; from our siblings we want recognition; from our partners, unconditional love; from our children, adoration. And what do we get? Human mixtures.

When we ask for advice, especially, we want to hear that we're right to do as we do. Or we may want to use another's advice as a pretext for arguing and testing our own reasons. We seldom want to be advised, especially if our adviser has different ideas about our problem than we do. Some of us have such strong needs for approval that we can't distinguish criticism from rejection.

Loved ones aren't always the best advisers. They're vulnerable to the same forces that can impair our own reasoning. At times we're well advised to seek counsel from wise heads that don't sit on family shoulders. If we always go for advice to those who agree with us, we're not being honest with ourselves. Like everybody else, we're right some of the time.

THOUGHT FOR TODAY: When I can accept my own imperfections, I can be generous with others. Like me, they're right some of the time.

There are pluses and minuses to each position in the family. Every child who becomes the next oldest loses the primary place of importance to the next person.
—Elizabeth A. Harris

Some students of the family believe that birth order or position in the family shapes our personalities to the point where we are drawn to and marry people with similar family configurations. (One of the authors, the eldest in a family that included two younger sisters, married a man with two younger brothers; the other, elder of two, married an elder of two.)

First children and onlies often have great strength and independence, but they can suffer from insecurities as well. After all, they were their parents' debut performance. Some of our feelings of comfort and uneasiness may stem from our occupying a certain family position and then having it change when a sibling is born.

Parents can attune to the pluses and minuses and try to balance the equation for each child, but in the end birth order is something over which we have no power. We can change our names, our hair color, even our gender—but not our position in our families of origin.

THOUGHT FOR TODAY: Every aspect of life has its pluses and minuses. I'll safeguard my chances for happiness if I devote myself to discovering the pluses.

Happy is the father whose child finds his attempts to amuse it amusing.

—Robert Lynd

Human fathers sometimes feel at a loss with their young children. Yet many social scientists believe that the only way to break down stereotypes of male and female behavior is for fathers to be caregivers for their children to the same extent as mothers. This means holding, rocking, feeding, changing, bathing, talking, scolding, incessantly *being with* babies and small children—not a couple of hours on a Saturday afternoon but an equal share in the absorbing, frustrating task of being a parent.

Fathers who do this are much more apt to amuse their children, because they have developed the kind of closeness that comes from trust. Whether parents live together or not, fathers can share the intimate tasks of child care with mothers, and discover the rewards of nurture: the unfolding of a human spirit.

Parents deserve their children's trust, but like anyone else, they must earn it. Happy is the child whose father is an equal parent.

THOUGHT FOR TODAY: What did I learn about fathering in my family? Do I want my children to learn the same, or can we do better?

No one tests the depth of a river with both feet.
—Anonymous (Ashanti proverb)

Compared with puppies or ducklings, human babies take a long, long time to reach maturity; they need to learn caution from caregivers who will curb their tendencies to fall off some things, bump into other things, and taste everything. When looking after young children, it's often difficult to steer a course between danger and excessive caution, and nobody guesses right all the time.

Most parents err on the side of caution. But some parents are great risk takers who put their children in jeopardy. Such children learn mistrust, and they can also learn a love of risk for its own sake. Adults who survive a hazardous childhood may have difficulty trusting others, and they may also be drawn to self-destructive behavior. They exchange emotional caution for physical recklessness, jumping into unknown depths with both feet, yet unwilling—or unable—to risk sharing intimacy.

For such people and for those who love them, risk and safety must be redefined. But it's helpful to uncover the family bases for these attitudes in order to deal with them fully.

THOUGHT FOR TODAY: What am I willing to risk? What makes me feel safe? I'll use soundings both from myself and from those I love.

Say you are well, and all is well with you
And God will hear your words and make them true.
                                        —James Russell Lowell

In some families, parents give their children a strong
unspoken message: Just tell us the good news, please.
These parents don't feel able to cope with troubles,
and they subtly discourage their children from con-
fiding them. Grown-up children from such families
tend to be ashamed of their negative feelings. They
believe they're not supposed to have any, and if they
feel frightened, sad, or hopeless, they think they've
done something wrong.

   Real optimism is different from feeling you have
to act cheerful all the time. Real well-being comes
from strong faith in a benign destiny. No matter
how depressed or fearful we may be, we still know
that in a larger scheme, all is well. We can't ever see
the big picture, and our small corner of it may look
bleak at times. But if we turn over our feelings of
inadequacy or despair—if we remember what a very
small corner we're seeing—we can truly say all is
well.

THOUGHT FOR TODAY: Once we bring our feelings out into the light of acknowledgment, they will
shrink to manageable size.

Blissful parenting lasts only until the first conflict, but conflict can be considered an opportunity, a chance to learn and grow.

—Jordan Paul

Conflict has a really bad name in our culture. Conflict between people, especially between people who love each other, is essential; it's healthy, and it's basic to peaceful coexistence. Between parents and children, negotiating and resolving conflict is the only way we learn. Whether we're the parent or the child in a conflictual situation, resolving it successfully allows us to practice essential skills.

New parents may be shocked at the strength of a child's opposition. It's sometimes tempting to meet it head on, sharpening conflict and escalating it, often ensuring that the finale will be accompanied by tears. If parents could detach themselves from the situation of a red-faced baby shouting "No," they might perceive that a great deal of self-discovery is packed into that "No!" It's by opposing their parents that babies learn, in a practical sense, who they are.

This lesson is too precious to jeopardize. Part of parenting is helping our children to discover their identities and to build them securely, with opinions, styles, and language of their own.

THOUGHT FOR TODAY: Conflict can be a source of light as well as heat. Fires lit by conflict can be harnessed for creativity; I will not fear their power.

A family needs a family dream or family vision that can be articulated.

—Robert and Susan Bramson

Food, shelter, and clothing are a dream for too many families in our world, an impossible dream. Too many parents must watch their children die of starvation or disease. In families that have solved the basic problems of survival, it's less easy to articulate the vision, but the most successful families have given some time and thought to the question and have come up with a simple answer that dignifies the lives of all family members. Racial and economic justice is one such dream; peace is another; sanctity of individual conscience another.

Most of us live from day to day without giving much conscious thought to our shared vision. We may articulate the dream on special occasions, family reunions, holiday dinners, weddings or funerals. Sheer survival has been a powerful goal for many, and the children and grandchildren of families that have survived wars and persecution may need to refocus their sense of the family dream. Let us give thanks for our good fortune but set our sights beyond comfort and success, to a vision that will nourish us spiritually, even as our bodies are fed.

THOUGHT FOR TODAY: I'll do my best to ensure that my family dream is one worth living for.

There is no duty we so much underestimate as the duty of being happy.
—Robert Louis Stevenson

Chronic self-neglect is a condition that is easily produced in a troubled family. Family members learn to ignore their own feelings, their most basic emotional needs; they learn to put themselves last in any ranking of priorities. Their happiness, they come to believe, will lie in neglecting themselves. This pattern is most often seen in families where one parent is chemically dependent, but immature, self-absorbed parents can replicate it.

Nothing could be further from authentic self-forgetfulness than self-neglect. It is true that happiness begins when we learn to look beyond ourselves, but for this to happen we must first recognize ourselves, know ourselves, accept and love ourselves unconditionally. Only then can we successfully forget ourselves and truly live for others.

When the victim of chronic self-neglect tries to live for others, she or he makes a mess of it. Needs and resentments that aren't acknowledged will crop up in disguised, distorted forms and ruin the best intentions. For effective living, our first duty is to be happy; for happiness, acceptance, care, and nurture of ourselves are basic to a strong spiritual connection.

THOUGHT FOR TODAY: I will be sure that what I share with others is something truly precious: myself.

*An escalating arms race and nuclear proliferation
... steal the present from millions of the world's
children, whose principal daily enemy is relentless
poverty and the hunger and disease it breeds.*
                              —Marian Wright Edelman

An earthquake in Central America, floods in Asia,
drought in Africa, create great suffering for millions
of the world's poor, most of them children. If gov-
ernments really held the welfare of children above
the welfare of other concerns, most of their suffering
could be eased. In fact, if superpowers didn't play
war games with smaller nations as counters, the
world's abundance would ensure a good life for us
all.

What is our responsibility to the children of the
world? If we learn to take account of all the world's
children as though they were our own, we'll understand. Actions we take in this country, as consumers, entrepreneurs, or voters, have direct impact on
the lives of children we have never seen, but whom
we want to love, and to help. Their lives are much
more vulnerable than ours to changes in the envi-
ronment or fluctuations in markets. Yet we're all
members of one human family, and the ripples of
environmental catastrophes or falling markets reach
us all eventually.

THOUGHT FOR TODAY: All connections among
people are family connections—that's the theory of
relative-ity.

Sow an act, and you reap a habit. Sow a habit, and you reap a character. Sow a character, and you reap a destiny.

—Charles Reade

Growing human beings is not like horticulture; no one seems to understand exactly what importance to give to nutrients, growing conditions, or root stock. Clearly wealth doesn't produce the best specimens or poverty the worst. There is plenty of mystery in the process.

Some things seem fairly sure: children need both freedom and restraint, nourishment and discipline. But what's the best mixture? Are vitamins as important as grandparents? Can nursery school make up for an illness? Does a child ever recover fully from the death of a parent? Is divorce better than misery, or worse?

Faced with complicated questions and no sure answers, parents today must do what parents have always done—the best they can. Great spirits can bloom in humble surroundings. Love and trust lay a solid foundation for character development.

As for destiny—destiny is what we call the intersection of character and the world. Since the world is mainly beyond our control, we're forced to rely on our inner spiritual resources. Trust and serenity will accomplish our destiny.

THOUGHT FOR TODAY: All my endeavors are open-ended. For my own sake, I must surrender the outcome.

*Love is like singing. Everybody can do enough to
satisfy themselves, though it may not impress the
neighbors as being very much.*

—Zora Neale Hurston

Until recently, most people had to do most things
for themselves—bake bread, sew clothing, make music. People bartered and exchanged some of the things
they made, and they sold their labor if they needed
to, but when it came to recreation, people had to do
it for themselves.

We're losing the knowledge of how to amuse ourselves. Families don't often make music together, or
cook meals from scratch together, or build things,
or read aloud. Yet these are always possible. Games
or songs or just good conversation may not impress
the neighbors as being very much, but all families
can do enough to satisfy themselves.

Nowadays, when families get together we often
focus on things that come from outside, like sports,
movies, or TV. Sometimes we're afraid of silences;
other times, we're afraid of speech. We may not
trust our families to be self-sufficient, even in providing pleasure.

THOUGHT FOR TODAY: Today I'll concentrate
on what my family and I can do for ourselves.

Marriage is an edifice that must be rebuilt every day.
                                    —André Maurois

The strongest marriages are the ones that survive change. Partnerships that don't change are brittle shells, enclosing emptiness. Real strength in a relationship comes from shared experience, struggle, and compromise—an edifice carefully built from native materials, not a prefab thrown up hastily.

Children who grow up in homes where parents never disagree have an unrealistic picture of life. Adults may appear to agree because they never discuss anything; such parents are less married partners than roommates. Or they may agree because they genuinely don't care; in such a marriage at least one partner has left, in spirit if not in body. Any two people who are committed to each other will bring their own changes, however subtle, into the relationship.

If a marriage isn't a living, growing thing, it's dead or dying. Some partners allow their marriages to crumble out of boredom or depression, because their lives in general don't nourish their spirits, and they've become estranged from their spiritual source. All it takes to rebuild the edifice is a renewal of spiritual nurture. If I will agree to be present in it, my marriage is worth rebuilding every day.

THOUGHT FOR TODAY: Are my relationships unsatisfactory because of my spiritual numbness? I can direct my vitality anywhere I choose.

*It is not so much our friends' help that helps us as
the confidence of their help.*

—Epicurus

It would be marvelous if we could think of our
family members as friends—if we could count on
them as allies. We like to think that in the days
when families were more important social units than
they are today, families were friends. But perhaps
rivalry and mistrust interrupted those bonds much
as they do today.

We know our world didn't invent family disorders—
unhappy marriages, or drunkenness or drug taking, or
cruelty. There have always been people who felt alone
and estranged from their families, people who sought
new bonds in religious groups or in the army when
their family situation left them feeling friendless.
Everyone needs the confidence of help from friends,
and some of us just don't get that from our relations.

I can put together my own group of friends. But I
have so much in common with my family—shared
history, shared jokes, Aunt Mary's carrot cake, Uncle Leonard's love for Mozart—it would be wonderful to have them on my side. So we try to live and let
live, allowing each other our individuality but counting on our special bonds as family members. I can't
share Aunt Mary's taste for cacti or folk dancing, or
Uncle Leonard's fondness for Wagner. But I'm grateful for what we can and do share. I'm grateful, and I
count them as my friends.

THOUGHT FOR TODAY: Am I a good friend to
my relations? Today I'll start building confidence in
our friendship.

Patriotism is the memory of the food we ate as children.

—Lin Yutang

Most Americans have been lucky enough not to be displaced—though many of us have been migrants or immigrants, and most of us have family memories of displacement reaching back several generations. Whether our families were forced here by slavery or war or fled here to escape from oppression, they all came with bits and pieces of their old loyalties, the memory of the food they ate as children.

American culture unites us, but our ancestral identities keep us separate. Sometimes color or language or religion adds another piece to the puzzle of patriotism. When our family has a strong identity that's far from mainstream America, we may feel torn. We want to be ordinary citizens, but we love family members who wear dreadlocks or payis or headbands or saris, who dip snuff or make blood sausage.

Each of us must decide how much of our identity is bound up with our family loyalties. Breaking away from traditions, especially religious ones, can feel like betrayal. We need to clarify within ourselves our real differences in belief. Blind patriotism is never wise; liberty of conscience challenges us to think for ourselves. We may need to change in ways our families can't understand.

THOUGHT FOR TODAY: The food we ate as children may please us in adulthood, or it may not. I have a right to nourishment; I'll learn to feed myself.

We live in a culture that hates children. Children remind us of our need for nurturing. Unfortunately, many of us believe that when we are the most in need, we are the most "bad."

—Connie Abbott

When our children act needy, when they mope and whine and cry "for no reason," we try to change their mood. If the neediness goes on for a long time, we may become exasperated: "I'll give you something to cry about!"

I remember saying this to a miserable four-year-old whose tantrums had spoiled an afternoon. I heard what I was saying; I was proposing to punish a child for the crime of being unhappy.

I don't remember how we got out of that bind, but I know what I'd do now, if I had the chance: I'd take her in my arms and rock her in a rocking chair, telling her I know how it feels to be unhappy. I'd ask if she can think of any special thing that's causing the misery, and what might help her change her mood. And whatever she thought might do it, I'd be willing to try.

When I feel sorry for myself, some music or a hot bath can help me feel cared for, or I'll take myself out for a cup of cappuccino, or buy flowers. In punishing my daughter for her melancholy I was trying to bury my own needy, childish self under a load of anger. I'm grateful that I recognized what was going on before I did any more injury to her spirit or my own.

THOUGHT FOR TODAY: My heart understands naked feelings. Accepting my own neediness, I can accept my children's.

You may be interested to know that the wolves have a different version of Little Red Riding Hood than we do.
— F. Forrester Church

Children see the world differently from adults. It makes sense to a child to scratch an itch, even though parents may know that scratching will spread the irritation. It makes sense to a child to let a whining dog go out, though we may know the creature's in heat. To punish children for such reasonable responses teaches them nothing except that we're bigger and stronger.

A friend once brought my family some large bronze-colored chrysanthemums. I was fascinated when a few petals dropped off. I touched them, and a few more slender petals fell. One by one, I picked off the rest. It took a long time to get to the interesting spongy yellow part that was left after the petals were all gone.

I got scolded for this, and made to feel ashamed, which puzzled me, because I felt my curiosity was perfectly reasonable. Punishing children for such behavior teaches them that it's shameful or dangerous to explore the world. This isn't what we want to teach. They'll learn better from patient explanations of our arbitrary rules about insect bites, and dogs, and flowers. Anger and shame they will remember, but they'll also send these punishing feelings on in their own families. We have the chance to help them feel good about the world.

THOUGHT FOR TODAY: I'll be gentle with children and others whose assumptions are different from mine. Perhaps they have something to teach me.

When saving for old age, be sure to put away a few pleasant thoughts.

—Anonymous

Pleasant thoughts can be elusive in old age. Our friends are dead, dying, or feeble; our own health isn't what it was. The world moves incomprehensibly into new patterns of violence. Old struggles, both in the world and in our hearts, erupt anew. It's easy to feel pessimistic, especially if we're isolated from our families and from the cheering presence of young children.

It's harder to be depressed around babies and children, unless you feel enslaved to them. One of the advantages of old age is having grandchildren or great-nieces and great-nephews, one's own or adopted —children you can enjoy without feeling fully responsible for them. Babies are like the whole world's pleasant thoughts: if you have none of your own, someone else's are almost always available.

Foster grandparent programs can give even isolated old people the company of children, and both will benefit. Old people may be poor and frail, but they have rich stores of information and experience, more valuable even than books. Young adults especially can be grateful for their living family history, the old people whose memory connects them to the past. If blood relations aren't available to you, borrow some.

THOUGHT FOR TODAY: The most valuable asset to keep in old age is an openness to experience, a capacity for joy.

There was nothing like a worthless weed. Nothing was of no use. Everything was loved and cared for.
—Meridel LeSueur

Families are little systems in which every part works to sustain the whole. Sick families may cast their members in undesirable jobs: it's in our families that people learn how to be bullies or victims. Unlearning such roles can be difficult, indeed.

When one part of the system ceases to function, however, the whole system changes. If some family member has learned the role of the "bad kid," or the scapegoat, then she or he also has the power to refuse to play that role. It is hard to change, not least because family systems reward us for keeping the system going. But when we realize that it may be unhealthy for us to play a certain role, we can summon help and guidance from our spiritual center. We have the power to initiate change, by changing the only thing under our control: our own behavior.

Transformation of a sick family system to a healthier one can cause some pain, of course; all growth is painful. But people are blessedly resilient. Believing in our power to change ourselves will help us live each day to the full, discarding old habits. Loving and caring for our own spirits will show us the path to healing.

THOUGHT FOR TODAY: Everything I do becomes part of some greater whole. Am I directing my family toward health?

The modern family satisfies a desire for privacy and also a craving for identity.

　　　　　　　　　　　　　—Philippe Ariès

In privacy our sense of identity develops, our own special sense of self. In family life this sense of our uniqueness sometimes gets lost. The family that nurtures us can also invade our privacy and wound our sense of identity.

We learn to share by being shared with, and our identities are strengthened when we are granted privacy and respect. Parents sometimes fear to leave their children alone, with unprogrammed time; they sometimes fear "secrets," as though privacy were something evil. These fears reflect parents' own fragile or damaged sense of identity, rather than real risks to children.

The supple framework of the family can be a cage—or a launching platform. Respect for one another, faith, and trust can help children build spiritual strength that will sustain them in their future lives. A firm sense of identity and privacy costs nothing, yet it is a priceless gift, within reach of every family member.

THOUGHT FOR TODAY: I will remember that everyone in my family has the same right to privacy as I do.

I realized that if what we call human nature can be changed, then absolutely anything *is possible.*
                                    —Shirley MacLaine

When I look at the miraculous transformations in the lives of my family and friends, and in my own life, I agree that anything is possible. People with grave sicknesses of the spirit, addictive disorders that controlled their lives—alcoholism, drug dependency, eating disorders—have been able to reach recovery. Through surrender, faith, and love, they have been able to remake their lives creatively.

The first step toward positive change is letting go—letting go of the attitudes and beliefs that keep me stuck, and admitting I'm not in control. When I can wipe clean my spiritual slate, I have prepared myself for miraculous change.

All I need to do is open myself, and the miraculous is simple. If I truly let go of my old behaviors and ask for help from my source of spiritual comfort and nourishment, I'm sure to succeed. Life will reward me with growth and change. I can't predict the direction of this change, but I can receive it gratefully, in the knowledge that in its turn, it too will change.

THOUGHT FOR TODAY: "Human nature" describes an infinite range of possibilities. I can choose how I'll live, and I choose miracles.

A little rebellion now and then is a good thing.
                              —Thomas Jefferson

We're all characterized by twin desires, for security and for adventure, for stability and for growth. A good life is one in which we balance these conflicting urges, so that we can have satisfying relationships as well as change in our lives. Devotion to one at the expense of the other unbalances us; either we grow stiff and calloused with familiar routines or we sacrifice human warmth in our quest for change.

It's important to remember that change is often for the better, although it shakes us up and can be distressing, especially if we're a little overbalanced on the security side. Adolescents undergo rapid changes in the decade between twelve and twenty-one; these changes are all necessary, and their outcome is almost always better than anyone could have foreseen. After adolescence the rate of change slows down, but it never ceases altogether. Every few years, "a little rebellion" changes the shape of our lives: a new job, a move, a change of partners.

Every change is both loss and gain. In old age, it may appear that changes are only losses. If welcomed, however, they can be opportunities for spiritual growth. Much wisdom has taught that detachment leads to serenity. If we trust that the outcome of change will be positive, we will gain from it.

THOUGHT FOR TODAY: Peaceful revolutions in my life are a sign of health.

To be emotionally committed to someone is very difficult, but to be alone is impossible.
—Stephen Sondheim

Love inscribes circles within us, and in these circles we include those we love. Our innermost circle embraces ourselves and the spirit that dwells within us; here is our source, the inexhaustible well of love that powers creativity and enhances our lives. Outer circles embrace our family, our friends, our fellows, then all humanity.

Emotional commitment means letting another person into our innermost circle. We can give this person the power to exalt us or wound us; because of this power, commitment feels risky and difficult. If we love unconditionally, as we wish to be loved, then we will take the hooks from our hearts. Removing conditions truly means letting go of consequences. We're thankful for the joys of intimacy, but its failure can't destroy us.

In varying degrees we commit ourselves to all those we love. The key that transforms love from needy and dangerous to self-renewing and creative is detachment, the inner unhooking. When we feel loved enough to love another unconditionally, then we are ready for emotional commitment.

THOUGHT FOR TODAY: When I become skilled at touching my own spiritual source, I will know it is truly impossible to be alone; I am always accompanied.

Few people know how to be old.
                          —Duc de La Rochefoucauld

Until very recently, little was known about old age.
Most people assumed that the old stopped changing:
one arrived in old age, if one was lucky, and stayed
there until one died. Only now, as large numbers of
people live into their eighties and nineties, are we
beginning to realize that old age includes the same
kinds of stages as the rest of life. We know that
middle age isn't a flat plateau stretching from forty
to seventy. Why should old age be a term without
nuance?

In our families we tend to think of age as a
pyramid, with one or two old people at the very top
and lots of babies at the bottom. This shape is
changing; many more of us will live to be very old,
and we're having fewer babies. We're not prepared;
we need to make sure that old people have as high a
quality of life as the young and the middle-aged.

When our social values catch up with our family
realities, perhaps more of us will know how to be
old, because we can be comfortable with old age.
Each of us will discover for ourselves what the late
changes are, the delicate differences between, say,
eighty-five and ninety. Every change of aging isn't
loss; for every weakness or blunting there is a potential gain in wisdom and detachment, if we know
how to find it.

THOUGHT FOR TODAY: Let me live now so as to
prepare myself for a good old age.

Childhood is the kingdom where nobody dies.
— Edna St. Vincent Millay

A death in the family shocks some essential part of our identity. When a parent or sibling dies, or a child, we feel as though we have lost a part of ourselves, and this loss affects us permanently.

For a child, the death of a parent is an irreversible loss that changes the nature of childhood. Healthy children unthinkingly believe their parents are immortal, and when this belief is cruelly overturned, a shadow is cast over the early years.

Those of us who encounter violence or death too early—and extreme poverty is also violence—may grow up hard. This hardness serves us well, protecting us from the terrors of death or abandonment. But when we're grown, we may find it shields us from tenderness as well as threats. Having had to leave childhood's kingdom too soon, we forget its language, the eternal language of loving desire.

Only we ourselves can recover this loss, and only gradually, by opening our spirits to the love that streams through all of creation. We cannot change the past, but we can ease its grip.

THOUGHT FOR TODAY: If I harden myself against grief or disappointment, I prevent joy from nourishing my spirit. Today I'll be open to all my feelings.

Experience is in the finger and head. The heart is inexperienced.

—Henry David Thoreau

Before we ever learned to talk or walk, we were acquainted with deep love, with rage, and with grief. We loved our caregivers passionately, for the warmth of their arms and the nourishment they gave us, and every love in our lives will call up that first deep, helpless, wordless passion.

When the adults in our lives couldn't pick us up, change our diapers, or feed us as soon as we wanted them to, we were filled with a rage as total and as helpless as the love we felt when we were held and fed. Every strong anger in our lives will tap a part of that infant rage.

When we saw, as babies, that someone important could leave us, we knew grief. And all the inevitable losses in our later lives will bring forth echoes of that old grief, that feeling of utter abandonment. Our hearts keep the purity and fervor of those early feelings, though our heads and hands learn to control their expression.

Family members call up these ancient feelings with particular intensity. When a family member dies, we may find ourselves helpless with grief or rage—or love. All we can do to heal ourselves at such a time is understand that our strong feelings cannot harm anyone—not ourselves and not our living loved ones. We can let ourselves feel them fully, and then we can let them go.

THOUGHT FOR TODAY: My head knows; my hands do; but my heart feels. I can control my head and hands. I treasure my heart.

When I play with my cat, who knows but that she regards me as a plaything even more than I do her.
　　　　　　　　　　　—Michel de Montaigne

Perspective is all-powerful. Take the case of a grown son who calls his mother every week and silently groans and rolls his eyes at her endless list of complaints. "I love him to call," she thinks, "but I wish he didn't expect me to complain all the time." Both are doing what they think the other expects. Shifting perspective might realign their relationship.

Suppose the son called at a different time and asked his mother's advice about something. Or asked her something about his childhood. She might talk about feelings, for a change, instead of arthritis.

Of course, this is risky. Perhaps this mother and son depend on a fixed relationship; maybe they need to be frustrated and annoyed with one another so that they can feel patient and generous. "If I can put up with her complaints," he thinks, "I'm not such a bad guy." A conversation that deals with their real feelings would upset this equilibrium.

But the rewards of a real relationship—even if it turned up some resentments—might compensate them for the loss of the unreal one. A shift in perspective might begin a realignment of family feelings. We can't resolve problems until we acknowledge them, and the false facade may be a way of protecting the problem and preventing its resolution.

THOUGHT FOR TODAY: I can use my family relationships to help me grow. A broader perspective, and possible change, is a vital part of my spiritual program.

Don't love anything that can't love you back.
               —Noreen Briggs

Single people who keep cats and dogs live longer than single people who don't. One person and a cat can be a family unit, sharing love and shelter and protecting each other from emotional isolation. Caring for a fellow creature keeps us in touch with our own basic needs.

Someone whose spirit has hardened from neglect or despair may have distorted patterns of expressing love. Such a person comes to value things more than people, order more than warmth or creativity. Most of the great makers of things, scientists and engineers as well as artists, loved human beings as passionately as they loved their work.

Love for things doesn't nourish us. Our spirits can't be refreshed by them, however precious or beautiful they may be. If we have no creatures to love us back, we need a very close connection to our spiritual source of love and nurture. We are infinitely loved, but we must learn to avail ourselves of this richness, by quieting and surrendering our spirits so that the current can flow through us.

Spiritual practice through meditation and prayer can strengthen our connection. Here is love that comes back, here is care that sustains us. In isolation or sorrow or in the midst of family clamor, here is the consoling love, the source of peace.

THOUGHT FOR TODAY: I know I'm constantly loved; I have only to open myself to return the blessing.

What really matters is what happens in us, not to us.
—James W. Kennedy

Suffering seldom ennobles us. Yet there are people who survive dreadful experiences and transcend them. Something happens within them, and they learn not to employ their tormentors' tools but to soften and use compassion and surrender.

This transformation occurs more easily when there's at least one sympathetic guide, one loving person to redeem experience and sweeten its bitter taste. Can I do this for myself? Can I transform the suffering that has shaped me? My first step is to let go, to surrender any obsessive concerns that stand in the way of my spiritual growth: money, success, jealousy, infatuation, shyness, anger. Then I must learn to meditate, to reach the deep pool of stillness within that connects me to the source of all love and serenity.

When I have mastered some spiritual practice—and the letting go and reaching within take time and patience—I'll be able to pray for what I want, and my prayers will be answered. For I'll want only what's meant for me, and in the slow unfolding of my spiritual wealth my needs will be supplied.

THOUGHT FOR TODAY: No matter what my past has been, love and faith can help guide me to the future I deserve.

No matter how much you love your children, there are times you slip. There are moments you stutter, can't give, lose your temper, or simply lose face with the world, and you can't explain this to a child.
—Louise Erdrich

We want to be perfect parents, to give our children not just love but absolutely the best of everything, and when we do less than our best, we can feel bitterly disappointed. We tell ourselves we don't mind so much for our own sakes; it's for them that we regret our lapses of patience, stamina, or grace.

If parents truly try their best, children know and have compassion for our human flaws. If we've treated them with openness and respect, our mistakes don't have to be explained. There are no absolutes in life, and no perfect human beings. There are firm steps and slips, acceptance and forgiveness, joy and sorrow.

Most often parents feel worse about their lapses than their children do. Children need the models of adults who can accept themselves, who aren't daunted by slipups or setbacks but who can let go of the past and face the future with zest. If we put our trust in a power greater than ourselves, we need never be disappointed.

THOUGHT FOR TODAY: Imperfections prove I'm human. My slips and stutters add luster to my progress.

Culture is roughly anything we do and the monkeys don't.

—Lord Raglan

Most of our contemporary family forms—single parent households, adoption, fostering, blended and stepfamilies—are variations on what the monkeys do, or at least the great apes. They seem new, because we've all learned the image of a sort of four-square family as the norm, but these family variations have always existed; our laws and our cultural images are just catching up with them.

The biggest difference between us and the monkeys is that we can use language to reveal or conceal our feelings, to simplify our lives or to complicate them. Our language for family relations leaves many things unsaid—like the feelings of grandparents, when divorce and remarriage blend their grandchildren into a family in another part of the country. Or the bond between former in-laws when the marriage that linked them ends. Or the ambivalence of birth parents when adopted children seek them out.

The process of acquiring or losing stepchildren, stepparents, and other relations often happens faster than our feelings can adjust. There's nothing wrong with us; we have a right to our feelings, whether we have words for them or not. Prayer and patience will help us feel congruent. Our family is part of an intricate mosaic, and if we trust in the rightness of our ultimate destiny, all will be well.

THOUGHT FOR TODAY: I'm part of culture and it's part of me, and both of us are constantly growing and changing.

*I never think about my limitations, and they never make
me sad. Perhaps there is just a touch of yearning at
times; but it is vague, like a breeze among flowers.*
                                          —Helen Keller

The woman who wrote these lines had extraordinary limitations: she was both deaf and blind; but
she also had extraordinary advantages—wealth, talent, and a developed capacity for giving and receiving love. Her spiritual journey, as recounted in her
book, *My Life,* is an enthralling mixture of struggle,
strength, and the transforming power of love. Helen
Keller became one of the outstanding women of her
time, a brilliant activist for peace and justice as well
as the benefactor of many with the same apparent
handicaps as herself.

Helen Keller's story invites us to think differently
about our own advantages and limitations. Especially when our lives are touched by special circumstances—differences in physical ability—we too may
feel a touch of yearning, a vague breeze of longing
for a different way of being. For some, this yearning
is deep and bitter. We're unreconciled to our lives,
and a sense of deprivation blots out any gratitude
for the advantages we enjoy.

Our choice to hang onto bitterness means we're
probably closing the door to happiness. However we
perceive our personal limitations—and everyone has
limitations—it's in our power to choose differently.

THOUGHT FOR TODAY: I can't feel grateful and
bitter at the same time. I'll choose gratitude, and it
will help me find the happiness I deserve.

*Man is an animal that makes bargains; no other
animal does this—no dog exchanges bones with
another.*

—Adam Smith

Exchange of gifts is built into family structure. In
some cultures the bride is seen as a gift, and the
groom's family pays a price in money, land, or jewels for the bride. In other cultures the groom is the
gift and the bride's family give her a dowry to
exchange for him.

Some husbands give their wives gifts for bearing
children. Grandparents, aunts, and uncles bring gifts
to a child's naming ceremony, and in return the
parents give a feast. Gifts are exchanged on birth-
days and anniversaries; gifts mark a marriage; they
solemnize these events.

The earliest gifts were not kept. In some tribal
societies still, a gift must be passed on. To halt it in
its path is to court bad luck. This meaning of gift
exchange survives in us as the impulse to reciprocity,
to give back equal value for the things we receive.
Yet we are happiest when we give in total freedom,
with no expectation of return. When we nourish our
spirits with giving, we're always amply repaid.

THOUGHT FOR TODAY: I'll take care that my
gifts are freely given, especially to those I love.

If you're not feeling good about *you, what you're wearing outside doesn't mean a thing.*
                                                    —Leontyne Price

Feeling good about yourself usually includes wearing clothes you feel good about—comfortable, becoming, *suitable* clothes. Expensive garments can't make up for poor self-image; they just distract our attention from it, so we fuss about clothes rather than facing what we don't like about ourselves.

When I see young children who look like models, overdressed and fussy, I know their parents must be terribly anxious about a lot of things they can't control. So they spend time and money on the superficial, temporary things they *can* control—like their children's appearance.

At one time or another most children will choose some look that upsets their parents—hair, dress, makeup, jewelry, something that parents feel is wildly inappropriate. It's too grown-up, too sloppy, too cheap, or too expensive; it's punk, it's freaky, it's pretentious or plain ugly. But young people need to experiment with their appearances. Mistakes are good; if you make them, you can learn from them. People who never make mistakes don't take enough chances.

THOUGHT FOR TODAY: Serenity makes me beautiful, no matter what I wear.

A child deserves the maximum respect.

—Juvenal

The decision to have a child is a momentous one; it should involve serious self-examination on the part of the parents, as well as faith in the future. When we make a child, we're extending a part of ourselves into the unknown. The time to develop respect for the child is well before it's born.

Do I have the emotional preparation for parenthood? No one is a perfect parent, but I want to be good enough. Do I know myself well enough to understand my flaws, and do I know where I'll need help in caring for a child—from my partner, from professionals, from books, and from my spiritual source?

Peanut butter and oranges can nourish a child's body, but the spirit needs nourishment, too. Do I have spiritual abundance and self-respect enough to share with a new life? It's more important than mortgages or trust funds; property can't repair defects in self-respect.

THOUGHT FOR TODAY: Self-respect is basic to my success in everything I do. I'll make sure, if I want a child, that this is congruent with it.

Nothing in life is to be feared. It is only to be understood.

—Marie Curie

Fear is a primitive response that evolved over thousands of years to help our species cope with danger. Chemicals flood our bloodstream; our heart beats faster; our breath comes quicker. We have extra strength and energy to either fight an enemy or flee. It isn't appropriate for most of what we have to face in our lives.

What's the fantasy behind fear? I'm fearful when I confront people I've invested with authority—when I stick up for myself, and ask for what I want. Gradually I've come to understand that this fear masks another feeling. I may be "afraid" to ask for what I want because of a deep, hidden sense of worthlessness that's too painful to feel directly. By masking my despair with fear, at least I get some energy to fight.

When I understand what's going on, I won't need to think of life in terms of a battle. Despite those ancient messages, I have the right to ask for what I want. I deserve fair treatment from others, and I deserve to live without fear.

The physical dangers we face as a species aren't hostile tribes or wild animals—they're acid rain, poisoned water, hazardous workplaces, drunk drivers. Understanding is a more effective way to meet such dangers than either fight or flight. We need to understand the measures we can take *as a species* to help us toward reconciliation and serenity.

THOUGHT FOR TODAY: My understanding protects my vulnerable self better than fear. I can choose how I respond to what I perceive as danger.

You can't measure time in days the way you can money in dollars, because every day is different.
                                        —Jorge Luis Borges

Clocks and calendars give us standard measurements: twenty-four hours a day, thirty days a month: a square of paper, regardless of whether the day was sunny and full of love and music or dull or filled with pain. The world often measures all people by the same standards, even though we're all different, each of us unique. Children take standardized examinations in school, and their growth is measured by percentage points against the growth of other children.

In our families, we don't relate to one another in terms of measurements, even though children may compete to see who's tallest on the kitchen doorframe. Yet sometimes we allow these measures to influence the way we think or feel about each other. Our children may pick up on this; they may begin to think that grades and scores are important in and for themselves.

Measuring and standardizing tempt us because they seem to make the world manageable, packing and wrapping it for easy handling. But this temptation falsifies the richness and variety of individuals. We're all different, all excellent in distinct areas. Our excellence is needed in ways that can't be measured, and we'll be happier once we stop trying.

THOUGHT FOR TODAY: I want to be known and valued for my unique qualities, and I owe others respect for their rich individuality.

It is in changing that things find repose.

—Heraclitus

Ours is a world of shifting, glittering transformations. The cells in our bodies change completely every few years. Our towns and cities change, our language changes; the clothes we wear, our music, all change, not just from generation to generation but from one decade to the next, sometimes from year to year. Although we believe the pace of change has speeded up, it's always been this way. Plato wrote of the disturbing sensual music of the young in the fourth century B.C. Louisa May Alcott deplored the frivolous new fashions of the 1870s.

Our family patterns change. As more people live longer, more of us have—and are—healthy grandparents, great-grandparents, great-great-grandparents. And as we live longer and healthier lives, more of us get married and divorced more often; women have children both earlier and later. More of us are only children; more of us are single parents. We may choose partners of the same gender, or our children may. Family life comes in a dazzling array of patterns.

Just as one may have an unquiet spirit in a strictly regulated life, in the midst of this variety it's possible to find repose. Serenity comes from inner peace, from the resolution of conflicts, from knowing that we're living in the way that's best for us. Openness to change balances us.

THOUGHT FOR TODAY: Inner peace gives constancy to the change that flows through my life.

It is not a bad thing that children should occasionally, and politely, put parents in their place.

—Colette

We learn in our families all the gestures, the tones of voice, that we'll ever use. We learn to cooperate and command, to admit and deny, to express love and anger. Even very young children play around with these emotional gestures. Two-year-olds who discover how to say "No!" will experiment with their parents: "No, *you* eat your cereal!" "*You* go to bed!"

In later years, parents and children may find their roles reversed in earnest, not in play. At the end of life, parents may need their children to care for them, as they were cared for, in intimate bodily ways. Failing eyesight or hearing, physical frailty, or the effects of catastrophic illness can leave parents as dependent as babies.

When the roles are totally reversed, children may find they resent their parents' demands. They feel called upon for nurture they didn't get, and they may become deeply angry at what they consider the unfairness of life.

Caring for aged parents is a burden only so long as we think of it that way. We can choose to change our way of thinking about care: to think of it as a gift, a gift we freely choose to give. Then our generosity will enrich us, not deplete us.

THOUGHT FOR TODAY: Giving of myself joyously can nourish my spirit, so I receive more than I give.

Our moment of history is unique. We—those of us with a tittle of sense—live with one purpose of all others: the preservation of the planet Earth.
                                        —Howard Fast

Every moment is unique. Throughout history, people have believed in their generation's unique destiny, and many times the call has sounded to save the world. Our present technological capacity to split and fuse the elements of matter and to release the energy that holds them together appears to be the most dangerous trick we've played yet. And as we struggle to learn to live together, we learn also that every choice we make has consequences that may dictate later choices. Global thinking is complex and difficult, and we're increasingly called on to do it.

But while we're considering the fate of the earth, which no one of us can control, we must hold on to what we know we can do. We want to preserve whales and butterflies and all living creatures, but our first responsibility is to ourselves; next, to our human family. Our single purpose has a dual focus: the planet earth and the human family. Neither can exist without the other, and all our goals must address both together.

THOUGHT FOR TODAY: I'm called on to play my part as well as I can, nothing more—but nothing less.

Freedom is not worth having if it does not connote the freedom to err.

—Mohandas K. Gandhi

How do we respond when someone in our family makes a mistake? Suppose it's an old person. Do we say, "Oh, Aunt Anne has lost it, better put her in a home," or do we help her find a way to arrange her life so she won't lock herself in the bathroom or set her stove on fire?

Suppose it's our partner. Do we go into a tizzy over an unbalanced checkbook, or can we let it go? Or our children: does the first scraped fender mean they can't ever drive our car again, or do we work out a payment plan within their allowance and tell them how glad we are they weren't hurt?

Patterns of dangerous accidents are another matter. If Aunt Anne really can't look after herself, she probably needs closer supervision. If our partner is chronically in debt and can't ever seem to reconcile income and outgo, some financial counseling is definitely in order. And we make sure our children get the best driver training available.

Other people deserve our trust, especially our loved ones. The leeway we grant to others indicates our level of trust in them, in ourselves, and in the world. Do we have such high expectations of ourselves that we don't permit errors? This is inhuman. We deserve better, and so do those we love.

THOUGHT FOR TODAY: We must accept errors, our own and other people's, if we are to learn from them.

Humility is the fruit of inner security and wise maturity. To be humble is to revel in the accomplishments or potentials of others.

—Cornel West

I can't be honestly delighted by anyone's accomplishment—even my own children's—if I have a lingering sense of personal inadequacy. Either I'll feel unjustifiably proud, as though their achievement were a credit to me instead of them, or I'll vaguely resent it, as though we were competitors.

Many of us have feelings of insecurity or inadequacy that flicker across the screen of our consciousness. These feelings are intermittent; they don't unbalance us or interfere with our appreciation of others. But some of us feel so damaged by our insecurity that we cling to our egos, as though we were afraid they might be taken away from us. When we're so personally insecure, it's difficult to set ourselves aside, to achieve the true humility that lets us enjoy our children's accomplishments.

Such a wounded spirit keeps us stuck in a place of conflict and competition, preventing us from balancing our needs and desires. With the help that flows unceasingly from our personal source of spiritual refreshment, we can heal the wounds of insecurity. We're essential members of the human family, loved and accepted despite our fears. When we nurture a healthy self-love, it will bear the precious fruit of humility.

THOUGHT FOR TODAY: I am worthy of the strength to grow and to love, and prayer will help me toward inner security.

*You grow up the day you have your first real
laugh—at yourself.*

—Ethel Barrymore

When I was about six I was taken to visit some
cousins who lived in another state. Their parents,
my aunt and uncle, laughed a good deal—at them
and at me. They laughed at my accent, my clothes,
and my ignorance of their ways, and they poked fun
at my cousins, who teased back. Teasing and ridicule were their family language.

I hated it. They asked, "Where's your sense of
humor?" and I didn't know how to answer. I think I
do now: Teasing is a civilized form of cruelty. In
families that tease and make fun of one another, anger
and other negative feelings are disguised—hidden—in
jokes. Children who grow up with this habit learn that
it's okay to meet new things and new people with
mockery rather than understanding. And in defending
themselves against ridicule, they become callous.

These people don't really laugh at themselves. To
find yourself sufficiently ridiculous to merit a good
laugh, you have to have a strong sense of your own
worth, and people who grow up defending themselves against teasing have a rather fragile sense of
worth, under the callus. The need to laugh at others
is a sign that you are frightened and insecure, not
acknowledging your own anger or vulnerability. The
ability to enjoy a joke at your own expense is a real
sign of self-confident maturity.

THOUGHT FOR TODAY: Laughter should be a
bridge connecting me with others, not a wall that
shuts me out.

May you like all the days of your life.
                              —Jonathan Swift

A friend told me she realized after psychotherapy that she'd been depressed most of her life. Her childhood was unusually full of pain and loss, and she felt she had shut herself down. "It was as though I'd been living in black and white," she said, "and then the color got switched on."

She began to like her life. Her young daughter contributed to her newfound enjoyment, as did her career. She found a stable, satisfying primary relationship. Her life wasn't perfect; no one's is. But it was likable.

No one can love everything in life. We all encounter our share of sadness, horror, and boredom. But with or without therapy, we can keep the color switched on and the energy flowing. My friend grew up fatherless, but her childhood pain doesn't have to be lifelong. She has it in her power to take what comes, to appreciate its vividness, and to like all her days. Her daughter will have a different family and—she hopes—a full spectrum.

THOUGHT FOR TODAY: I wish this for myself, my friends, and my family: May we like all our days.

When the elephants fight,
It is the grass that suffers.

        —Anonymous (Swahili proverb)

When adults are violent, they hurt their children even more than they hurt one another. They pass along an image of grown-ups who believe in solving disputes by hitting others or throwing things, which is pretty poor preparation for life.

Hostile adults who don't fight but who sulk or freeze aren't much better role models. They too are a scary living demonstration that angry feelings are so powerful they can control one's whole life. Children desperately need to know there are ways of controlling anger, for if anger isn't transformed but rather driven inward, it will return in some destructive form.

Talk—respectful, responsible talk—is the greatest transforming agent known. Talking about anger lets me have my feeling without acting on it. I can express my resentment, and I can hear my partner's, without anyone's getting hit, without any broken crockery or glass.

Some angers can't be resolved; some partnerships dissolve when they yield more rage than pleasure. But our greatest good fortune is that we can choose what we do with our feelings, and our children learn emotional freedom with emotional responsibility when they observe our good choices.

THOUGHT FOR TODAY: My anger can be a source of strength or a source of destruction; I choose how I use it.

I am not young enough to know everything.
                              —James M. Barrie

Some people never seem to lose the rummaging curiosity of a two-year-old child. When faced with something new, they try to understand it as eagerly as a child pesters its parent—how do you make cheese? Where does a flower bud go? Why do you wear clothes?

Some of us reach a point where we feel we do know everything—we know the chemical action of rennet on milk and the life cycle of plants, and why our hominid forebears first draped their bodies in animal skins. At nineteen or twenty we may feel that life has lost its mystery. We understand the world *much* better than our parents did, and we believe that everything important has already been discovered or invented.

In middle life we may come to another realization: the things we know are merely details. The big, important things in life remain as mysterious as ever: the power of love, the miracle of faith, and other secrets of the heart and spirit.

Old age brings us, if we're lucky, detachment from details. We may also come to accept our ignorance. Cultivating our spirits is more important, finally, than seeking to know everything; we come to believe that serenity holds more answers than information.

THOUGHT FOR TODAY: Some knowledge may be power, but spiritual tranquillity is a greater power.

The commonest fallacy among women is that simply having children makes one a mother—which is as absurd as believing that having a piano makes one a musician.

—Sydney J. Harris

I learned to play the piano from Mrs. Hansen, who wore burgundy crepe dresses and smelled wonderful. She taught dozens, maybe hundreds of pupils in her life. The only preparation I had for parenting was the way I was raised; and my brother and I were the only training our parents ever had.

They in turn knew only how they were raised, and their parents had only their own experience. There are books, of course, and videos and experts and controlled scientific studies, and we all pick up some information from relatives and friends—but when the chips are down, we're on our own. That baby, that toddler, that fourth-grader, that teenager, will present us with problems for which no one has prepared us.

Good doctors say they're successful if they work themselves out of a job. Good parents could say something similar. We'll always be parents, but if we're successful, our children will take over the job of caring for themselves.

THOUGHT FOR TODAY: Good parents, like good piano teachers, prepare children to make music on their own.

Twenty thousand years ago, the family was the so-cial unit. Now the social unit has become the world, in which it may truthfully be said that each person's welfare affects that of every other.
                                              —A. H. Compton

Our families give us the rewards—and sometimes the punishments—of intimacy, and we may feel entitled to breach some of their boundaries. If our social unit and our family were really as wide as the world, we would treat everyone the same, rudely or politely. Our family deserves at least the courtesy we show to our fellows. Yet we'll interrupt them, vent our frustrations on them, invade their privacy, some-times even push them around. Why can't we show them the common politeness we give to strangers?

   Love should not involve emotional abuse. We give back the treatment we receive, but if we've been treated more harshly than we deserve—especially if our loved ones have violated our personal bound-aries—we can still choose to return courtesy. What a peaceful, harmonious world we might have, if every-one were able to make that choice.

THOUGHT FOR TODAY: Do my family and I treat each other with the same courtesy we show our friends? We should.

*Cleaning your house while your kids are still
    growing
is like shoveling the walk before it stops snowing.*
                                        —Phyllis Diller

In a strictly unofficial survey, I found that house-cleaning accounts for more ugly memories than any other aspect of growing up. We do well to introduce children gradually to reasonable standards of cleanliness—picking up after themselves, helping us with simple tasks, learning in a safe and pleasant way the techniques we use to keep order in our households. If we do this patiently and cheerfully, our children will learn to think of housecleaning not as a hideous chore but simply as part of independent life.

It may surprise us to find how much disorder we can tolerate when the cause of the mess is a beloved child. We can overcome our unpleasant childhood memories of housecleaning and turn it into an occasion for closeness with our families, a shared activity that will leave everyone with a feeling of accomplishment, and a reasonably clean house.

THOUGHT FOR TODAY: I'll be sure my desire for order isn't creating problems for those I live with and love.

The same heart beats in every human breast.
                              —Matthew Arnold

Human hearts, stars, seashells; all the same, yet each unique. Human families—all the same, yet all different. To grasp our kinship, the ways in which we're all the same, is the key to serene acceptance of our place in the universe.

Every family is a minor variation on the theme. All family troubles—conflicts with authority, abuses of power, crises of identity—are more the same than different, and so are family rejoicings. We all have intimate knowledge of these events from our growing up. We can understand and empathize with all human feelings, because we're capable of feeling them all.

Every child is uniquely special; yet every birth evokes the same emotions. Our life paths are individual, yet thickly traveled. The same rain falls on us, the same sun shines, yet each of us is a unique and indispensable part of the whole.

THOUGHT FOR TODAY: Although I can rejoice in my individuality, my similarity to all human sisters and brothers is a great comfort.

The dead might as well try to speak to the living as the old to the young.

—Willa Cather

Sometimes I find myself wishing I could spare my children the pain of learning from their errors. But I can't: their mistakes are tailor-made, and every experience brings its lesson.

"If youth only knew; if age only could!" Yet youth must discover limitations and boundaries for itself. We can't learn from others' experience, no matter how wise they are. And by the time we've acquired wisdom, we seldom want to repeat the trial-and-error fumblings of our youth.

The lucky middle-aged, who have learned from their youthful mistakes, seldom really want to trade places with the young. As we age, we find we grow more reconciled to the limitations of our bodies if our spirits are well developed. The old don't need to speak to the young; the young must learn for themselves.

THOUGHT FOR TODAY: My own mistakes will give me ample lessons. In old age I'll have a treasure of experience to reflect upon.

Love is the water of life—receive it in thy heart and soul.

—Rumi

Because it flows like water, to receive love is to give love. We can see this in our families: the most loved are the most loving. But anxiety and fear can stiffen love and prevent it from flowing. Sometimes parents' anxieties mix with love for a child, and the mixture produces what the world calls a spoiled child. Because the parents' wishes and fears interfere with the expression of the real love they feel, the spoiled child never feels loved unconditionally.

When parents lavish material gifts on their children, the children confuse love with things. Real riches of the heart and soul, which flourish with unconditional love, can be inhibited by material wealth.

Other kinds of mixtures can spoil love, like parental violence or jealousy. A child who experiences love along with abuse or manipulation becomes spoiled in another way, fearing deep and spontaneous feelings because love has been confused with pain.

Healing is slow. Yet opening oneself to the unconditional love that streams through the universe, flashing in the stars and uncurling in the pale green buds of spring, can ease the heart and soul. We are refreshed, brimful, and love flows outward from us again.

THOUGHT FOR TODAY: Pure love is an ideal; in the world it will always be mixed. I can begin today to remove conditions from the love I feel for others, and my heart will be eased.

Silences shared with good friends or loved ones can be rich with meaning and understanding, needing no audible expression.

—Betty Yarnall

Family members and old, intimate friends often share a language of common references, gestures, memories. When we meet someone sympathetic, we may have the feeling that we understand one another without words. This silent sympathy can also be a sign of full acceptance of another's being.

What a gift is such total acceptance! It surely is the most important part of love, the welcoming of another's spirit, without judgment, without conditions. Total acceptance of others is possible for all of us when we have totally accepted ourselves. We are imperfect creatures, mixtures of qualities, and the only certain thing about us is that we will change.

Too often, family relations are roughened by disapproval, disappointment, or rivalry. If we can let go of these and accept all the members of our family, all the people in our lives, imperfect and changing, like ourselves, then we will have nourished our own spirits and helped theirs toward that self-acceptance that is the basis of selfless love.

THOUGHT FOR TODAY: You and I may not be perfect, but we're the best there is.

No fathers or mothers think their children ugly.
—Miguel de Cervantes

Unfortunately, some fathers and mothers do have deep dissatisfactions that they take out on their children, just as many seem to have inflated notions of their children's intelligence, ability, or good looks. How difficult it is to see them simply as they are—like other children, imperfect and lovable.

Distorted perceptions most often come from inner needs that we're not aware of—areas of our lives in which we feel dissatisfied. We attribute to our children the ability to satisfy us—or perhaps to confirm our disappointment. You can hear this in the words of people who say, "No one in our family ever wins prizes," or "Your mother's family can't run to save their lives"—using family identity as a kind of damper to discourage youthful enthusiasm.

At the other extreme are parents who live through their children—the mother who wants her son to make up for what she sees as his father's failure, or who pushes her daughter to achieve the things she wants, rather than what the daughter wants. Children are what they are. Their identities unfold best with a minimum of interference.

THOUGHT FOR TODAY: Children need love and care. Unrealistic expectations are too heavy for them to bear, no matter how light we think they are.

We need a world in which it is safe to be human.
—Arthur Goldberg

We're frequently asked to consider the welfare of whales, seals, wolves, eagles, and other creatures that are endangered by our industrialized world. But what about us human creatures? In our zeal to develop weapons that will protect us from one another, we've made our world an unsafe place for all. We've mortgaged our children's welfare by investing our wealth in destructive products. Nuclear technology, even in its "peacetime" applications, threatens our future.

Today is the anniversary of the day on which the United States dropped a nuclear bomb on the civilians of Hiroshima, killing and maiming many thousands of fathers, mothers, brothers, sisters, grandparents, and children. Since that time, the Bomb has been a member of all our families, looming over our lives with the mysterious power to change our future in hideous ways. We can't go back to a prenuclear world, but for the sake of all our families, immediate and global, we must use our creativity to clean up our postnuclear act.

Each of us has power to influence this aspect of our lives. It's the strongest pro-family gesture we can make—working in whatever way we can for peace, and for the containment of our dangerous relative.

THOUGHT FOR TODAY: Today I'll remember the families of Hiroshima and Nagasaki, and pray for the safe future of our human family.

To ignore evil is to become an accomplice to it.
                            —Martin Luther King, Jr.

We all know evil when we see it: evil is what hinders
growth, what distorts the unfolding of our bodies
and spirits. Good and evil are intimate relations in
the world, especially in family situations. Sometimes
people do evil with good intentions.

People do evil things to one another out of fear as
much as ignorance. If we believe that evil is being
done, we have the duty to find out; and if our
suspicions are accurate—if a child is being terrorized
or an old person is receiving abuse—we must find
out about the possibilities for intervention, for our
own sakes as much as others'.

When we ignore wrongdoing and become accom-
plices to it, we hinder the growth of our own spirits.
It takes great courage to confront evil, but we can
rise to the occasion.

THOUGHT FOR TODAY: Among the things I pray
for today will be the strength to confront evil when I
encounter it.

Families teach us how love exists in a realm beyond liking and disliking, coexisting with indifference, rivalry, and even antipathy.
—John Updike

Love has no single, simple meaning. Even between the same two people, the stream of love flows in many different ways, through affection and exasperation and disappointment. "I wouldn't be so angry if I didn't love you," our parents said when they punished us, and we got the idea: love is commitment, a sense of belonging together, no matter what.

We may not experience our family love as love at all. It may give us pain or shame. Only those we love have the power to shame us and hurt us, because we feel associated with them. Our commitment to them makes us vulnerable; we hook in to their feelings, sometimes, and neglect our own.

Of course we want love to be a source of pleasure and not pain. Yet our families have the power to make us suffer more keenly than friends or even lovers, because our commitment to them is rooted in the helplessness we felt as young children, when they did in fact have tremendous power. Recognizing this may help us to free our love for family members from the negative feelings that so often cloud it. We have a right to love our families happily, with detachment, for our deeper commitment to them can't be broken.

THOUGHT FOR TODAY: I can choose to love my family in the way that makes me feel most whole.

*Genuine appreciation of other people's children is
one of the rarer virtues.*
                                        —Harlan Miller

Sometimes we look at people and things enviously,
as though having them or being close to them could
make us happier, as though we didn't hold the seeds
of happiness inside us all the time. Sadly, we com-
pare other people's children with our children, using
some imaginary measure of talent, beauty, or brains
to make ourselves—and our children—unhappy, regardless of who benefits by the comparison.

Children are like us: they're developing just as
they should. We make sure they're well fed, clothed,
and housed, but after that, they're unfolding according to a plan that's beyond our understanding. Our
children's schedule of blooming has to do with them,
not us; we may not understand or appreciate their
timing, yet they're coming into their own.

When we love and trust ourselves, when we feel
good about our lives, then we can appreciate all
children for the marvels they are. Our guests for a
brief time, they leave to take their places in the
never ending hospitality of birth and nurture. This is
true of all children—our own, our friends', strangers'
—on all continents. The world's children aren't in
competition with one another: they're learning to
cooperate for future mutual survival.

THOUGHT FOR TODAY: Appreciation for my own
children teaches me kinship with parents and children everywhere. We deserve a harmonious life, not
one driven by competition or envy.

Ye are better than all the ballads
That ever were sung or said;
For ye are living poems,
And all the rest are dead.
                    —Henry Wadsworth Longfellow

Regret must be the most unproductive emotion, yet it's one of the commonest, especially after the death of a loved one. Almost everyone regrets lost opportunities. "I never told my mother how much she meant to me"; "Grandpa was such a joker, I never got to talk to him seriously"; "Now I'll never have a chance to tell Aunt Jessie about—"; "Now my brother will never know how angry I was at him."

The only lesson regret can teach is an indirect one: that we should seize the time, open up, tell our near and dear ones how we feel before it's too late. Those who are living now are part of our growing, changing lives. For them to get full value from our personal growth, we must include them. Too often, we freeze our relationships at an early age, not wanting to change the balance, or else we make outrageous predictions for other people: "She's too old to learn," or "He'll never change."

What we really mean is that *we* don't want to risk changing our relationship, with Cousin Paul or Brother Ted or Mom. But if we don't do it now, it'll never happen. We owe our family members as much trust as we can bestow, as much honesty as will spare us useless regrets.

THOUGHT FOR TODAY: Today I'll risk sharing myself with those I love.

*My view is, that the most important thing in life is
never to have too much of anything.*

—Terence

Too much of something always means not enough
of something else. Too much money usually means
not enough simplicity or humility; too much sunshine means not enough rain. But just as different
climates have their own proportions of hot and cold
or wet and dry, different families have their own
styles of behavior. "Too much discipline," thinks
the liberal humanist about an Amish child or a little
Orthodox Jewish scholar. "Too much laxity," thinks
the traditional parent about the progressive family.
Too much makeup, too much allowance, too much
studying, too much dirt; in our pluralist society we
have wonderfully different ways of caring for children and educating them, feeding and managing our
households. When sane parents love their children,
the growing conditions are pretty good no matter
what techniques are used.

As a nation mostly of immigrants, we come in
many colors, shapes, and styles. What may seem
excessive to Nordic people or to Native Americans
might appear barely adequate to Latinos or Hungarian
Americans. One secret of living successfully in a
multicultural society is to respect differences while
preserving our own distinct characters and traditions. Balance is the key; we respect and love others
when we respect and love ourselves.

THOUGHT FOR TODAY: The one thing I can
never have too much of is unconditional love.

When face to face with oneself—there is no cop-out.
                              —Edward Kennedy (Duke) Ellington

We put on a face for the world that looks better than we feel—luckier, richer, more hopeful. But to ourselves we admit without fear that we make mistakes and that life could be better. Children pick up fast on the difference between public and private realities, but sometimes they get confused. And sometimes children come to believe that it's wrong to admit mistakes or dissatisfactions, so they develop a habit of concealment—even from themselves.

A parent's job is to let their children know everyone has failures as well as successes. There's no joy without some sadness; whatever they're feeling is right for them to feel. Young people sometimes believe their own thoughts are monstrous; no one else ever had such hideous ideas. They need to know that everyone has felt that way, and that they're loved no matter what.

We all need to know that. The only way we can be sure is to be honest with ourselves. There's no cop-out because we don't need one. We accept ourselves—sad, happy, lucky, depressed—as we are.

THOUGHT FOR TODAY: It's always the right time to be honest with myself. If I'm not, who am I fooling?

*O who could have foretold
that the heart grows old?*

—W. B. Yeats

Bodies grow old; eyesight dims, hearing fades, joints crack, skin wrinkles. Gradually we adapt to the aging process. Our tastes change, and our activities. If we retire from work, we may find our days a desert of boredom or a rich expanse of leisure and chosen activity. The heart need never grow old.

We can love as strongly in our eighties as in our sixties or our twenties, though the way we love may change. We can't make love—or dance—all night, or play four games of tennis back to back, or eat or drink as lustily as we could when we were young. (Perhaps we couldn't then, either; memory is a great braggart.)

But the heart? Unchanged. Age introduces us to moderation, whether we've ever been moderate in our habits or not; the wisdom of the ages is easier to accommodate when our senses are less insistent and our muscles less elastic. Then we welcome patience, practice detachment, and cultivate our inner resources.

THOUGHT FOR TODAY: Just as my feelings can stay fresh and strong all my life, so at any age can I acquire the wisdom of moderation.

Praise is an earned thing. It has to be deserved, like an honorary degree or a hug from a child.
—Phyllis McGinley

We're in the world to encourage one another, to support each other's creativity, and to help our fellow beings express their special gifts as fully as possible. We're not here to give praise without merit, or to distort our judgments.

Different kinds of family feelings can warp our appreciation for our loved ones' accomplishments. Jealousy leads us either to belittle their achievements or to give them undue weight. Pride leads us to overvalue them; shame makes us disparage them. It's hard to see our siblings, our children, or our parents clearly enough to appreciate them simply for what they are.

Yet we know ourselves that the words of family members carry great weight. We all hunger for love and appreciation, especially from our intimates; if they give praise cheaply, we can feel betrayed. We don't want extravagant false praise; we want our due. We want to know that our efforts were seen and appreciated; above all, we want support from those we love, and falsehood is never supportive.

THOUGHT FOR TODAY: I deserve encouragement for my sincere efforts; no more, but no less.

You adults really "adopt" each other in the wedding ceremony ... feel closer to your mate than to the blood brothers and sisters with whom you grew up.
— George Crane

A marriage is strengthened by reciprocity. The parent–child relationship, on the other hand, should be characterized by trust on the child's part and unconditional love on the parent's. In a family that includes both chosen and biological children, it's important to make no distinctions. Neither way of entering the family entitles a child to special intimacy with its parents.

Children need to know they're loved, no matter what. We all do; unconditional love strengthens our spirits and teaches us to love ourselves. We all have access to an endless source of love and understanding. When we learn to tap it and use it in our family relations, we make this source available to our children—the richest heritage we can bestow.

THOUGHT FOR TODAY: Loving families are true democracies, where all children are loved equally and no one is more equal than another.

Happiness is like jam—you can't spread even a little without getting some on yourself.

—Anonymous

When you do a really good job with jam, there's some on everything you touch—on your fingers, in your pockets, on the soles of your shoes. Radiant happiness will stick to everyone who comes within its range. Anxiety and depression are like this, too. Remember Li'l Abner's unlucky friend Joe Bftsplk? He walked around under his personal cloud; it was always raining on Joe. We make our own emotional weather, and our loved ones share it in part, however good they may be at detaching from our moods.

Moods are contagious. It's hard to stay worried when you're in the company of a gurgling baby or a chatty toddler, or a young adult shining with requited love. The contagious quality of happiness and hope makes sure that someone else's good fortune reminds us of our own. The same is true for unhappiness; it takes a strong spirit to withstand the contagion of sorrow.

Reflecting on this makes me realize how much my moods are within my control. Since I can choose more or less how I feel, shouldn't I opt for happiness always? I'll need support from my spiritual source, but my efforts will be richly repaid. Happiness is that place inside myself that I can reach, with practice, by clearing away anxieties.

THOUGHT FOR TODAY: Today and every day I'll remember to pray for happiness, a duty that is its own reward.

Never fear shadows. They simply mean there's a light shining somewhere.

—Ruth E. Renkel

Just as light lets us see shadows, so happiness lets us perceive its complement, sorrow. Everyone is sad from time to time; knowledge of sadness is part of growing up, and it's important for parents to set this in perspective, both for our children and for ourselves.

When children come to us because they're sad, we offer them comfort first—a warm lap to sit on and arms to hug them. Then we try to find out if something's "the matter."

Sometimes there is no matter. A child or teenager is simply sad. Perhaps the child has glimpsed mortality in a way that makes it vivid to her or him. Or perhaps self-doubt overwhelms confidence for the moment.

Life is a pattern of contrast and complement, light and shadow, happiness and sorrow. Our pulse has a double beat; we breathe in and breathe out; each half depends on the other. We don't need to feel responsible for other people's feelings—even our children's, much as we wish we were. They too have shadows on their paths, and sunlight.

THOUGHT FOR TODAY: I can't cause or cure another's sadness, but I can share the wisdom I get from my source of spiritual strength.

*The only moral lesson that is suited for a child—the
most important lesson for every time of life—is this:
"Never hurt anybody!"*

—Jean-Jacques Rousseau

Moral lessons come packed in actions. Children may
not listen closely to our words, but they're keen
observers of our behavior. Children who see adults
treating others rudely learn that rudeness is okay.
Children who see adults living by Rousseau's lesson
learn consideration.

It's possible to get what you need without hurting
others. Sometimes the world may seem to be a cold
and hostile place, where beasts compete with fang
and claw—but this is an illusion. Our world is what
we make it; if our goals are appropriate, and we
approach life in a spirit of friendly cooperation, the
world will be warm and bountiful, and our efforts
will be successful.

That's the lesson our children need to learn from
our behavior—that gentleness and generosity can
succeed. Morality begins in the family, with a baby's
inborn sense of justice and parents' loving response.
Wouldn't it be a pleasant world if we all behaved
more like what we are—members of one family?

THOUGHT FOR TODAY: Am I living in such a
way as to hurt no one? What about myself? I deserve love and respect from everyone, myself included.

*It's not how busy you are—but why you are busy.
The bee is praised. The mosquito is swatted.*
                                    —Marie O'Connor

Some of us have parents (or children) who call or
write frequently, telling us everything and spinning
minor decisions or events into lengthy discourse.
Mothers save coupons for us; sons clip newspaper
articles. Yet in important ways they may not offer
the support we need. The same can be true of spouses,
who may shower us with evidences of their affection
yet aren't emotionally accessible to us when we need
them.

We have a right to ask our families for the treatment we want. If we feel we're getting a lot of hectic
busyness, without any productive outcome—if our
parents, children, or spouses agitate our spirits without nourishing them—we have a right to ask for
more. It may be merely an incompatible style; it may
be a mutual failure. But whatever the cause, if our
intimate relations aren't satisfying our emotional
needs, we owe it to ourselves to confront the problem. Part of our self-worth is seeing that our own
needs are met. Rather than swatting mosquitoes, we
should help ourselves to some honey.

THOUGHT FOR TODAY: We deserve the highest
quality of relationships with our families and partners, and all relationships need maintenance and
repair.

The most beautiful experience we can have is the mysterious. It is the fundamental emotion which stands at the cradle of true art and true science.
—Albert Einstein

"The mysterious" awakens our sense of wonder. This "fundamental emotion," as Einstein calls it, is at the glowing core of our being; it fuels our feelings of holiness, awe, and deep, yielding love. Our industrial society leaves little room for awe and wonder; we're expected to cram these beautiful experiences into an hour or two of formal worship, music, or art.

Daily meditation can help us to cultivate our sense of wonder. A silent three quarters of an hour, when we contemplate a sacred text, a stone or poem, or whatever else we choose, is enough—if we concentrate on freeing ourselves of preoccupation—to put us in touch with our center, where the sense of beauty and mystery resides.

Meditation as a spiritual practice also lets us touch the child in ourselves. We can recapture the time in our life when mystery was our daily companion. We'll feel closer to our own children as we recover more of the child within us. The contemplation of beauty softens our spirits and releases our capacity for love.

THOUGHT FOR TODAY: I humbly accept the mysteries in life, the greatest of which is love.

Kids' needs are best met by grown-ups whose needs are met.

—Jean Illsley Clarke

A starving person isn't a fussy eater; people will try to meet their basic needs however they can. Besides food, we humans need loving intimacy and emotional support. Sadly, when we don't get these from other adults, we may try to get them from our children.

Adults who abhor the notion of incestuous abuse can still harm their children by involving them in inappropriate relationships. Emotional invasion and manipulation may be milder than outright physical abuse, but they leave lasting scars. Children who are treated as escorts or mock lovers by their parents— "He's such a little man"—or leaned on or manipulated by thwarted adults don't get a chance to develop according to their own inner time clock.

If our adult relationships don't provide emotional satisfaction, we risk harming the children we love. We deserve happiness, and they deserve to grow at their own pace. We can't get adult emotional fulfillment from children, and if we try, we interfere with their healthy unfolding. Neediness is communicable; we owe ourselves emotional health.

THOUGHT FOR TODAY: If I don't put my emotional and spiritual welfare first, I'm cheating more than myself.

Who of us is mature enough for offspring before the offspring themselves arrive? The value of marriage is not that adults produce children but that children produce adults.

—Peter DeVries

The arrival of children certainly changes a relationship. You may have resolved most of your differences and worked out a comfortable, pleasant life, and now there is a third party with needs and demands that must be met around the clock. Both partners at times feel jealous of a new baby, because it's a rival for the other's attention. Dealing creatively with these feelings—jealousy and resentment clashing with deep love for the baby and the fierce desire to protect it—is a maturing experience.

Sometimes the challenge posed by the arrival of a child—or children—is more than a relationship can bear. Couples break apart because they're unwilling to change in the necessary directions. True maturity means the ability to order your priorities in such a way that you can see past your own immediate comfort and pleasure; you aspire to a higher level of comfort that encompasses the needs of all family members. This doesn't mean placing someone else's needs before your own, but it does mean redefining your needs so that caring for your children becomes as vital a source of well-being as caring for yourself. Not *more* important, but *as* important.

THOUGHT FOR TODAY: Breadth, generosity, and a sense of proportion; these make me an adult who can deal compassionately with my children.

*Do not remove a fly from your friend's forehead
with a hatchet.*

—Anonymous (Chinese proverb)

Have you ever greeted a tiny frustration by bursting
into tears, or lost your temper at a child for some
minor mishap? Responding appropriately to the challenges of family life is never easy, but it's made
easier by the regular use of a spiritual connection
that lets us step back, take a deep breath, and surrender our anxieties to a power greater than ourselves.

When we have such a connection, we're less likely
to fly off, blow it, or overreact. However difficult
our circumstances may be, we always have occasions for gratitude. By acknowledging that we can't
control others, we discover the power we do have.
Overreaction is often triggered by feelings of fear
and powerlessness; once we admit life's uncontroll-
ability, we've met the problem halfway.

Success means giving up the notion that we're in
control, even of our children. We're partners with
them in this adventure called living. Our share of the
bargain is tender care and unconditional love; we're
rewarded by their share, which is achieving their
fullest growth. Together we learn to meet each day
as it comes. We needn't reach for the hatchets; tools
for each task will be at hand.

THOUGHT FOR TODAY: When my spirit feels
calm and refreshed, I'm most patient and loving.

One of the delights known to age and beyond the grasp of youth is that of NOT GOING.
—J. B. Priestley

Can you recapture the blissful anticipation you felt as a child before some planned celebration—a party or an outing? The sense of promise was so much more delicious than any fulfillment could possibly be. Perhaps some of us can hold on to the belief that *this* party, *this* picnic, *this* movie or concert will be the best yet; but I suspect most of us, as we grow older, often find that celebrations aren't all they're cracked up to be.

The secret of that eager anticipation was our own readiness, the capacity for enjoyment that we brought with us. We made our own good times, or bad times, if that's what we had. And as we age, we bring our capacity for pleasure to different occasions. We've changed, from looking outside ourselves for ecstatic happiness to recognizing that joy comes from within. Happiness is a response to life, and we don't need outside events to evoke it.

So *not going* to a celebration can be more pleasant than going. True celebration is within us, like our pulse, like our ability to love. And like these, it's part of our spiritual connection, source of all love, life, and joy.

THOUGHT FOR TODAY: I'm good company, and I can enjoy myself wherever I am.

Why are other people's children so well-behaved?
—Alice Silverman

Every parent has felt some twinges of inadequacy when other people's children seemed immaculately dressed, poised, and polite. But if these feelings become a real source of anxiety, we need to ask ourselves some honest questions.

First, do our children behave badly, or just like children? Perhaps we're embarrassed because they don't stay clean and neat. Do we really want to devote ourselves to coaching them for public appearances?

The next question is about us, not them: Do we tend to belittle or devalue anything that's ours, because deep down we doubt our own worth? This is an area where parents can really harm their children. If we believe unconsciously that we're failures, that nothing we do can succeed—including our family life—we'll communicate that to them. If we feel hopeless about our own lives, we probably despair of theirs as well—or else we use them as a sort of life preserver, counting on their success to redeem our failure. Either way, children get loaded down with a lot of baggage they don't deserve.

Most of us can soothe those twinges by reminding ourselves how wonderful our children really are. But the deep hopelessness is a more serious problem. To heal this, we need help, maybe from outside, certainly from within—the loving help that comes to us whenever we invoke our higher power, our spiritual connection to universal harmony. Our children are who they are; our growth is proceeding as it should; all is well.

THOUGHT FOR TODAY: Children behave like themselves. I will accept them joyously.

Don't do nothing halfway, else you find yourself dropping more than can be picked up.
—Louis Armstrong

A small girl and boy were playing house at day care. They trotted back and forth, picking things up and putting them down, mixing things in bowls, and feeding stuffed animals. She told him to put up new wallpaper in the living room, and he got a stepladder and made some passes at the playhouse wall, while she opened and closed the oven door on the toy stove and answered the doorbell. Watching them, I realized that their gestures were stylized. They'd seen adults do these things and they were imitating the way they *looked*, not what they did. The boy didn't color on the wall, for example; the girl didn't put anything in the oven. They were practicing the moves, like dancers.

Many young people go through a phase of stopping and starting projects, trying out different moves, before they find activities that fully engage their energies. This is part of learning how to work well. But sometimes dropping things half-finished can reinforce a sense of failure or inadequacy. We all need to succeed once in a while. The key to success is doing, and completing, one thing at a time, no matter what pictures we have in our heads.

THOUGHT FOR TODAY: Some loose ends are unavoidable, but I'll make a practice of finishing every project I can.

If one is a greyhound, why try to look like a Pekingese?

—Edith Sitwell

Children accept more variety among their pets than among one another. A child who is out of the ordinary—strikingly tall or short, freckled, large-nosed, big-eared, eyeglassed—may be teased mercilessly during the preadolescent years, when youngsters tend to run in packs. The solitary standout is penalized for just the qualities that make her or him outstanding.

Parents need great compassion to help their children accept themselves. Some children seem not to notice teasing; others take it in stride or good-naturedly turn it back. But many, especially when their distinction is physical, feel shamed and miserable and have no way to put such thoughtless cruelty into perspective.

The creation of mass markets in our society has made possible a fantastic variety of consumer goods, but it also reinforces pressures for conformity. Knowing that our children's peers are responding to pressures outside their ken, or their parents', helps us to accept and forgive their thoughtlessness. What we must do as parents is to show our children that we love them for what they are. Their difference from their peers is precious to us.

THOUGHT FOR TODAY: Knowing I am loved strengthens me to face ignorance or ridicule. I can strengthen others with my love.

If you have an unpleasant neighbor, the odds are that he does, too.

—Frank A. Clark

Do you have family troubles? So do your relations. It's partly a matter of perspective. When you're very close to a situation, your view is narrow and distorted, but when you step back you can see your share in the problem.

Many family troubles are bargains. Our children become picky eaters and bedtime rebels in exchange for our attention—angry attention, to be sure, but lots of it. Or our brother-in-law will write bad checks in exchange for our exasperated tolerance. If we change our behavior—if no one covers the bad checks, or insists that children clean their plates—the problem behavior will have to change, too. It takes a while, but when I stop delivering my end of the bargain, so do the others. Their behavior is only a problem for me if I buy into it.

There are troubles that detachment can't resolve—deep disturbance, addiction, illness. These require more than our own sanity and prayers. But if we're faced with such troubles, a wider perspective helps us cope. It helps us to survive the threat of injury or loss and to give thanks for our family's strengths and graces.

THOUGHT FOR TODAY: It takes more than one to quarrel—and to harmonize.

*Life was a good show to her; it arranged itself well,
and she was clever at picking out the best scenes.*
                                        —Rose Macaulay

We each write our own life script, although we're all
actors in a collaborative effort. Every single one of
us is the central player in our own comedy.

   Young children play endlessly at families. "You
be the father; you be the mother; I'll be the baby."
"No, I want to be the baby; you be the father."
Sometimes the baby gets to marry or murder the
mother, or the father; sometimes the parents are
loving, and sometimes they're viciously cruel to each
other and to their children. Like other role-playing
games, these let children fantasize about their families and also at least pretend to share family power.

   One key to picking good scenes for our life's
drama is the ability to choose among many different
ones. When we have no choice, we feel trapped in
someone else's script, speaking lines out of character. We deserve the starring role in our own life
story.

THOUGHT FOR TODAY: I'm simultaneously play-
wright, actor, and audience at the long-running hit,
life. I'll do my part to help bring about a happy
ending.

It is wisdom to believe the heart.
                                    —George Santayana

It took me years to realize that my uneasiness around a friend stemmed from the faint odor of hospital disinfectant that clung to him (he's a doctor), arousing painful memories of a childhood hospitalization. My response to the scent is instantaneous; my heart has information before the rest of me, and I need to deal with my feelings, not suppress them because they're "silly."

My feelings respond to smells, and I'm responsible for what I do with my feelings. Once I know what they are, I can act accordingly; but while they're suppressed, they influence me without my knowledge.

The doctor is a friend. A stranger who smells of lavender might not be. Knowing the basis of my response is at least the beginning of wisdom in dealing with people.

THOUGHT FOR TODAY: I have a right to my feelings, and a need to understand them.

The young man knows the rules, but the old man knows the exceptions.

—Oliver Wendell Holmes

Most of us are going to have only one or two chances to do the job of raising children. We may not have had the benefit of growing up in large families; we may live far enough from our relatives so we can't ask for help with a colicky baby. Our lack of experience may mean that our precious one-and-only gets treated strictly by the rules, because in our anxiety to do what's best, we don't relax enough to discover any exceptions.

We can learn a lot from friends and books, and the best books, like the most sensible friends, will pass along some exceptions to the rules. Babies shouldn't sleep with their parents, but if an infant falls asleep in the parent's bed after a middle-of-the-night feeding, the exception is more gracious to parent and baby than waking everybody up. The rule against playing with matches might be bent for a responsible seven-year-old who loves to build rockets.

We follow rules when we're unsure; it's safer. With children, though, we aren't baking a cake or assembling a model, we're involved in flexible inter-action with human beings who love us, whom we love. Asking for guidance from our steadfast spiritual companion, we'll find the strength to do our best.

THOUGHT FOR TODAY: I'll surrender my inexperience, trust my instincts, and in humility learn all I can from all sources.

Most of the adults who sentimentalize their schooldays are like veterans who romanticize their war years. What do they mean—"It wasn't that bad"?
—Melvin Maddocks

Are we afraid to pay full attention to our children—afraid we may hear something we don't want to hear? If we truly listen, we're apt to hear the truth.

Their experience, like our own, is probably a mixed bag: some pleasure, some anger, some fear, some triumph. Even the brightest, best-behaved child has squabbles, jealousies, and shames. These negative experiences help prepare the growing person for a balanced attitude toward adult life. Our feelings, like our minds and bodies, develop when we're young.

If adults deny that there's some pain among these developing feelings, either for ourselves or for our children, we are denying their reality—and denying ourselves the power of growth. War is hell; soldiers may have soul-transforming experiences in it, but that doesn't make it a good thing. Schooldays are tough. Children deserve respectful attention from adults who acknowledge that pain and sadness inevitably accompany satisfaction and achievement.

THOUGHT FOR TODAY: My spirit grows whenever I truly listen to another.

*In every one of them dwelled the unappeased child
with her rights and her claims, and they were being
forced to remember her, and how much it had cost
each of them to subdue her.*

—Doris Lessing

Human infants, like all animals, are born with claims
to food, warmth, and nurture—and in growing up
we learn to subdue these. Though most of us can't
recall the power of our early desires, it costs us
dearly to teach ourselves to settle for less than everything. So we live unappeased, with a hunger just
below our consciousness that's easily awakened—by
loneliness or pain, or sometimes by happiness. How
can we satisfy these desires that come from our very
earliest self and last at least until we die?

Some people find that living for others nourishes
the child within. A life of selfless service paradoxically strengthens the self. Others accommodate their
hungry children in other ways, gentling and nurturing themselves. Intimacy means acknowledging our
own child and someone else's, and sometimes we
will accept from others what we can't give ourselves.
In loving relationships we learn how lovable we are.

THOUGHT FOR TODAY: Repressing my desires
won't quell them. Learning to satisfy myself creatively turns hunger into power.

"Is Johnny not to be taught to read because he does not like it?" "Johnny must read, by all means," would the doctor answer. "But is it necessary that he should not like it? . . . may not Johnny learn, not only to read, but to like to learn to read?"
—Anthony Trollope

Many voices in our lives claim, "This is good for you." "I'm doing this for your own good," parents may say when they punish a child, and we hear the same line about shots, dentistry, food we don't like, and the multiplication tables. No wonder many of us grow up firmly convinced that "good for us" means painful or nasty.

All living things want what is good for them, unless they have been taught somehow to dread it. Were we terrified by school, church, or whole wheat bread? That doesn't mean these are bad for us, or that video games and junk food are good for us because we enjoy them. We have a right to wholesome nourishment for our brains, spirits, and bodies, and we have a right to enjoy it. Learning should be joyous, and so should health and worship. What is bad for us is the dread we learned. If we've made bad connections with these sources of power, we can break them and make new ones.

THOUGHT FOR TODAY: Today I'll claim my right to a good life. I'll work on breaking through the fears that block me from having what I deserve.

"Aunt Sarah, does Thee really think any slaves were Freed because thee did not use sugar or cotton?"

Perfectly tranquil was her reply: "Dear child, I can never know that any slave was personally helped; but I had to live with my own conscience."

—Florence Kelley

We learn valuable lessons from growing up in a family with strong spiritual practices. We learn that observance of these practices is important in and for itself. We also learn that our own timetable doesn't govern the workings of the universe. When we pray, we don't expect immediate results. When we follow the dictates of conscience, we don't imagine we're changing the world.

This precious gift we receive: the knowledge that we're part of a larger picture, a broader reality that has its own laws, its own rhythms. The most we can hope for is to live harmoniously within our broader human family, neither colliding with necessity nor crushed by it, and connected to a source of spiritual nurture. It's said that in our journey through life we are responsible for the effort—that is, the effort to be as good as we can—and not the outcome of our endeavors.

THOUGHT FOR TODAY: I will try to live by my conscience and detach myself from the outcome. I can't heal the world—at least, I can't do it by tomorrow.

If you stand in a meadow, at the edge of a hillside, and look around carefully, almost everything you can catch sight of is in the process of dying, and most things will be dead long before you are.
—Lewis Thomas

Long ago, Hindu and Buddhist thinkers realized that what we call death is merely a change—a physical change of form, a chemical change of recombination. The individual leaf, star, bird, or human being ceases to exist in that form, and its elements recombine to form other beings.

We understand a great deal about the biochemistry of plants and animals; we can imagine flesh and bone, teeth and hair and organs becoming simpler compounds, entering into the earthly processes of decay and growth that nourish grass, insects, ruminants, birds, and human beings. But the elemental components? Of them we know very little.

When our loved ones die, we pray for the health and integrity of their spirits. We don't know what happens to the soul when the body dies. For many of us, not knowing can be a comfort. We may not understand immortality, but we know that when those we love die, their spirits dwell among us for a time. Grief softens us and helps us to accept what we cannot change. But grieving, too, gives way to the next stage in our eternal progress.

THOUGHT FOR TODAY: All lives, all deaths, affect me, and my death will change the world as my life has. Yet I'll always be connected to the people and things I love.

Creation is everything you do. Make something.
                                        —Ntozake Shange

I wish I could do something with the care, pride, and easy skill of a five-year-old making a drawing. All children are gifted children; all are born artists. Yet in the necessary ranking and regimentation that most schools impose, their creativity is quashed. Lucky children have parents who let them express their creativity at home, at workbench or kitchen table, but many of us had parents who were discouraged creators themselves, and they discouraged us, too.

We can keep our creativity healthy and growing by being gentle with ourselves and especially with our children. Making something is easy; making something good is hard. A cake, a poem, a birdhouse, a quilt, a garden—everyone can tap into the well of inspiration that kept us so absorbed when we were young, and irrigate some useful, pleasant project.

It's important that we overcome the discouragement we learned—in school or from our parents—and give ourselves and our children lots of room to make mistakes, to try different things, to go slowly. Not all adults are great artists or skilled crafters, but we're all able to make things that will please us—if we let them.

THOUGHT FOR TODAY: The only barriers to my creativity are within me, and I can surmount them.

*My parents lived most of their lives at the edge of
poverty or over it, but the richness of their political
commitment was more than adequate compensation; their politics gave meaning to their lives and
comprised their proud gift to their children.*
>   —Henry E. McGuckin

Many of us can look back on childhoods spent
under pressure of not enough money. If we're lucky,
we can also recapture a sense of values that provided more than adequate compensation: spiritual,
political, or moral. Fortunate are the children who
grow up in a home where possessions of the heart
and spirit are more prized than mere commodities.

When we have children, will they be able to look
back on a rich heritage of commitment to ideals—
like justice, equality, beauty, or spiritual wholeness?
If not, they will never have the opportunity to raise
their sights above the things of this world. We owe
all children the chance to develop strong spirits,
along with strong bones and teeth. If we stretch
ourselves, we'll have proud gifts to hand on to them.

THOUGHT FOR TODAY: Perhaps my upbringing
never led me to see beyond my own comforts; still,
within me is the capacity for spiritual grandeur.

We sometimes forget the amazing capacity of the human being to speak. The tone of voice, the calm example, produces discipline. Children want to be like loved adults.

—Gisela Konopka

Parents shudder at the role models their children choose—James Dean, Elvis, Marilyn Monroe. Are they truly beloved adults, and do children really want to *be* like them?

As their personalities are formed, from family influences, life experiences, and their own bodies, many young people try on various styles. They let their hair grow or cut it in new ways. They wear clothes their parents would never have chosen—and for just that reason. This period of experimentation, though it's hard on parents, is a sincere attempt to be like them. Young people admire strength, independence, and originality. Parents whose own styles and values are firmly traditional may not appreciate their purple-haired children's homage to their steadfast characters, yet that's what it is.

Most generations face what looks like a revolution in personal style and values, and most young people who have a firm and loving upbringing aspire to be like the caregivers they love. In the process of finding out how to live, they explore paths that seem to lead to power and creativity, and if their sense of these things has a solid foundation, they'll learn to tell the genuine article from its glamorous counterfeit.

THOUGHT FOR TODAY: When today's children have children, their role models will seem bizarre or dangerous to them, too.

Dispensing advice is always easier than biting one's own tongue.
> —Richard Stillerman

How do we know so clearly what's right for other people? Parents especially feel they understand exactly what their children should do; children often have the same feeling about their parents. Brothers and sisters are sure they understand one another's jobs and relationships much more clearly than the persons concerned. If you took the advice of all the people who dispense it, you could open an advice shop.

Other people's advice, of course, is based on only part of the whole picture. The part we all see is the obvious part; what we don't see are the feelings of the people whose lives we're prepared to straighten out.

Some advice is valuable: "Try to detach from the problem"; "Buy low, sell high." But most of it isn't useful; the well-meaning friend or relative who says "Don't act hastily" may not know you've been mulling over the problem for months and are finally ready to do something about it.

So it's usually wisest for would-be advisers to bite their tongues, or at most to say, "This worked for me" in a similar situation. The urge to give advice comes partly from a genuine desire to help, but part of it comes from a need to control another person— child, parent, or sibling. We can't control others, only ourselves.

THOUGHT FOR TODAY: Real care for others includes respect for their privacy. Even when asked for, advice isn't as useful as love or listening.

*Most adults develop amnesia for their own traumatic
teen years. Parents have to try hard to think back.*
— Morris Sklansky

What do we dislike most in others? Often the very
traits we dislike in ourselves. Parents are apt to react
most severely to the same behaviors in their children
that troubled their own growing up. Many grown-
ups struggle with old shames and anxieties about
sexuality or self-image that date back to their
adolescence.

Adolescence, like toddlerhood, is a time of trial
and error. But the stakes are higher for teenagers;
they can get drunk, and they can get pregnant. They
drive cars; they ride motorcycles. No parents are
willing to stand by while youngsters make mistakes
that can have disastrous consequences. Yet experience is the best—sometimes the only—teacher. It's
one of the ironies of life that our children don't
learn from our mistakes.

All adults have survived their adolescent experi-
ments. Why is it that we forget—what are we afraid
of? Are we afraid of remembering the sadness and
the fears that went along with excitement in those
years? If parents can think back to their stormy
adolescent experiences, they'll realize that love and
trust are needed much more than preaching or punishment. Compassion can help us through our
children's teen years—so like our own.

THOUGHT FOR TODAY: Today I will strive to
accept myself fully, including my secret fears and
shames. If I embrace them, I can let them go.

One can light a fire with fragments;
After that, one can burn the large tree.
                              —Bostan of S'adi

When there is a problem in our families, we sometimes let ourselves think about it in ways that are as
unproductive as trying to start a fire with a large
tree. "How can I get my mother to leave me alone?"
"How can I get my teenager to shape up?" "How
can I get my father to stop drinking?"

The fragments that will kindle a change, in any
one of these unmanageable situations, are the bits
and pieces we can control—mainly, our own attitudes and behavior. The problem, in other words,
isn't really Mother's prying or Father's drinking or
Teenager's sloppiness and incivility; the problem is
our attitude toward these things. If you don't want
Mother to pry, don't give her access to your intimacy. Close the door to Teenager's room. Go to
Al-Anon or Alateen, the groups for families of alcoholics, and learn that alcoholism is a family disease.

If we start with our own selves, at least we're
addressing the problem realistically. By changing ourselves, we change the situation. Sulking and nagging
lead to frustration, not action. Broad changes can
follow a modest beginning, as a whole tree burns on
a fire kindled with twigs.

THOUGHT FOR TODAY: I'm part of every problem that affects me. I may not be able to change
others, but I can change myself.

You can't chew with someone else's teeth.
                    —Anonymous (Yiddish proverb)

Someone else's pain or loss may give us pain because
we love them and wish them well, but it's not our
loss. Similarly, we may be happy for another's
achievement—especially a family member's—but it's
not ours. We get into trouble if we feel other people's feelings, or try to. Sympathy and compassion
aren't the same as borrowed feelings.

If all our tears are for others' sadness and our
laughter for borrowed joy, we're hurting ourselves,
stifling our own emotional responses. Those of us
who are most at risk for vicarious feelings are people with tightly disciplined emotions. We may start
on a career of borrowing others' feelings just because we're out of touch with our own.

We pretend to chew with someone else's teeth
until we can hardly taste the bread in our own
mouths. But we can offer ourselves the bountiful
compassion we show for others. If we put our trust
in our own source of spiritual strength, and have
patience, we will begin to feel the difference between
our own feelings and our loved ones'.

THOUGHT FOR TODAY: Does anyone in my fam-
ily take over my feelings? I'll pray that they learn to
get back in touch with their own.

I can live for two months on a good compliment.
—Mark Twain

What is a really good compliment? It's an appreciation of our qualities that lets us know we're valued for ourselves—that another person sees our uniqueness and upholds it. This very personal warmth we can give in our families, to our children or our brothers and sisters, setting aside the daily flow of bicker and banter, and singling them out for applause.

It doesn't need to be a big or public demonstration. Just some kind words that let a child or sibling know we *notice* them, we pay attention to them, their life's journey matters to us. If we know that someone has been working hard on a personal goal, self-control or spiritual growth or weight loss or broad-jumping, our notice, our appreciation, can reward their effort.

Loving attention is our most precious gift to one another. We can easily give it, for it comes from an inexhaustible source—our own hearts. If we grudge the good compliments, we need to ask why. We deserve to be happy enough within ourselves to spread happiness for others.

THOUGHT FOR TODAY: Appreciation nourishes the spirit, as bread feeds the body.

For fast-acting relief, try slowing down.
                                        —Lily Tomlin

To a child, a week is a long time. As we get more weeks and months under our belts, time seems to speed up more and more, until we're old, and the years slide by like base runners stealing home.

Parents of young children can borrow some techniques for slowing down. Napping is a wonderful way to stretch the day, because I feel refreshed when I get up, not frazzled from the effort of staying awake. Do I pay attention to how tiring it can be to play with my friends? Overscheduling is a constant temptation, but if I practice clearing from my calendar everything that doesn't contribute to my health and growth, I'll find I have time to do everything I want to do.

Babies, children, and adults all need some empty time, time to play in the bathtub, go for walks, stare into space. This time is healthful and restorative, and much better than pills. Developing a creative relationship to time can ease the stress we feel at balancing our family commitments, work, and social life. Reaching into ourselves can't be rushed, and what we touch there is irreplaceable: our source of spiritual health and nurture.

THOUGHT FOR TODAY: I deserve all the time in the world.

When my friends lack an eye, I look at them in profile.

—Joseph Joubert

Some old friends introduced their teenage daughter to me. The mother said abruptly, "She's very short."

I could see the girl was short, and I could see a tension in her jaw when her mother said that. She was also bright and charming, and I enjoyed our visit.

After she left us, I asked the mother, my old friend, "Why do you comment on her height?" She explained that it was much on her mind and she couldn't help herself, although she knew her daughter hated to have her say it. She's short herself and clearly feels responsible for her daughter's stature.

Many parents overstep the bounds of their children's privacy and identify with them physically, constantly offering comments on their hair, skin, height, or physique, as though dwelling on an imagined defect could change it. Families where such boundary blurring is an ordinary occurrence risk deep estrangements or enmeshments—children who either can't separate themselves from their parents or break off contact completely. Stewardship, not ownership, is a healthy relationship.

THOUGHT FOR TODAY: Real love includes respect for differences; my family deserves as much respect and compassion as my friends.

We get our parents so late in life that it is impossible to do anything with them.

—Anonymous

This nameless child phrased a common exasperation particularly well. Parents are set in their ways—they'll never understand pop music, or jokes, and their rules are so harsh. Many children feel powerless and hopeless about communicating with their parents.

Children also feel sometimes that their parents are acting out of habit, without taking account of special circumstances. It's a mark of respect for parents to tell their children how they make certain decisions, how they change their minds, what influences them, and how they evaluate the children's behavior. Parents who discuss decisions with their children find that they feel less manipulated as well.

Not only is it possible to do something with parents, it's even possible to talk to them. In some families, parents and children informally contract with each other to get what they want—for chores, for schedules, for special privileges. Even children as young as eight or nine can make simple agreements and stick to them. Parents may not ever enjoy their children's music, but they can keep two-way communication going.

THOUGHT FOR TODAY: I'll learn to be most open to those I love the most. As long as others have something to teach me, I can keep on learning.

We are all like Scheherazade's husband in that we want to know what happens next.

—E. M. Forster

At any age we can be struck with despair, in which the world seems chaotic and cruel, but it's most common in adolescence. Some of us respond to the chill feeling of hopelessness with suicidal thoughts. Just at the point when we're preparing to enter the grown-up world, when we have the greatest need for self-assurance, we're overwhelmed with a sense of wretched absurdity.

Tragically, some adolescents do kill themselves—but what prevents many more, I think, is that beneath our pain, we're all terribly curious to know what happens next. Many young people have thoughts of suicide, and relatively few act on them. The current of life pulls us along; we want to know how our young siblings will turn out, what will happen in soap operas and comic strips and in our own lives.

Unhappy though we may be at any given moment, we're part of life, enmeshed in its texture. We'll never see the whole pattern of which we're one tiny, irreplaceable part. Our pain is as real as anything else in the larger picture, but this picture changes constantly. Our faith in a power greater than our own lets us know that whatever comes next, it will be different. New colors are always appearing in the vast, shimmering web of life. We may be in pain, but we know joy awaits us.

THOUGHT FOR TODAY: Despair at times overwhelms me, but I know some new turn of events will call me forth, and life will seem worthwhile again.

There is nothing new in the world except the history you do not know.

—Harry S. Truman

The other night a woman I know described a visit to her parents: "As soon as I walk in, my dad starts tearing me down. 'Streaked your hair, eh? No wonder you can't hold onto a boyfriend. Where'd you find those pants?' Blah, blah, blah. Then my mom comes in. 'Oh, you look so wonderful, how's your new boyfriend, I love your hair.' Blah, blah. After a couple minutes I realized *he's* cutting *me* down to get at *her; she's* building me up to get back at *him*. They did that to us all through our childhoods, and we never knew it. I could just walk out of the room and leave them to it."

My friend is the youngest child in a large family; the parents have always spoken to each other through the children. After many painful years of feeling it was somehow her fault that her parents argued over her, my friend has learned to take care of herself.

She'll never receive the unconditional love we all crave from parents who are locked into a distorted relationship, but she is learning to supply it through a spiritual connection to a power greater than herself. And if she—and her brothers and sisters—can get out of the middle, the parents may have to confront one another directly, get to the bottom of their conflict and bitterness. My friend is helping them in the only way she can, by ceasing to play the game that has scarred all their lives.

THOUGHT FOR TODAY: In my journey toward self-discovery, I am constantly learning aspects of my history I didn't know.

Being a husband is a whole-time job.
—Arnold Bennett

To husband means to preserve, to care for, to manage well. Sharing responsibility for a family household *is* a whole-time job, even if the family consists of one person and a goldfish; it's whole-time in the sense that this responsibility to care for one's share of the household becomes part of one's identity, part of the answer to the question, *Who are you?* A married man is a husband, whatever else he may be.

We can all be good husbands, whether or not we're married or male. Good husbands care for what they have. Maybe what you have is an inquiring mind and a restless foot. Caring for them properly means paying attention to the needs of your mind and spirit. Settled family life doesn't suit everyone, yet everyone can husband well her or his own resources.

Our most important task is knowing who we are; then comes our responsibility to care for what we have. True husbanding of our resources will always bring us rewards, for our actions will be in harmony with our needs and desires.

THOUGHT FOR TODAY: Since caring for my spirit and body is a whole-time job, today and every day I'll strive to do it fully and well.

Parents can only give good advice or put them on the right paths, but the final forming of a person's character lies in their own hands.

—Anne Frank

Each of us at times would like to blame our parents for what we think they did wrong. Yet life is too thickly textured, each of us is subject to too many different influences, for us to be able to make simple correlations. We may start our journey with handicaps or advantages, but what we are and do, finally, is up to us.

Sometimes we're afraid to accept responsibility for our lives. It's much easier to lay it off on our parents—yet how disrespectful, to them and to ourselves. They did the best they could with what they had. Their parents, too, made inevitable mistakes, while doing their best. Perhaps they struggled with illness or with grave personal shortcomings. It's up to us, now, to seek and find the real spiritual power that will guarantee success in our lives.

Each of us is a vital part of a picture larger than we can see. We're connected to all the other parts, yet free to determine our own destiny within the larger whole. Our task is to accept our freedom along with our connectedness.

THOUGHT FOR TODAY: The power to shape my life lies in my own hands. I'll be careful not to give it away.

*[In the seventeenth century] apart from the lives of
little saints, schoolchildren were given as subjects of
edification accounts of the childhood years of full-
grown saints—or else of their remorse at their mis-
spent youth.*

—Philippe Ariès

Remember the improving stories we read as children? Remember rooting for the bad kids? Everyone
loves a charming rogue, because the child in us
keeps hoping to escape the grown-ups' laws: thou
shalt not, thou shalt not, thou shalt not.

Children often disobey as a way of asserting their
individuality. That's what the "terrible twos" are
about, usually; the child discovers that it can say
"No," and that this word has power in the world.
The parent, who has struggled to meet an infant's
needs for two years, feels that the child has plenty of
power. But the child doesn't see it that way. All the
child has done is yell when it's hungry, cry when it's
hurt; this isn't the conscious exercise of power, like
saying "No," even though parents feel controlled by
those cries and yells.

We all survive the terrible twos and become trac-
table threes and fabulous fours. We learn to tie our
shoes and go to the store and clean up, pass tests, get
jobs; but inside each of us is still a child, thrilled to
discover we can say "No" and shock our parents. The
best stories always include some triumph for the child
in us, even though the grown-up may win in the end.

THOUGHT FOR TODAY: Maturity means doing
the right thing for my own reasons.

*You don't tell people your troubles when you are
still in the midst of them, otherwise it makes them
bigger, more insoluble.*

—Buchi Emecheta

Some troubles seem to get bigger when we talk
about them, but this may be because we're not saying
the right things. People in the midst of trouble have
the right to a sympathetic hearing from someone
who can see around the problem. When we're caught
up in trouble, usually we see only our own distress.
Wise counsel can help us find our way.

Family members may not be the best listeners or
counselors, because they're partial. Either our troubles become fodder for gossip or they're taken
personally—neither of which helps us very much.
Yet the big troubles of life—illness, death, violence—
are too heavy for us to bear alone.

Luckily we can seek people whose job it is to help
with such troubles. Professional counselors listen without any of the history a family member attaches to
our words; professionals can also offer solutions
without trying to shame us. What magnifies and
complicates our troubles is for others to take them
on. We deserve better in our lives.

THOUGHT FOR TODAY: When I need advice and
counsel, I'll consider carefully where I seek them.

For fear of what it might do to me, you never paid a compliment, and when others did, you beat it away from me with a stick. "He certainly is looking nice and grown-up." "He'd look better if he did something about his skin."

—Garrison Keillor

Many of us lack the confidence that we know what's best, either for ourselves or for those we love. We're fearful that if we give in to our soft and loving feelings, we won't prepare our children for life in the hard, cruel world. Hardness and cruelty, however, are qualities we'll find more often if we go looking for them.

Our fears can keep us from expressing the love and support we feel for family members. Most often, we fear that our children or our parents or siblings will invade us emotionally, smother us, if we reveal our vulnerable, loving spirits. Goodness knows, there are times in family life when boundaries are violated and privacy is invaded, and most of us carry some scars. Sometimes we let this scar tissue harden into an armor that keeps away all kinds of contact, caresses as well as blows.

The work of maintaining our personal boundaries is important work, with great rewards. When we respect ourselves and others, we are given respect in return. When our boundaries are firm, we're able to offer love and praise freely, and to give constructive criticism when it's appropriate. We're also able to hear the honest appraisals of others, without feeling endangered by them.

THOUGHT FOR TODAY: Today I'll pray for the serenity to show my appreciation to those I love.

The more I study the world, the more I am convinced of the inability of brute force to create anything durable.

—Napoleon Bonaparte

Any parent of a two-year-old can tell you that force creates rebellion, and that people obey orders better if they have helped to give them. Maybe it took Napoleon most of a lifetime to discover this because he never spent time with small children. People who do—and in Napoleon's day these would have been mainly poor women, who cared for their own families and worked as servants and nurses in the households of the rich—understand the weakness of brute force.

In families as in larger political bodies, the lasting decisions are reached democratically. Young children may approach family democracy in a spirit of play, but their innate feeling for fairness will soon help them to see that a process of debate, arbitration, and voting works.

Parents must be fair, of course, and willing to compromise. Phony democracy is like one-party voting, and children are smart enough to spot totalitarian tactics. The basic requirement for equity in a loving family is trust: trust in one another's essential goodness, and trust that the outcomes we desire aren't so different. We all want what's best for those we love, as for ourselves. Our disputes are usually over matters of degree.

THOUGHT FOR TODAY: If I'm to be heard, I must be willing to listen. If I'm to give, I must be willing to receive.

Think of the distressing contrast between the radiant intelligence of a healthy child and the feeble mentality of the average adult.

—Sigmund Freud

All children are geniuses; I was and you were. Our radiance was dulled by schooling, and by learning to accommodate to the world. In their time, our parents were geniuses, and they too became ordinary, like their parents and theirs, stretching back as far as the beginnings of human society.

Why isn't it possible for us to keep this radiance undimmed? The fresh intelligence of children can see all sorts of emperors that have no clothes. They would never put up with bureaucratic delays or political corruption, endless business meetings, routine jobs, forms in triplicate, legal jargon. In short, the world as we know it would crumble before the clarity that we could bring to it, if all our childhood luster shone forth.

We can see our children's intelligence; can we protect them from growing into ordinary people? More, can we rescue ourselves within the lives we lead? Today I'll seek to recover some of my early radiance and turn it on the dark places in my life. The gift of clarity is mine, to use as I wish.

THOUGHT FOR TODAY: If I can nurture the child within me, I can retrieve a spark of genius.

Home is not where you live but where they understand you.

—Christian Morgenstern

Conflicts of belief or behavior may drive a wedge between family members. One of us may feel drastically different from the rest—or excluded. We may seek the benefits of family living—intimacy, shared growth, self-discovery, and the opportunity to live for others—elsewhere, with a friend's family or in a community of friends.

As we grow older we may find ourselves returning closer to our original family, especially if we've been successful in making a new home, a place where we feel fully understood. No matter how deep the connection to our chosen home, there's a resonance to the family where we grew up, the parents and siblings who shaped our early lives, that impels us to reforge our links with them. They may not understand us any better now than they did in our youth, but it matters less. We understand ourselves better, and our love for them is unconditional.

Acceptance is often a gift of age—acceptance of what we don't understand and of those who don't understand us. If we find a loving family and understanding of our special qualities in the same place, we're blessed with great good luck. If we find them separately we're still blessed, because we have them both.

THOUGHT FOR TODAY: When I've achieved self-understanding, I'll be at home everywhere.

Mobility is our ethos. We take it for granted. And because we do, we have perhaps neglected to tell our parents . . . that our leaving home was never a choice, just happenstance.

—Mark Patinkin

When young adults leave school and work at their first real jobs, the old intimacies of parents and siblings can feel shabby and outworn, like an ancient leather jacket. Still comfortable, maybe, but not something you wear to work. You need another garment, something cut to your own style. And so young people leave, for homes of their own where they may start new families.

Home means emotional intimacy to most of us, far more than lath and plaster. If we're at ease with those we love, we can feel at home in a camper or hotel room. Home may mean another country; home can be a language or style of cooking. We've all had the experience of meeting a stranger and immediately feeling at home.

Most of us leave home many times, and most of us return—to our families. Shared food, shared jokes, the framed photographs, the battered chest of drawers. If we're at ease in the world, we are home away from home. If we're lucky, we carry home with us when we go.

THOUGHT FOR TODAY: Home is where I am loved. When I quiet my spirit, I feel the love that streams through the universe.

As those we love decay, we die in part,
String after string is severed from the heart.
                                        —James Thomson

One thing about growing old: you live through the deaths of a lot of friends and relations. If you live to be very old, you sustain the loss of younger loved ones, perhaps even your children. Sometimes an old person wonders, "Why me? Why am I alive and a younger person dead?"

Suppose the heart were like a dirigible, held down by earthly attachments to family, work, friends, and property. Suppose further that as we age these attachments, these strings, are cut one by one, and when we cut the last ties our hearts rise up and sail, free at last of the bonds that held us to earth. Now we are ready, if we choose, to attempt the highest serenity, the detached peace that passes understanding.

If we are gifted with long life, we have the pain of losing those we love. In exchange, we are offered the opportunity for spiritual transcendence, for the replacement of earthly love with cosmic love. Then we will have attained wisdom; this is what we understand as bliss.

THOUGHT FOR TODAY: Freedom from bonds never means I will stop loving.

The answer to your dreams is inside you.
                              —Lorna Ozman

Since we are the dreamers, all the challenges, questions, or beauties of our dreams come from within us. It's only logical that their answers can, too. When our children or other family members set their sights on a goal that seems fantastic, our role is not to mock or discourage them but to help them reach it, if we can.

Young people sometimes dream impractically— "And I'll be downhill skiing champion and a brain surgeon and a movie star"—but there, too, we can help. If dreams stay impractical, they'll never turn into goals, but when we take the dreamers seriously and help them convert their fantasies into possible future identities or skills, they'll be able to decide which are really life goals and which are the stuff of daydreams.

Our sleeping dreams use themes and images from our waking experience to tell stories about our fears and desires. Our waking dreams can lead us to solid achievements. Both kinds come from inside us, and what we do with them is our choice.

THOUGHT FOR TODAY: My dreams can lead me to what I want most in life, and I can encourage all those I love to dream.

An easy task becomes difficult when you do it with reluctance.

—Terence

My small nephew was in his terrible twos when he dropped a peanut butter sandwich on the kitchen floor. He began to howl; the word *raisins* could be heard among his lamentations.

"Fine," said his father, who was washing dishes. "You can have some raisins after you pick up the mess. Come on, I'll help you."

"No!" shrieked Jeffrey. "No, no, no, no, no!" The father kept his temper, but the little boy threw a full-fledged tantrum, stamping his feet and kicking sandwich scraps all over, in corners, under the table, and in the cat's dish, and smearing peanut butter into the linoleum.

"Come on," repeated his father. "We'll do it together."

"No!" sobbed the child. In the end Jeffrey did pick up half a dozen bits of crust, while his father searched out the rest and the cat licked up the peanut butter.

Jeffrey was so exhausted that he didn't want his raisins; he retreated to his blanket and fell asleep. I think of him whenever I catch myself postponing a simple chore, or complicating it with reluctance.

Jeffrey is lucky, because his parents offer cooperation and don't interfere with his expression of his feelings. I need to accept my own feelings as calmly as they do his.

THOUGHT FOR TODAY: Am I making things hard for myself? I need freedom from resentment, with the help of my source of spiritual strength.

All truths are half-truths.
> —Alfred North Whitehead

This notion, that every truth is only a part of the truth, comes from a mathematician and philosopher, but it echoes the experience many of us have had. All the wise words our parents, grandparents, aunts and uncles, and guardians laid on us turned out to be partly wise. A penny saved is sometimes a penny earned, but in severe inflation it can be a halfpenny.

There may be family voices still ringing authoritatively in our ears—the voices of people who never admitted doubts, at least not where we could hear. As we grow in our knowledge of the world, we find that to be honest we must admit most things are part good and part bad; part true and part false. We're thrown back on our own judgments and powers of discrimination, and—since we too are mixed and partial—we need guidance from a source of spiritual strength that blesses our limited powers.

We do well to go gently in our search for truth, being patient with our slow pace. We can be faithful to a family legacy of high moral purpose by admitting our limitations and surrendering ourselves to the creative power that has no limits.

THOUGHT FOR TODAY: My part of the truth lies in my search for consistency. Today and every day, I seek to be fully myself.

Say not, when I have leisure I will study; you may not have leisure.

—Hillel

For infants, time has only one tense—the present. Although they love games like peek-a-boo that use repetition—playing with time—they have only primitive notions of past or future. Soon babies' memories develop, and they learn to anticipate. Then they enter the time structure of adult life, where a lot of energy is bound up in remembering the past and planning the future.

Though we may make plans, neither future nor past is within our grasp. The only time we have is now. Our family is not what it was two generations ago, or when your grandpa was alive, or what it will be in twenty minutes or when your sister gets married. Memories may bring joy, and anticipation or dread can quicken our pulse—but the only time in which we can act is the present.

Because our only real time is now, what we do now has the most importance. Not what we did last year or what we're planning to do when Bud graduates or when Aunt Ruth dies. Now is the only time we have to show our love for one another, to take the risks we've been putting off, or to say the words we've been rehearsing. If it's ever going to be worth doing, it's worth doing now.

THOUGHT FOR TODAY: If I could predict the future or change the past, I would lose the gift of the present. I can concentrate my powers fully here and now, for now is all the time I have—or need.

*It is easy finding reasons why other folks should be
patient.*

—George Eliot

A little boy was playing doctor with his doll. "Sshh!"
he whispered sternly. "Dolly's being very patient
with me."

Patience really is loosening of control, a relinquishment. When we're patient with small children,
we encourage them to explore and experiment, to
take ten minutes to brush their teeth or half an hour
to walk a hundred yards. Our patience is a double
declaration—one, that we can't control their movements, and two, that we believe in the rightness of
what they're doing.

When we're impatient, we pull others along in our
wake. "Don't dawdle," we say to our children, "let's
get going." This too is a declaration—that our plan
is all-important.

Sometimes impatience is unavoidable; some schedules must be met. But the double declaration of
patience is welcome to children's developing spirits.
They learn to feel confidence in their own projects if
we've been patient with them in their investigations
of the world. And we're helped to be patient when
we have a strong connection to our own spiritual
source, our connection with the vital essence of life.

THOUGHT FOR TODAY: The reasons why others
should be patient hold true for me, too. Am I patient
with my growing, changing self?

I live in that solitude which is painful in youth, but delicious in the years of maturity.
　　　　　　　　　　　　　　　—Albert Einstein

Solitude can be painful at any age if it's not a chosen condition. Young people seldom have the wealth of inner resources to enable them to choose solitude. We all want to be able to choose our companions, or no companions.

Families can solace our loneliness, providing a refuge when we feel bruised by the world. We're fortunate indeed if we grew up with loving, supportive family members. Some of us come from households that were colder and lonelier than any isolation we could imagine, and we fled from them—more to avoid them than to join another.

Such families damage us, and our great search in life is to heal ourselves, to open ourselves to love. Solitude can be blessed, when we choose it because our thoughts are rich; because we amuse ourselves best; because our spiritual practice shows us we are never really alone. Prayer and meditation develop the inner wealth that heals us and enables us to make such choices.

THOUGHT FOR TODAY: Today I'll seek the balance of solitude and companionship that complements my needs.

*In the family sandwich, the older people and the
younger ones can recognize each other as the bread.
Those in the middle are, for a time, the meat.*
—Anna Quindlen

Strength and wisdom come in middle age, but so do
heavy demands. The generation in the middle, people in their forties and fifties who still have responsibility for children and may also have aging parents,
can feel these gifts as burdens. In the cycles of family
life, responsibilities shift. Parents who cared for us
when we were helpless need our care when age or
illness saps their strength. Children we raised may
care for us in our old age.

The trouble with this orderly picture of genera-
tional cycling is that it ignores the multiple patterns
in the real lives of families. Children may live with
one single parent or share time among several complex households, with step-, half-, and foster siblings. People die and divorce at any age. Long
distances may separate family members.

We can find serenity in the family sandwich—
though sometimes the bread may feel like millstones,
crushing us with need. We are not alone. Spiritual
comfort is ours for the asking. We need to let up on
ourselves and not expect perfection; we'll do the
best we can.

THOUGHT FOR TODAY: The other side of every
strength may be a defect, but the other side of misfortune is a blessing.

Good, to forgive;
Best, to forget;
Living, we fret;
Dying, we live.

—Robert Browning

We may recognize the wisdom of detachment—most saints and sages have recommended it as a key to serenity—but achieving it is another matter, especially when family members are the source of our grudging and fretting. How can we detach from the troubles of our spouses, parents, or children? We live with them, rub up against them daily; their crazy habits shape our day-to-day existence.

The answer is to tend to our own spiritual health. We're responsible for our own actions, our own lives; we can care for our families without hooking in to them. "But—but—" we say, "my daughter calls me up all the time to ask for money"; "My wife doesn't speak to me"; "I can never forgive my father for the way he treated us."

Holding on to old wounds ensures that they won't heal. Reacting to destructive behavior is a way of encouraging it. Our creativity and love are so much more powerful than our resentments and injuries that we can find a way to detach from them, if we choose. Begin by acting "as if" we had detached from our problems; detachment suddenly brightens the prospects for life and growth.

THOUGHT FOR TODAY: Detachment begins with self-worth, the foundation of all self-forgetfulness.

There are few places outside of his own play where a child can contribute to the world in which he finds himself.

—Viola Spolin

Children need to feel they're important to the big, powerful adults in their lives. Everyone is born with a sense of her or his own importance, but a child who is always hushed, ignored, or hustled out of the way soon learns to express it in devious ways.

A firm sense of our own importance is necessary before we can turn our energies outward. In their play, children mirror behavior and concerns from other areas of life; the difference is that they get to make up the rules that govern their play. Parents who encourage their children's play and take it seriously are contributing to their children's sense of self-worth.

With healthy love and nurture and plenty of imaginative play, a child's inborn sense of importance will find expression in achievements—in sports, arts, school work, social interaction. Adults who are happy in their work and in their lives can call on some of the imaginative powers of play they had as children. Our playful self continues to enhance our self-worth, whatever our age.

THOUGHT FOR TODAY: Play can nourish and renew me; I owe it to myself to tap some childish energies.

Next to the very young, I suppose the very old are the most selfish.

　　　　　　　　　　　　　　—W. M. Thackeray

Look in any bookstore at the shelves upon shelves of books devoted to early life, babies and children, their health, emotional development, care and feeding, training and education. Then look for books about old age. You'll find a handful about death and dying, and maybe a couple on physical fitness; but nowhere in our culture do we recognize that old people have emotional and psychological needs that are different from younger people's. "Old age" isn't one thing; there are stages in growing old, as in other times of life. No wonder the old appear selfish! Nobody else seems to care about them at all.

　Surviving into old age is quite a heroic achievement, yet we have no way of celebrating it, beyond the same annual birthday observance that we make for children. To grow old is to come to terms with many losses, in one's world and in oneself. Shouldn't there be some ceremony that recognizes this heroism?

　In old age, we hope to reach some understanding of change and constancy—what we call wisdom. If we can couple this with serenity, which is the product of a good spiritual connection to a power greater than ourselves, then we will achieve a peaceful spirit. We'll be ready for the next stage in our journey.

THOUGHT FOR TODAY: Serene old age comes with detachment from the world. I'll learn to tell the difference between serenity and selfishness.

Anger is often more hurtful than the injury that caused it.

—Anonymous (Yiddish proverb)

Children feel violent anger—violent enough to make them want to do harm. If death enters a young child's life, especially the death of a parent or sibling, the child may believe that her or his anger was involved in—or even responsible for—the death. Many people whose childhoods bear the scar of loss have harbored this primitive belief, that their anger was lethal. Unless children are surrounded by loving, understanding adults at such a time, they may well grow up with the unconscious belief that their anger can kill, and in adult life they may have an unreasoning fear of anger, their own and others'.

If we suppress it, anger comes out in other ways. Sometimes anger turns against the self or leaks out in our jokes and conversation, like a poison gas; or else the energy we use to keep it repressed leaves us permanently exhausted. We need to have access to our anger, to understand that it's a shared human feeling and not our own horrible secret.

When we accept our anger, we can turn it to good uses—channel it into activities of various kinds, convert it into energy for writing letters, starting groups, challenging unjust authority. Far from killing, anger can be used for healing.

THOUGHT FOR TODAY: Properly balanced, my anger is a necessary part of my humanity. I'll pray and work for the power to use it wisely.

To speak a true word is to transform the world. . . .
Consequently no one can say a true word alone—
nor can one say it for another.

                                        —Paulo Freire

Before we can speak, those who care for us speak
for us. In families where individual growth is nurtured,
adults encourage children to develop their own voices,
to speak their minds and to say what they want and
don't want: long hair or oatmeal, soccer or ballet
lessons or tattoos.

When our desires become larger than our personal
lives—when the concern is with social justice, rather
than with raisins in the oatmeal—then we join our
voices with others who have the same concerns. If
we've learned respect for differences in our families,
we carry this over into our social lives. I will say "I"
rather than "we," unless I have explicit permission
from those whose names I invoke, whose desires I
speak to.

When I want to use my energies to help transform
the world, I need to find my allies. In whatever
group I join, I will remember that love for my fellows includes respect for their voices. If I'm chosen
to speak for others, I'll do everything in my power
to merit their trust, and I'll be fully responsible to
myself when I agree to let another speak for me.

THOUGHT FOR TODAY: Whether I'm alone or in
a group, I won't confuse my desires—or my voice—
with others'.

Only one person in a thousand knows the trick of really living in the present.

—Storm Jameson

Infants have no choice; the demands of their bodies anchor them firmly in the present tense. Gradually, children develop their sense of memory, their trust in the future. These become our tools for understanding the world. Perhaps it's to escape the knowledge of our extreme vulnerability that so many of us choose to live lives of planning and control, or of memory and regret.

Living fully in the present is a matter of attitude and habit. It means doing what we can at every moment to nourish our senses and our spirits. It means releasing the past, not letting a frown sit on our faces after whatever provoked it has passed. It means also admitting we can't predict or control the future. We may put money in the bank so we'll have it in the future, but we don't starve today in order to eat tomorrow.

The only time we have for sure is right now, this moment. If we're not fulfilled by it, something is askew. Let's look at our lives, our families: Are we harmonious, or are we twisted with contradictions and denials? This moment is my whole life. I'll pray for the strength to make it radiant.

THOUGHT FOR TODAY: What I can't change, I accept or surrender. What I can change, I will.

I believe in getting into hot water; it keeps you clean.

—G. K. Chesterton

Everybody worries about children who are constantly in trouble—hurting themselves, hurting others, disobedient, exuberant, noisy, restless. We all despair of adults who are constantly in trouble—getting into fights, getting into debt, getting into trouble with the law. But what about the child or adult who's *never* in trouble? That can be a danger signal, too.

Life is richly fulfilling if we live it to the full, but discovering our limits often leads us into trouble of one kind or another—trouble we recover from, and are better for. Trouble, often, that we learn from.

Someone who never steps over a limit may be afraid to live fully. Have we scared our children into occupying only a small corner of their potential lives? Breaking rules can be healthy; we need to let our children know that our love for them stretches to cover their mistakes.

THOUGHT FOR TODAY: Did I learn from the mistakes I made when I was young? Or will I have to make them all over again?

It is always a fascinating problem to consider who we would have been if our mother (or our father) had married another person.

—Gwen Raverat

When I was a child, it was quite thrilling to think that my identity depended on my parents' genes. What if I'd had blue eyes? But those of us who are children adopted by our parents or guardians, rather than born to them, have a less pleasurable sense of possible alternatives.

We spend a lot of fantasy time wondering how our lives would have been different if our birth parents had raised us. We make up stories about their lives, endow them with wealth and health, and imagine that we'd have none of our current dissatisfactions, if only . . .

By the time we're grown, we know that most people's lives are more alike than not. Once our basic needs are met, we all face similar problems: children need schooling, adults need work; everyone needs security and a sense of community. Rather than wasting our energies on might-have-beens, we can come close to realizing our dreams. Of course, we'd be different if we'd grown up with different parents, in different circumstances. But we can be all we dream of, if we put our minds and hearts to it.

THOUGHT FOR TODAY: Dreams and wishes are as real as I want to make them. The decision to take them seriously is mine.

"Oh," was all he could say—the thin plaintive sound made by a small boy who has suddenly understood that there are some ills Mommy cannot cure.
                                                    —William Murray

When we were small, the touch of a loved and trusted hand had the power to take away pain. "Kiss it and make it better," we demanded when we stubbed our toes or bumped our heads, and someone did. And then we encountered the pains too great to kiss away.

Those of us who had plenty of loving nurture have a healing power within ourselves, enabling us to survive pain and injury. The healing power is made up of love, trust, and faith: love we can feel, that envelops and softens us; trust that the powerful forces in our lives are looking out for us; and faith that our place in the universe is secure and we'll come to no harm.

Many of us have experiences that challenge our healing powers of faith and trust. But the knowledge that we're loved still can heal us, if we know how to tap it within ourselves. If our self-love is strong, we can surrender our mistrust. And this strength we can give our children, knowing that they too will face great challenges in their lives.

THOUGHT FOR TODAY: I am grateful for the healing powers I received from those who love me. With them, I'm equal to any task I choose to undertake.

To die will be an awfully big adventure.
—James M. Barrie

All the world's religions include belief in some form of immortality or resurrection, some continuity for the human spirit. Yet we have the habit of looking at death as the end of our story, rather than the termination of one chapter.

When children die, parents' deep sadness usually includes a sense of profound injustice along with grief. The child was torn out of the web of loving relationships before life had a chance to fulfill its pattern. It's rare that grieving survivors can think of the adventures of the soul.

Yet everything we know on earth teaches us that when one door closes, another opens. Frustration in one direction always includes opportunity in others. Whatever our personal beliefs, we know that on a sheerly biological level, there's no such thing as final death; there is only change, the recombination of elements into ever-changing series of compounds. Who can say what may happen on a spiritual level?

Of course, we grieve the tearing of our web. Our grief is for ourselves, our own loss of a loved one, a familiar voice, the touch of a small hand. That change may be the entrance into a new phase, an existence we can't imagine. Whether we can use this image for consolation is up to us.

THOUGHT FOR TODAY: Where life and death are concerned, all we know for certain is that we don't know everything.

Today things change so fast that the experience of the last generation is increasingly irrelevant, and the bottom has dropped out of the market for venerable sages of either sex.

—Elaine Morgan

Styles change and language changes, but human kindness doesn't change. A venerable sage who understands human motives will be an asset to any endeavor, even if the techniques or the vocabulary are newfangled. True, technology becomes obsolete pretty fast, but wisdom doesn't go bad. Young people may think their parents or grandparents have nothing useful to impart because they don't understand arbitrage or lasers. Our tools may be different, but we use them for the same jobs.

Things appear to change very fast, and speed can be frightening. Fear may cloud the perception of even the wisest elder. Sages themselves may get sidetracked by details—the way a good cook might despair of learning to use a microwave oven.

If parents and grandparents are truly wise, they'll wait to be asked before sharing their rich experience. But if young people wish to enlarge their world and add to their perceptions, they'll find the sages in their families and humbly learn from them.

THOUGHT FOR TODAY: The movements of the human heart and spirit don't change very much over the centuries, and knowledge of them is timeless.

Hybrids are what make the world go forward.
                                    —Luther Burbank

Most of us are hybrids. A few of us may come from
families where all our known ancestors married within
the same ethnic group—Chinese, Eastern Europeans,
native American Indians—but most of us have hy-
bridization in our family trees. And most of the
partners with whom we choose to have children
have similar varied ancestry. For humans as for plants
and animals, new genetic combinations increase the
potential for high-quality descendants.

It's highly unclear what role inheritance plays in
any given individual's makeup. We know something
about hereditary potentials for disease, but not for
health. Human growth and upbringing are too complex to allow for speculation beyond a general sense
that new combinations are usually desirable. We can
say for certain only that difference is to be welcomed—differences in style and belief as much as
differences in color or national origin.

When family members enrich our future by choosing varied partners, we have occasion for rejoicing.
We're widening our circle of intimacy, as when we
adopt a child. Differences stretch our spirits, making
them resilient and strong. When we embrace difference, we grace ourselves while helping to heal the
world.

THOUGHT FOR TODAY: I will seek out the gifts
of diversity wherever I can.

My daughter is lesbian. She is also the light of my life. . . . If society has some false notions about her, that is all the more reason she needs and deserves my support.

—R. Bernstein

When children choose partners from an unexpected color, gender, or class, parents may find their notion of family stretched. A same-sex lover can change our idea of who we are, of just who's meant when we say "we." We may give a kind of automatic assent to the notion that humanity is one family, but that's different from finding gays or lesbians at our family dinner table.

Same-sex partners can be more difficult to accept than other colors and classes, partly because of the question of granchildren. Most parents of lesbians and gays either have or acquire enough information to get rid of any lingering shame or stigma around the question of sexuality. But the notion that they may not have grandchildren can be distressing. Today many lesbian and some gay couples are choosing to bear or adopt children. Like other assumptions about family, this barrier to parenthood (and grandparenthood) is turning out to be illusory as well.

Parents of lesbians and gays learn some hard lessons in acceptance and courage, like everyone who faces the "false notions" of prejudice. Loving, accepting parents are a lifelong asset to their children—especially when they believe that the breadth of experience lesbians and gays bring to a family is a precious gift.

THOUGHT FOR TODAY: I welcome challenges to my world view; they help me to grow.

A child by his very existence makes a parent feel older, nearer death.

—E. B. White

My father called children "hostages to fortune," meaning, I suppose, that once he had them he was no longer free to do battle with the world; he had to conform, get a job, wear a tie, pay the rent. I think of my children differently, as messengers of hope. Because of them, I'm involved in their world; I want to do what I can to make it a safe and decent place for them. They encourage me to widen my world view, to think more of my human family and less of myself.

Yes, children make us feel older; we *are* older, suddenly—caregivers, rule makers, the older generation. But in exchange we're given the immense privilege of the future. We glimpse the slowly turning wheel of time, in which birth and death are merely points on a curve, and our lives are the fulfillment of our special destinies.

My children bind me firmly to my life, to my world. For their sake, I love all the world's children, and I want for them the peace and harmony my children deserve. They lift me out of myself and my life, uniting me with my parents and ancestors, with grandchildren and remote descendants. They bring me close to the elements of life—one of which is death.

THOUGHT FOR TODAY: The spiritual dimension of parenting broadens my view of death, as it has of life.

*It is far easier to be wise for others than to be so for
oneself.*

—Duc de La Rochefoucauld

When should young people move away from home?
"When they go to college"; "When they get married"; "When they get a real job"; "When they're
eighteen." There are probably as many right answers as there are different families.

These days, young people marry later. "Real jobs"
are hard to find, and so is low-cost housing. There are
plenty of reasons for young people to live with their
parents, and convenience ranks high. Why duplicate
cars, stereos, laundry equipment, or VCRs? If parents
can make these amenities available, why move out?

There are good and bad reasons for staying at
home. The best reason to leave is because we need
independence, the personal autonomy that no amount
of material goods can supply. We all need to separate from our family of origin, though no one can
tell another how, or when. As parents, it's easier to
see what's best for our grown children than to look
at how we may be clinging to them or pushing them
away. As children, it's easier to see how parents
ought to behave than it is to own our part in the
family interaction.

The right time to move away, as for other important transitions, will come when we communicate
openly and lovingly with our family members, naming problems and discussing possible solutions. Parents and children can be wise together, for themselves,
if they will be open with one another.

THOUGHT FOR TODAY: Today I'll remember that
I need all my wisdom to guide me—and my children.

Fans don't boo nobodies.

—Reggie Jackson

When something we do attracts unfavorable attention, it can stir up old feelings—we feel guilty for attracting attention even more than we feel ashamed of the negative comments. These feelings may come from early childhood, from caregivers who smacked the squeaky wheels and rewarded the quiet ones. They taught us not to stand out from the crowd.

Any strong position will meet opposition, on any question: political, social, why you liked a certain movie, or the best way to make hash browns. But if you take a public stand, you need to be serene within yourself to endure the boos as well as the applause. I'm the same person, whether other people praise or blame me. Their opinions don't change me, any more than the wind changes grass.

It isn't wrong to stand up for our beliefs, even if they're unpopular—maybe especially if they're unpopular. When we know we're doing what is right for us, we'll be strong enough to hear the reactions of others without being swayed by them.

THOUGHT FOR TODAY: My source of spiritual guidance will steady me when I feel blown about by opposition.

Nobody ever forgets where he buried a hatchet.
                                        —Kin Hubbard

Have you ever found yourself arguing with a spouse or family member and suddenly dredging up an ancient quarrel? Or had an old grievance flung in your face? Most of us have. We may believe we've let go of the fight, laid it to rest, buried it deep. Still, something rankles within us, a jealousy or dissatisfaction, and when we're looking for weapons in a new fight, we dig up the old hatchet.

The truth is, it's probably the same old fight. Between family members, conflicts seldom are truly resolved once and for all, truly let go. We bury them for the sake of peace but the underlying source remains a live coal, ready to flare up.

It is possible to let go completely—of a sibling who got the attention we craved, or of a parent who punished us irrationally—but we have to want to, with all our hearts. Some old angers are as precious as old friends, but we'll never achieve serenity unless we can release ourselves from their hold. First, we must acknowledge and accept them fully, including our own pain; then we must recognize that we're different people now, and that we want to be different. Our families did the best they could with what they had; now our lives belong to us.

THOUGHT FOR TODAY: Taking full responsibility for my life may mean abandoning some old maps—like the one that shows where the hatchet is buried.

In her eyes I see the force of her love. It is bulky and hard to carry, like a package that keeps untying.
—Louise Erdrich

Family affection changes over time, as we grow and develop. Parents' love for their children always includes remembered love for the children's younger selves. Love between siblings always holds memories, too, of jealousies and angers as well as affections. All of us become confused at times about whether our feelings have to do with present-day reality or with the remembered past, and some kinds of love can be as inappropriate as resentments.

The way to heal the past is to accept it fully, to accept our own past acts and feelings, to forgive ourselves and others for what can't be changed. A parent who loves a grown child inappropriately may be clinging to shame or regret that had its origin long ago. An adult child whose love for parents is bulky and hard to carry may be sharing the parents' guilt or self-absorption in ways that stymie future growth.

Basic to our spiritual health is self-love that permits us to respond to people and situations in the here and now. Our feelings aren't parcels, to be neatly packed or stored or carefully untied; they're living streams that flow through us. Love should comfort, not bring with it memories of shame or pain. Letting go of pain will let us love each other lightly and well, and spiritual surrender will teach us to let go.

THOUGHT FOR TODAY: I will learn to let go of my pain so that love can nourish me and my family.

Parents are the bones on which children sharpen their teeth.

—Peter Ustinov

Parents or caregivers are our first love objects because they feed us, caress us, keep us warm. They're our first hate objects, because they say "No." Inevitably, there comes a time when they deny us gratifications. When we become parents or primary caregivers, our children go through the same emotional developments with us, and their children will with them, as long as families exist.

When there are two parents, or other adults in the household, children will try to get from another what one parent denies. Rules must be firm; children soon learn who will cave in if nagged or wheedled. When parents live separately and share child care, they need some basic agreements, too, or children will learn to exploit the situation. "Mom lets me," or "Dad always says yes," is not pleasant to hear. If parents can work out shared guidelines and stick to them, everyone will benefit.

THOUGHT FOR TODAY: Behavior needs limits to give it shape; like bones in the body, parents should offer some resistance.

*The company of a mere child is infinitely preferable
to that of a mere adult.*

—Fran Lebowitz

Mere means "nothing more than," yet when we say
"a mere child" we're often expressing admiration
for unchildlike qualities of courage or wisdom. The
word "mere" comes to mean almost its opposite.
But mere adults don't sound as if they could claim
the eager creativity of children. In fact, "nothing
more than an adult" sounds pretty dull.

For me to explore my fullest potential I need to
keep in close touch with my childhood self, the
small person who faced the world with wonder. I
had to be told to get out of the water because my
lips were blue. I ate myself sick, sang myself hoarse,
and traced my favorite pictures dreamily, lovingly;
and somewhere within the responsible grown-up I am
today is this passionate, gluttonous, dreamy child.

Do we make our children ashamed of being
childish—do we tell them, "Act your age," and mean
"Act like adults"? We want them to have access to
childhood's enthusiasms; we want them to be able
to nurture the child within, not to deny it. Trust in
wisdom beyond our control can help us to respect
our unfolding selves.

THOUGHT FOR TODAY: Every stage of growth is
right for the one who's growing.

One of the best ways to persuade others is with your ears—by listening to them.

—Dean Rusk

We teach our children how to treat others by the way we treat them, and we teach them to listen by listening. If we give them a full hearing, and respond to their desires and concerns in a way that lets them know we've listened, they'll respect our decisions more. If we continue to listen and to show that we've listened, our children will learn in a very practical way how we make our decisions. They'll also feel respected and included in our decision making.

Agreement is never guaranteed, but this method will produce closer harmony than some. Besides, listening to our children gives us a fuller picture of their lives, and this in turn gives us a better basis of information for making our decisions. When we show we respect them, we nurture their self-respect.

THOUGHT FOR TODAY: Today I'll resolve to listen carefully even to those I believe I've already heard.

*A singular disadvantage of the sea lies in the fact
that after successfully surmounting one wave, you
discover that there is another behind it.*
—Stephen Crane

Life seldom allows us time to recover from major
events. A new baby easily doubles the stress of ordinary life; death, divorce, moving, changing—or
losing—jobs, all double it again. And when we're
overcome with the combined effects of family, economic, and emotional strains, what happens? We
get sick, which adds to the stress (although it may
permit us a day or two in bed).

To cope with the tidal regularity of stress in our
lives, we can learn to ride the waves. When we're at
peace, in harmony with the world and nourished by
our source of spiritual guidance, we're spiritually
buoyant. Centered within ourselves, we can bear
life's stresses without capsizing or cracking apart.

But during especially stressful times, and in our
families that means at new arrivals as well as death,
illness, or divorce, we need constant refreshment
from our inner source. Frequent meditation and the
habit of prayer can help us to turn over our worries,
entrusting our lives to the care of a power greater
than ourselves. We will grow as we strengthen this
connection.

THOUGHT FOR TODAY: If I'm too buoyant to
sink, the waves will lift me up.

Instead of loving your enemies, treat your friends a little better.

—E. W. Howe

Most of us distinguish our friends from our families; friends we can choose, family we can't. Yet *friends* is an old term for relatives. Friends are those who are on our side, whom we can count on. "Enemies" are those we believe are against us. Loving our enemies is an abstract exercise for most of us, having to do with charity and forgiveness and not very much with our feelings.

We tend to show our worst behavior to those we love the most, because we know it's safe to pout or scold or lose our tempers; our near and dear ones won't leave us even if we're infantile or unpleasant. So we allow ourselves sharp words, sometimes channeling other frustrations into our domestic anger just because we feel safe expressing it at home.

Intimacy allows us to reveal ourselves. But am I always revealing the same aspect of myself, and is it always the disappointed, nagging, impatient self? Do I make amends to my partner, my children, my parents, for the hard words I dare to speak to them—perhaps to them alone? Those I don't trust, I often treat politely. My family deserves at least as much, for they're my closest friends—or should be.

THOUGHT FOR TODAY: When I forgive myself, I can ask the forgiveness of those who love me.

I always see that the universe is rich, if I am poor.
—Margaret Fuller

The gift of serenity lets us detach from immediate personal trouble and see it in perspective. No matter how desperate we may feel, the universe is full of hope. Light returns every morning. Rain and winds cleanse the air. The world is fully occupied with its own maintenance and repair.

Sorrow may bow down our spirits temporarily; we have a sense of loss, of confusion, we don't know where to turn, and all paths seem equally unpromising. But trust in a power greater than ourselves will let us turn over our fear and pain and give us courage to continue on our path, our own path, whatever it may be. Our choices are right for us; trust lets us know this, and courage helps us to face our lives.

Children's sadness feels total, global—their young spirits feel crushed because they lack the perspective we can lend, as adults who've weathered some storms. With loving patience we can help them to accept pain. We know that all change causes some pain, and every sorrow is also an opportunity for growth. If we're gentle with ourselves and with our children, they'll come to appreciate our serenity.

THOUGHT FOR TODAY: My poverty will be enriched when I let myself be hopeful.

No wise man ever wished to be younger.
—Jonathan Swift

Children often wish they were older than they are—old enough to go to school, to cross the street alone, to own a watch or a knife; old enough to drive, to vote. But when adults wish they were younger, it may be because they feel they missed some stage in their growing up and they don't know how to compensate for it. People who marry young may feel they missed out on a wider range of romantic experimentation. People who spend many years educating themselves for a profession may feel their singleness of purpose has made them narrow, and they miss some breadth of experience.

No one who has lived with children going through the difficult years of dating and trying out different styles of life would wish to be in their shoes. When you're a novice, the opposite sex can be terrifying. You don't know how the experiment will turn out; you don't know what you're doing; and you don't know whom to trust.

Wise adults realize that what they *really* want is an occasional fantasy: to have the youthful experience without its consequences in terms of emotional and financial ties, jobs, partners, aging bodies. Part of wisdom is understanding how much we have achieved in our real life.

THOUGHT FOR TODAY: Real dissatisfaction can spur me to change. Today I'll concentrate on the satisfactions in my life.

People have to work, but they don't have to work in the old way and for the old reasons. We can't look for a new way or for new reasons unless we believe that there are human reasons for not working.
                    —Grace Lee Boggs and James Boggs

Some young people seek training and education so they won't have to work at unskilled jobs. But many educated people choose such jobs, in preference to skilled professional work they feel is spirit-destroying. Parents may find it hard to accept their children's decisions not to work as engineers, lawyers, or chemists, but there are human reasons for making such choices. Our social structure rewards a few people with wealth while forcing many to work irregularly and to struggle for goods, while a large minority remains workless and poor. This is the old way; young people are looking for a new way.

Most parents wish their children to have an open, questioning view of life, unprejudiced and fresh. All we can do is to help them prepare themselves for happiness; we can't control their decisions or the outcome of their efforts. If they've been given good tools, their construction will be sound, whatever shape it takes.

THOUGHT FOR TODAY: Respecting children's choices of what to do with their lives is a difficult, important part of loving them.

Has anyone supposed it lucky to be born?
I hasten to inform him or her, it is just as lucky to
die, and I know it.

—Walt Whitman

Some babies are born to parents who long for them and cherish them. Others come as an unpleasant shock to people who have no particular desire to be parents. Most of us grow up in families that are somewhere in the middle: sometimes loving, sometimes neglectful; selfish, human, imperfect.

Do we understand the consequences of our early childhood experiences? Some people whose spirits are wounded by early neglect or cruelty grow up to be unhappy people, and in their own families they perpetuate suffering. Yet on the other hand, great saints and benefactors of humanity have survived wretched beginnings. One outcome seems to be as lucky as another.

Birth and death are mysteries as great as growth, and our meager human notion of luck can't begin to express their vastness. We have the power to deal with the here and now, whatever our experiences have been. Real life is in the present; all the rest is guesswork. I'll pray for "the serenity to accept the things I cannot change, the courage to change the things I can, and the wisdom to know the difference."

THOUGHT FOR TODAY: Whatever my family did is now beyond reckoning. What counts is what I do with my life today.

We all know what the American family is supposed to look like. We can't help it. . . . The striking point, in the face of all the propaganda, is how few Americans live that way.

—Louise Knapp Howe

I used to feel weird, in first grade, reading about Dick and Jane and Baby Sally, because my family didn't fit. We were Jewish and urban; we lived in an apartment, like the families of most of the kids in my class, and we didn't own a car or a cat or a dog. My grandparents lived in an apartment and played pinochle instead of golf. Our family fell outside the cheerful stereotypes we read about, and many of my classmates must have felt the same—Filipino, Chinese, Japanese, and African Americans, European refugees (for this was during World War II), children who lived with one parent, poor children, only children.

Did we all feel some shame about being different from the way Americans were "supposed" to be? Did we feel it was our fault that our families were different? I don't remember. What I do remember is that we learned to mistrust those images. American families come in all sizes, styles, and colors; whatever ours is, it's the one we have. All up and down the spectrum of family styles there is happiness and unhappiness, families that work and families that break down. We need to find satisfaction in our own family, no matter how "different" it may be.

THOUGHT FOR TODAY: All kinds of families are American families, whether or not we find ourselves reflected in media images.

The family is the smallest political organization possible.

—Jacques Donzelot

Politics is the use of power. How power is used defines a political system: Is power exercised by one over many, or shared among a few, or distributed more or less equally among a representative sample? These are useful questions to ask about families. Is one parent a benevolent despot? A tyrant? Do both parents reign as monarchs? Is one family member "the leader of the opposition"? Or does the family follow a democratic model, in which every member has a vote and everybody's interest is represented?

Different political models may be appropriate for different stages in family development. Small children need firm leadership, but a family of adults may get along in peaceful anarchy, where each decides for herself or himself. A family may find enduring comfort in the authority of a supreme spiritual source.

If family politics are causing pain, children can't impeach a parent; nor can parents exile a child. But together they can try to change the system. All rulers stay in power with the consent of the governed. If a family needs a peaceful revolution, the governed must first withdraw their consent. Tyrants, including domestic ones, are lonely and fearful. They can be shown that love is more effective than oppression.

THOUGHT FOR TODAY: Today I'll remember that all politics is personal. We learn about authority and punishment long before we ever learn the words,

[Shopping malls] offer a low-stress oasis of human scale, where the age-old activities of walking and gawking are permissible.

—William S. Kowinski

Critics point out that most stores in most malls carry goods no one really needs. "They're driving out the hardware stores and shoe repair shops," people say, "and what do we get in exchange? Candles. Chocolates. Another boutique." Yet malls serve an essential social function, like parks, providing a clean, safe place for old and young to sit, to meet, to read a newspaper or drink a cup of coffee.

For parents of toddlers, they provide a place to meet other young families. A parent is likely to spend many hours in the company of one or two young children. Even a well-balanced adult can develop a skewed perspective in the exclusive company of pre-schoolers. Having a place to go and meet others is a valuable outlet.

For old people, isolation is more devastating. A mall is one of the rare places where the old can interact casually with the very young. Wouldn't it be nice if shopping malls in busy communities opened free play centers? Old people could contribute their skills as volunteers, reading to children, rocking babies, or talking with parents. In our age of far-flung families, we can find creative solutions to bring different generations into closer contact.

THOUGHT FOR TODAY: New developments will show me opportunities as well as obstacles. Change can enhance growth as well as disrupt our lives; a shake-up blends ingredients.

Birds will get vicious when they're fed and then rejected. People as well.

                                    —Toni Cade Bambara

People can go literally crazy when they're treated with capricious cruelty. We all need to know what to expect. Whether it's food or rejection we're given, we need to be certain of it. If a parent is depressed or otherwise suffering and treats a child with systematic cruelty or neglect, the child learns to cope better than if the parent is intermittently loving and rejecting. Neglected children learn to fend for themselves; abused children learn to survive. But children who never know what kind of treatment they'll get become fearful, depressed, and sometimes schizophrenic.

Absolute consistency, of course, isn't possible for human beings. Everybody has some degree of mood swing, and family members learn to adjust to mild variations in each other's temperaments. Love and trust will get us through the ordinary changes in emotional climates. But people who show severe, unpredictable swings in behavior destroy our trust. They need our help, and our prayers.

THOUGHT FOR TODAY: I will pray for the ability to be consistent with my family and friends in both my prayers and my deeds.

Drawing on my fine command of language, I said nothing.

—Robert Benchley

Silence is always better than hurtful words. But silence is a language of its own. There is the child's resentful silence; the parents' silent coldness to a naughty child; the lovers' peaceful silence. Saying nothing often says a good deal.

In our family relations we need clarity. If we're lucky, we give and receive love unconditionally, and there's nothing we mean that we can't say to our parents, our children, our siblings. But most of us aren't that lucky. There are areas of feeling and experience that we can't share, or won't, and we fall silent rather than risk pain.

You are the only judge of when you should speak, for you know your own feelings. Perhaps it's been a victory for you to learn to hold back screams or insults. But after learning to keep silent, there may be a further lesson: how to speak appropriately.

Some things I may never say; but I hope there are no unhealthy silences I won't break. I'll learn to say what is in my heart. Silence is open to many interpretations, and I will strive for simplicity and understanding.

THOUGHT FOR TODAY: When I'm silent, I may not be saying what I mean.

You cannot imagine how stable and firm and fixed your body looks to me. You cannot imagine that I can feel my molecules moving around, wondering what miraculous shape they will prefer next time.
—Barbara Rosenblum

The woman who wrote these words has cancer, and she is engaged in the long process of treating her disease. It has changed her. Confronting the changes wrought in our self-image and identity by a disease like cancer is a task many of us will face in our lives. Many of us will belong to support groups for family members going through this process.

Coping with a chronic disease means including it in our most intimate self-definition. We become not "healthy Barbara who has a temporary illness" but "Barbara who has cancer," or diabetes, lupus, MS, or AIDS. Our disease affects every aspect of our lives, setting in motion things we thought were fixed and freezing things we thought were fluid. In such a welter of shifting perceptions, we need to call often on our source of spiritual strength. We need help, more help than other people can give. Surrendering ourselves to a greater power can help us to accept our changes and flow with them.

Those who support the person with a disease need their own support, from their own spiritual connection. Such a source of strength can help us to accept whatever changes we go through.

THOUGHT FOR TODAY: Disease makes extraordinary demands on everyone who is touched by it. Attention to the needs of my spirit will help me to meet those demands.

*Little children do not lie until they are taught to do
so.*

—Sa'adia ben Josef

Dreams and fantasies are different from lies: a lie is
always meant to deceive another person. Children
learn to lie only when they're punished for telling
the truth. Children understand very well the sorts of
lies that may be necessary for survival. They don't
confuse personal honesty with expediency—unless,
as the Babylonian philosopher pointed out, they are
taught to do so.

Parents who are honest don't say "I'm busy" when
they mean "I'm angry" or "I'm tired." They don't
manipulate their children or their spouses, and they
deal fairly—with chores, allowances, and treats, not
playing favorites or lightly breaking promises. They
demonstrate honesty every day, while parents who
do the opposite teach lying. Part of a parent's spiritual progress is realizing the power our children
invest in our behavior. Here is the source of humility.

THOUGHT FOR TODAY: I will respect my loved
ones enough to offer them my honesty.

There is no good arguing with the inevitable. The only argument available with an east wind is to put on your overcoat.

—James Russell Lowell

The beautiful and popular Serenity Prayer says, "Grant me the serenity to accept the things I cannot change, the courage to change the things I can, and the wisdom to know the difference." All three are difficult, and well worth praying over, but accepting the inevitable may be the most difficult of all.

Death and grave illness are events over which we have no control. Accepting the death of a child or a spouse may seem impossible; we feel unable to come to terms with it; it changes everything. Our identity has been bound up in that other person: we *are* a spouse, a parent, a daughter, a son. When death breaks this attachment, we may not know how to go on being ourselves.

We're not given a choice or a chance to set more favorable terms. The wind of change simply blows. Our part is to pray for acceptance, letting go of any anger, guilt, or regret that might flavor our loss with bitterness.

THOUGHT FOR TODAY: Fully experienced, the pain of loss softens us, ripens us for compassion.

Growing pains are real.

—Morris Sklansky

Not only are growing pains real, we can have them all our lives. Each one of us is unique, blessed with special talents and gifts and unfolding according to our own schedule. No one else can tell me when it's time to take the next step on my lifelong journey.

Yet well-meaning others, especially family members, sometimes believe they know me better than I know myself. "You're too big/too small for that," they tell me; "You know you never liked/you always loved carrots"; "Isn't it about time you got married/got a job/had children?" Part of the pain of growing up, at sixteen or at sixty, is pain at setting aside such misdirected love and concern—seeing it for what it is, acknowledging finally that those who love us can't always see us with clarity. Yet we'll always have the love and concern of those we truly care about.

All pain is real, whether we feel it in our heads, our hands, or our hearts. Pain softens us, teaches us gentleness, helps us not to inflict pain on others. We have the power to soothe ourselves, to let go of much pain, to grow beyond it. Trust in the rightness of our choices is a balm for wounded spirits.

THOUGHT FOR TODAY: The pain of growth is like the cracking of an eggshell or the opening of a bud. I must experience it to become fully myself.

If we'd only stop trying to be happy, we could have a pretty good time.

—Edith Wharton

One human characteristic that's responsible for a great deal of unhappiness as well as happiness is our reluctance to leave well enough alone. We tinker with the world, flattening mountains and crossbreeding varieties of fruits. We leave our marks; we expect children will do better than their parents. And while we've achieved high levels of productivity and comfort, we've also poisoned the world's waters and deprived a growing proportion of our human brothers and sisters of work and shelter.

We all could have a pretty good time on this bountiful earth if we redirected our thinking—away from technological development and toward human needs. Technology has produced enormous changes in the past two hundred years, but it has helped to shift our attention away from the needs of families, parents, and children.

The world's future is made in today's families. How can we help our children to choose social priorities? By strengthening their ability to have a good time in simple ways, which means cultivating that ability for ourselves.

THOUGHT FOR TODAY: My spiritual commitment to people rather than things leads me toward acceptance and universal love.

The world talks to the mind. Parents speak more intimately—they talk to the heart.

—Haim Ginott

Our hearts took instruction from our families; it's there we learned to behave in ways that let us feel good about ourselves.

Some of what we learned may have been harmful. Many of us learned to suppress our own wishes for the greater good of a large family, or because our caregivers weren't able to cope with us. We got rewards for appearing to want what others wanted. When we grew up, we may have had difficulty even knowing what our own real wishes were. Our minds understood that we have wishes, but we lost touch with them.

If I'm out of touch with my real wants, life may seem slightly unreal to me, as though it were a movie I'm watching. I don't inhabit my life fully, and I'm only partly using my capacity for love. To reach my own wants, to occupy my own territory, may mean learning some new ways to feel good. My family's words are not the only truth; I can reeducate my heart.

THOUGHT FOR TODAY: I have a right to my feelings; my heart can learn to talk back.

I am not unbalanced in transition between the centering stability of a relationship. I am single. It is my choice of how to be in the world.

—Nett Hart

Balanced singleness is a rare choice today. At early ages we feel pressured to form couples, to live coupled. Architects, engineers, and the Internal Revenue Service all penalize singleness, and our society regards it as a temporary condition. Those of us who can't imagine life unpaired worry about family members who deliberately choose it.

For a person who is at peace with herself or himself, this may be the perfect choice. Singleness doesn't mean either selfishness or solitude; it may mean simply that one feels happy and fulfilled living alone. Those who chafe and worry about single friends or family members may have some unresolved difficulties about their own lives, their own coupledness or their place in the family. Rather than question their own uneasy balance, they project their woes onto someone else. Everyone has different spiritual needs and for some, serenity comes with singleness.

THOUGHT FOR TODAY: Other people's choices don't have to suit me; I can live only one life at a time.

There is nothing more enviable than to have an old head and a young heart.

—George Sanders

Lifelong marriage is rarer and more recent than we may think. In earlier periods, childbirth, war, and disease ensured that most old women or men had had several partners in the course of their lives. The world has always known many varieties of domestic experience.

Of course, as any partner in one knows, a long relationship goes through many different stages. One literally can't have the same partner for thirty years, because everything about us changes. (Perhaps not everything; my husband still folds his clothes the way he did in high school, and I still talk in movies.) The cells of our bodies have changed many times, as well as our jobs, our houses, and the way we touch one another.

A relationship is a living thing. Some may look dead, but that's usually a kind of suspended animation; if both partners are open to it, the trance can be broken. Our older selves are wise enough to know when we're stiffening ourselves against the challenge of growth. Our hearts can stay young and ardent; whatever brought us together in the first place still lives in them.

THOUGHT FOR TODAY: I am half of any relationship I enter. When I change, it changes, too.

Time is the only comforter for the loss of a mother.
—Jane Carlyle

Time, it's true, will blunt the sharp pain of such a loss, but we can help time along in its healing work. Our mothers are our earliest connections to the world. If we have warm and happy memories, these can help to console us for our loss. If we were lucky, they mothered us so well that we can take up the task where they left off. Everyone needs mothering all through life: warmth, approval, nurture, unconditional love.

If our connection to our mother was less successful, we need to face that. If we lie to ourselves about our unmet needs or our resentments, we're adding to the burdens we already bear. Learning to comfort ourselves, to help time in its healing work, we need to assess realistically what we got from our mothers and what we wanted but didn't get. The latter we'll have to give ourselves.

Part of our grief, when a mother dies, is knowing that now she will never give us anything but what she gave. Death takes away that possibility; on the other hand, it makes us face squarely our unmet needs. What are we going to do about them? It's important for us not to paint a rosy picture of a reality that may have had plenty of thorns—and pests—and unopened buds.

THOUGHT FOR TODAY: I'll try to be grateful for what I have and realistic about what I want. I'll find a way to give it to myself.

We didn't all come over on the same ship, but we're all in the same boat.

—Bernard Baruch

The man who said this was thinking, no doubt, of Mayflower ancestry and the snobbish pride that leads some people to boast of it. But his words can be understood in any context: whatever the family that brought us into this rapidly shifting world, we share it with one another. The great upheavals of this century created millions of immigrants; our culture is multiracial and pluralistic, and all our fates are intimately connected.

Some of us come from families with a kind of frontier ethic of self-sufficiency. Maybe on a real frontier a family needs to turn inward and provide for all its needs, but the geographical frontier is gone, and isolation isn't a good way of life. Our paths crisscross so many others; our special gifts enrich all who come in contact with us, as theirs do us. If we close our families off from the multicultural enhancement of our neighbors in this boat, we deprive our children and ourselves.

Wherever it began, our voyage provides us with a wide choice of shipmates. Let us choose those who have the most to offer, in terms of wisdom, strength, and harmony with our spirits. Each one of us is irreplaceable. Let's learn to value one another at our true worth.

THOUGHT FOR TODAY: My real family is all of humanity. We need each other as guides on our voyage.

Her desire to think well of herself always needs to be supported by proof.

—Henry James

When children's feelings lead them to do something they've been taught is wrong—tormenting small animals or pinching a new baby, for example—they may feel deeply ashamed and unable to think well of themselves. They may add to their shame the feeling that they're monstrous even to *want* to hurt the baby or the puppy, and this self-disgust can injure their self-love.

How parents deal with such episodes can be crucial to children's moral future. Everyone feels jealous; everyone feels curious. These aren't bad feelings, though they can impel us to do harmful things. Since we're blessed with the capacity to talk about our feelings, children can be encouraged to tell their parents about their anger and jealousy at a new baby rather than taking it out wordlessly on the baby or the family cat.

Parents need to reassure children of their love and of the utter normalcy of their feelings. Unconditional love gives just the right proof of lovability. Children who are helped through early moral dilemmas by understanding parents will be able to accept their own flaws and still think well of themselves.

THOUGHT FOR TODAY: In order for me to act well, I must forgive myself, as well as others, for our human imperfections.

*One way of looking at life is as a series of problems
to be solved by "experts." Another is to see life as a
journey toward meaning.*

—Robert M. Coles

Life sometimes seems so complicated that we long
for a strong leader to solve our problems—negotiating
foreign policy, balancing a checkbook, or telling us
what's right and wrong. We long to surrender our
own decision making to someone wiser and better
able to sort things out. With a sigh of relief, we let
our county commissioners decide where to put hazardous wastes; we let newspaper editors decide how
much we need to know about our government's
intelligence operations. More and more, we give over
our own powers, narrowing our fields of competence: "I don't know anything about economics/
nuclear power/censorship," we say. "I'm just a
housewife/tree surgeon/operations manager."

At one time we felt we knew everything—when we
were babies. Later, we believed our parents possessed
all knowledge, or our grandparents. Then, as we
achieved greater understanding, we came to believe that
no human being can solve all problems. Our search
for meaning becomes more coherent if we believe in
a source of wisdom from which all solutions derive.

"Experts" are only human beings. Leadership is a
technique that all can share. On the journey toward
meaning, our path will be smoothed if we travel in
company.

THOUGHT FOR TODAY: If I pray for guidance
on my own journey, I'll find companions; we can
share the tasks of breaking the trail.

Of late she had learned that happy people hate the unhappy.

—Rebecca West

It's not truly happy people who hate those less fortunate—it's anxious people, people with lingering feelings of guilt or shame, competitive people who feel their own good fortune came at others' expense. We can see this in families where older children who feel unsure of themselves behave cruelly to their younger siblings, or a set of prosperous cousins snubs their poorer relations. When people are genuinely happy—accepting of their limits, creative in their pursuits, and emotionally fulfilled—they wish only the best for others.

Such family resentments mainly stem from feeling unloved. The surest preventative is to let each family member, each child, know how important his or her place is in our hearts. We do this by paying rapt attention to our loved ones, showing them our willingness to open ourselves to them, and showing them also the joy such openness brings us.

Real happiness is as contagious as measles, for happy people can't help spreading some of their serenity and enjoyment wherever they go. And since happiness usually grows out of a strong spiritual connection, this serenity and enjoyment are limitless. The supply never runs out but is constantly replenished from the abundance of the spirit.

THOUGHT FOR TODAY: Unlike material wealth, gifts of the spirit grow as they're given away.

Society's eternal problem is the connection of parent to child, the transmission of experience from one generation to another.

—Vasily Sukhomlinsky

Sending experience from one generation to another has never been a simple matter; if it were, our species might have made moral and spiritual advances as great as our scientific and technical progress. Every family has to learn basic social wisdom for itself. We may believe abstractly in democratic principles, but until we're challenged to act on them in our families, they have no real meaning for us.

Justice and equality can't be left out of family relations. A man who is a public progressive and a domestic tyrant sends a mixed message to his children, and so does a woman who wields iron authority at home yet presents herself publicly as yielding and dependent. Their families believe their behavior, not their words, and when these are at odds, they produce inner conflicts.

All of us cherish an ideal of wholeness and harmony, and we can give this to our children, at least as an ideal. Parent and child are connected by love, and love can heal our inner conflicts.

THOUGHT FOR TODAY: I don't have to reinvent the wheel; I can accept the best existing wheels and let them take me where I want to go.

This land, my sister, has a fertile heart. It throbs, doesn't wither, endures. For the secret of hills and wombs is one.

—Fadwa Tuqan

In our eagerness for technical mastery, our culture has neglected our spiritual bond with the land that nurtures and sustains us. We build vast creations of metal and concrete, we irrigate deserts and pave over marshes, but however we remove ourselves we're still organisms of flesh and spirit that belong to the great world family system. All people are our kin, and the earth is our dwelling. We owe one another the same care and imagination we lavish on our machines.

The secret of life is its power of regeneration—the mystery at the heart of each family. This throbbing life is spiritual as well as physical; we're bonded to the earth by the chemicals in our body's cells and also by the warmth of love that streams through us. Each family, each individual, is precious and necessary to the whole, as each tree or fern or tiny herb has a part to play in the earth's unfolding. The care with which we tend our children and our old people belongs to the enduring cycle of birth and decay and rebirth.

We're all necessary, all accounted for. The fertile heart of the land embraces us all, and in return we owe it gentleness. Let us dedicate a part of ourselves to this holy connection and pass it along in our individual families, so our children and their children can feel it. Kinship, not mastery, is the key.

THOUGHT FOR TODAY: My spirit is renewed through my connection to the land and to my human family.

It is easier to stay out than get out.

—Mark Twain

This is true of quarrels, quicksand, drugs, and poker games. But in family quarrels, all the family members already are in.

When we're children, we can't take a neutral stance in family quarrels. By the time we're adults we can see, regardless of right and wrong, how family members keep quarrels alive or pick new ones. We understand how quarrels may work to keep families together, at the price of holding family members back in their personal growth.

Spouses who have fundamental, long-standing conflicts may find quarrels provide their only intimacy. If parents argue about their children, they can express strong feelings without having to touch on their own real conflicts—like emotional coldness or instability. By letting off steam in small recurrent quarrels, people protect their big permanent quarrel, ensuring at the same time that they can express some anger and that they won't be challenged to change.

When parents are fixed in a pattern like this, their children suffer the most. Often one will take the role of mediator, others may choose sides, still others leave home, emotionally if not physically. However one can, getting and staying out of a quarrel is a good way to foster one's spiritual and family growth.

THOUGHT FOR TODAY: Am I in any quarrels that serve as smokescreens? I'll get out as fast as I can and move on to the real issues

The children's duty of obedience is their right to be educated to the liberty of manhood.
                    —Georg Wilhelm Friedrich Hegel

Parents' authority is really their responsibility to their children, and therefore their gift to them. Children obey benevolent authority. That's how they learn to exercise it over themselves. This is the gift that just, wise parents bestow.

When parents are too strict or too lax, children don't learn as well how to discipline themselves independently. The strongest authority comes from love. When parents love children unconditionally, the children learn to love themselves. When children trust their parents, they learn to trust themselves. Loving guidance and firm authority give us the inner strength and security to manage our freedom. Authority should never chafe; obedience is as natural to the growing spirit as taking up water is to a tree.

THOUGHT FOR TODAY: Conscious contact with a source of spiritual guidance refreshes our powers and helps us to live responsibly and joyously.

Everybody is ignorant, only on different subjects.
—Will Rogers

One key to successful living is respect for others—
for other people's expertise in their own areas. You
may know internal combustion engines, or piecrust,
or soil pH, better than anyone you know, and still
respect others' knowledge as they respect yours—or
as you'd like them to.

Sometimes family members compete for territory
in each other's lives. A parent or grandparent may
tell obscure anecdotes to prove they know us better
than we know ourselves. Our own reality becomes
contested territory in a familiar struggle: "No, *I*
remember when you broke your ankle; that was the
year Donna was born—"

Entering the struggle isn't the way to end it. What's
really going on when family members invade our
lives, claiming bits and pieces of us for their own?
They're probably expressing love and pride. They
may be saying they don't know us so well, now that
we're grown up and moved away, and they'd like to
see more of us. They'd like credit for knowing us
when.

THOUGHT FOR TODAY: I'm the central character in my own drama, and my supporting players all
have their own dramas, in which I support them.

The earth's responses are limited. It's easy to forget that in a land of such abundance. But while we feast, others fast because they have no other choice.
—Harriette Grissom

The world's population is one family, though it may be difficult for us to think about it like that. If the family is fair, resources will be shared, and all will be treated equally. If some members grab an unfair share of the family budget, others suffer.

When some eat steak and lobster, others will have to eat peanut butter sandwiches. If one wastes money, the others will have less to spend. In our families this behavior makes us angry and sorrowful, yet it happens in the world, between rich and poor countries.

In our own hemisphere, the wealth of North America is used to increase the poverty of South Americans. Rich North American companies can influence economic decisions, bribing poor countries to cut down rain forests and graze cattle for export. Poor countries grow coffee and bananas instead of corn to feed their own people. Sometimes wars are waged to protect these unfair practices. And we let them continue, without sorrow or anger, because we don't yet think globally about our human family.

Harmonious living takes a commitment to generosity, maybe even the sacrifice of some of our pleasant habits. The future of our large and growing world family depends on fair distribution of resources. Do we want our comfort to depend on the misery of others?

THOUGHT FOR TODAY: Peace can be achieved only with justice. I need to understand how I'm related to my world family.

*Worry is a form of fear, and all forms of fear pro-
duce fatigue.*

—Bertrand Russell

Of all the unproductive activities humans have figured out for themselves, worry must be the most
popular. The brute fact is: worry is a waste of time.

Why do we do it, then? Perhaps we have a guilty
feeling that even our best efforts are inadequate, that
nothing we can do will ever be quite enough, so we
apply a little worry. Our children are so dear to us,
and they seem so fragile; we worry as a way of
proving to ourselves how much we care. Worry, we
must realize, has to do with us, and not with those
we worry about.

How can we protect our loved ones? First, with a
sense of proportion that distinguishes real hazards
from imaginary ones. We don't let small children
cross the street alone, or play with fire, but we don't
fill their little heads with improbable dangers like
rabid dogs or masked muggers. We try to teach
them to take reasonable precautions.

Next, we take good care of their health and teach
them to look after themselves, and we furnish a
limitless supply of unconditional love. Then we've
done our best. If we choose to worry on top of all
this, we're wasting our energy. We can stop, if we
can come to believe that we deserve serenity and not
anxiety.

THOUGHT FOR TODAY: When I am secure in my
love for others, I'll let go of unproductive worry.

Love lights more fires than hate extinguishes.
                                    —Ella Wheeler Wilcox

Love is powerful, because everybody wants it. The power of hatred is more limited—we all fear it, but nobody wants it. Hatred can destroy, but unlike love it can't create. Love, the force that powers all constructive action, never dies.

Love has different meanings and different faces. The love we experience in our families prepares the ground for all our subsequent ability to give and receive love. The most difficult love of all, love of our enemies, is possible only if we've reconciled our inner conflicts. We must love ourselves wholeheartedly before we can love those whose actions we deplore.

Everyone deserves love. Most of us feel we never get enough, and it's a human weakness to grudge the love we give. Yet the power of unstinting love is the greatest force available to us. When we love, we are radiant. Love is contagious; love gives itself unquenchably and asks nothing in return. The power of love answers prayers and heals hearts—it's our spiritual fuel.

THOUGHT FOR TODAY: My first duty is to love myself, for only then am I loved enough to greet the world as it deserves.

If you can figure when to stand firm and when to bend, you've got it made.

—Joseph Shore

The nuances of parenting are too difficult for me to handle alone. If I have to decide how to respond at every moment, I'll soon find the job's beyond me. Fortunately, I have help, in this as in every other aspect of my life; my direct line to a source of power greater than myself gives me access to unending supplies of wisdom, patience, and love.

Sometimes the line gets fouled, especially the patience and wisdom channels. There are days when I feel blocked from my sources—not because there's anything wrong with the transmitter; my receiver jams when I try to control the others in my life, imposing my own wishes and trying to have them carry out my agenda instead of their own.

When I remind myself that my partner, my children, and my parents all have their own spiritual connections, then I can slow down, step back, and detach myself from the situation. It's easier to stand firm or bend when I'm making my own moves and letting them make theirs.

THOUGHT FOR TODAY: My connection works best when I can get out of my own way.

Never think about any one thing for too long.
                              —Walter Bowers Pillsbury

When we have some sorrow or anxiety in our lives, a developmentally disabled child, a chronically ill spouse, a parent or sibling in trouble, we may find ourselves thinking obsessively. The anxiety plays constantly in our thoughts, like the bass notes of an organ. No matter how we go over it, we can see no solution, no way out. We've reached the limit of our ability.

Then our alternative is prayer—turning over our troubles to a power greater than ourselves. Prayer can't undo injury or defects or get our brother out of prison, but faith in a higher power can quiet the obsession that clouds our minds. We may have felt frustrated and frightened by our inability to solve this anxiety, soothe it, or make it go away. We don't have to. All we have to do is turn it over. Then we're free to think about the things in our lives that we *can* do something about.

Turning over our troubles isn't lazy; it's a gift from our source of spiritual strength, an acknowledgment that we're not alone. Our thoughts should lead us, not stymie us. When we've thought ourselves into a corner, it's time to reach out for the help that's always at hand.

THOUGHT FOR TODAY: My limits don't confine me, for I have access to unlimited powers of surrender and love.

The most complete revenge is not to imitate the aggressor.

—Marcus Aurelius

Marcus Aurelius was probably thinking of empires, and of how conquered peoples in spite of themselves come to resemble their conquerors, yet he surely was aware of the echoes of his words in private behavior.

Human aggression mainly stems from fear, and we can't handle aggression without addressing our sources of fear. Fears dwell in the childhood self that was formed when we were at the mercy of our caregivers. If the powerful adults in our early lives suffered from distorted thinking, we carry the effects in our deep-seated anxieties and terrors. Did we learn to stave off these fears by meeting the world aggressively, as they did?

We may never be able to remake ourselves completely, pray though we may. The fear–aggression connection may be too strong and central a part of ourselves. But we can choose how we express our aggression. Turning aggressive energy to creative rather than destructive uses, we can liberate tremendous power within ourselves, power to do good. The fear–aggression connection binds great reserves of energy, and when we succeed in owning our fears, and soothing some of them, we increase our powers. The courage to change ourselves begins with acceptance and gentle healing.

THOUGHT FOR TODAY: I want to use my energy creatively, not to imitate aggressors but to change myself.

By the time I'd grown up, I naturally supposed that I'd grown up.

—Eve Babitz

F. Scott Fitzgerald once wrote a story about a character called Benjamin Button, who was born old and got younger throughout his life until at his death he was an infant, small and helpless. How would it be if life proceeded that way? Perhaps we would be able in our "old age" to enjoy the fruits of experience with strong young bodies—or perhaps, if we were born with the wisdom as well as the frailty of old age, we would grow increasingly ignorant and limited.

Many thinkers have noted the similarities between infancy and old age, but how would it be to reverse the seventy or eighty years in between? Years have little enough to do with real maturity as it is. Some young people are gifted with self-acceptance and serenity, while many old people lack them; these are the real signs of "grown-upness." Babies have unlimited wants, and we all must learn to cut our desires down to manageable size. If we do a good job, we become happy with what we have; but we seldom manage to tame the wild child within us once and for all.

THOUGHT FOR TODAY: Growing up is a good life's work. By attending to the health of my own spirit, I'm doing the best I can for everyone whose life touches mine.

Not to know is bad; not to wish to know is worse.
    —Anonymous (West African proverb)

Anyone who's heard a four-year-old asking questions understands that children have a passion for knowledge—a passion that's often kindled for some reason in the supermarket checkout line. "But I want to know how to make a baby *now*." "Why can't you tell me what's inside a light bulb *now*?" Children understand that information is power.

Schools unfortunately do little to feed this natural hunger, and few parents have the time, the patience, and the teaching skills to satisfy it themselves. So the passion for knowledge, and the power that knowledge makes possible, can get channeled into other forms of curiosity. Gossip gives a child a sense of power, and some children become gossips or tattletales at least partly from frustration of their healthy thirst for knowledge.

Family gossip is important—it's one way we keep in touch, phoning each other about Jennifer's new baby or Uncle Mike's gall bladder. But family members can trample on our personal boundaries, using information to invade our privacy. In such a case, not to know is good; not to wish to know is sublime.

THOUGHT FOR TODAY: I'll satisfy my hunger, and my children's, with useful knowledge.

This I know without being told,
'Tis time to live as I grow old.
'Tis time short pleasures now to take,
Of little life the best to make
And manage wisely the last stake.
                                    —Abraham Cowley

It's often said that one should live every day as though it were the last. People with chronic illnesses can come to be very good at this, especially if their capacities are limited, and so can old people. One's own family is a good place to look for models of good living, for people who make the most of what they have and find pleasure and joy in the simple acts of daily life. When you can't walk far or fast—or when you can't walk at all, and learn to blend a set of wheels into your self-image—you see and feel the world in different ways.

If you have a wheelchair person in your family, or a very old person, you could spend some time learning what their life is like. Whatever the limits on our human powers, and we're all limited, the interior worlds of mind and spirit are always accessible. Wise management of life's stake, at whatever age we find ourselves, includes attention to our mental and spiritual growth. The pleasures of literature and the benefits of meditation are free to all, yet what they yield is the greatest wealth the human spirit can attain.

THOUGHT FOR TODAY: My life can always be enriched by the gift of another's attention, and I can pass along the gift.

A map of the world that does not include Utopia is not worth glancing at.

—Oscar Wilde

The idea of Utopia, a perfect place, is an important one, as important as our ideals of perfection for ourselves. No one really expects any country to be perfect. In the world, perfection is always unattainable. We'll never be perfect husbands, perfect daughters, perfect grandparents, because no family is perfect, and neither is any individual. In fact, if perfection could be achieved, we'd have to find other ideals.

We need ideals, but not to beat ourselves up with; we need them for direction, so we can see that we're growing in whatever directions we choose: honesty, intimacy, patience. We have the right to expect that we'll grow spiritually and that our loved ones too will grow. Along with growth, we need ideals of behavior to help us support one another.

We form our images of family from many sources, and those images should always include room for improvement. People change, and family relationships need the flexibility to accommodate our growth.

THOUGHT FOR TODAY: My ideals can serve me well, when I understand that they're guideposts and not trail markers.

We ask for our bread and not my bread, like we used to call God our papa and not my papa. To ask for bread is to ask for it for everybody.

—Ernesto Cardenal

Parents get used to stretching their egos like a kangaroo's pouch to include the little ones; you don't even think of going somewhere without knowing where the children will be. This habit persists. The pouch still wants to contain the child, even after the child's growing independence makes it unnecessary. I and my and we and ours can turn into fighting words.

We know we can't live others' lives or control their actions; yet when we see those we love forming harmful behaviors, it causes us pain. How can we resolve these contradictions? They're especially perplexing in families with children who can't yet take full responsibility for themselves.

One key to serenity in this confusion is letting go of consequences. We can include all those we love in our wishes for bread, for peace, for joy, while letting go of any expectation of how they will behave. I can control only myself, yet in acting responsibly I take care not to harm others. And my deepest wishes involve all my human family.

THOUGHT FOR TODAY: Sorting out what is mine and what is yours can take a lifetime, because we live through many changes in our boundaries.

It isn't enough to talk about peace. One must believe in it. And it isn't enough to believe in it. One must work at it.

—Eleanor Roosevelt

Peace won't come to a warlike spirit, nor will the making of weapons bring peace. Like love, peace involves risk, the risk of letting down one's guard, setting aside one's armor, removing one's missile bases, opening one's fences. Without vulnerability, there can be no peace, only armed truce.

Most people say they want peace. How many of us are willing to become peaceful? Peace must be waged, actively; we need to learn how *not* to fight and injure one another; how to resolve our most deeply felt conflicts without doing violence.

The best place to learn peace is at home in our families, but since so few of us know how to work at peace, most of us (and our children) grow up with the stale old strategies of competition and combat. Studying the lessons of the great peacemakers like Gandhi and Martin Luther King, Jr., can help us work at the peace we believe in, the peace we talk about, the peace we desire.

THOUGHT FOR TODAY: Peace, like love, is an active process. If we truly want it, we must learn to do it.

Consistency requires you to be as ignorant today as you were a year ago.

—Bernard Berenson

When we're in a relationship, the consistency I need from you is your commitment to that relationship. If we're partners, I need you to take me seriously, especially when our relationship comes to an end. I have no right to stop you from changing, only to ask that you treat our breakup as seriously as our coming together.

So it is with all relationships, including family ones. We may sometimes feel that our families stand in the way of our changing. But what our family members really need from us is our love and commitment through all our changes—and theirs. Change can be painful, but it's never as painful as rupture. The cruelest thing we could do in our families is to break with them.

We often hear that children need consistent treatment from their caregivers, and so they do; but not to the point of repeating a mistake or denying growth. The bottom line in family life is loving commitment, and we can hold onto this without being false to ourselves, through all stages of our spiritual growth.

THOUGHT FOR TODAY: Are my relationships giving me the consistency I need? I'll examine my part in them.

If you marry, you will regret it; if you don't marry, you will also regret it.

—Søren Kierkegaard

With the most positive attitude in the world, many of us find ourselves hooked into negative thinking by our family members. Often, this negativity plagues us because we persist in asking for things from our families that we're pretty sure we can't get. What we ask for isn't a *thing*—a lap-top computer or cashmere scarf—but a feeling, whatever it is we feel we didn't get when we were children. It's this consistent lack that depresses us or causes us to dread family get-togethers.

Ordinarily, we know better than to beat our heads against stone walls. One woman describes it this way: "Looking for certain kinds of appreciation from my family is just like going to the hardware store for a gallon of milk. *They don't have it.* But they have other things that I can't get anywhere else. So I just need to go to them for the things they have."

How many times would we ask for milk at the hardware store? Yet we go back to our families again and again with our unmet needs, setting ourselves up for disappointment, finding no cause for celebration and plenty for regret. Part of healthy self-love is learning to give ourselves what we don't get from others. If no one in our family can understand or appreciate our qualities, we need to praise and appreciate ourselves. In the family orchestra, we should pick an instrument we can play.

THOUGHT FOR TODAY: When I'm able to let go of regret and take hold of celebration, my family becomes a happier one. I'm grateful for the power to change my own attitude.

Promises are a uniquely human way of ordering the future, making it predictable and reliable to the extent that this is humanly possible.

—Hannah Arendt

A promise expresses a wish. We promise to be in certain places, at certain times; we promise to behave in certain ways. "Promise me you'll write"; "I'll be good, I promise." On a grander scale, treaties between nations are promises; contracts, prayers, vows, and resolutions are all promises. We enter into them because they express our wishes, our desires.

Sometimes we make promises idly, keeping a part of ourselves in reserve. "I promise I'll take you to the zoo on the next sunny day," we tell a child, reserving an unspoken clause: if I feel like it. Children take promises as seriously as grown-ups take legal documents. They're a pledge to the future, an island of certainty in a sea of the unknown.

Breaking a promise to a child is not a trivial matter. If you do it repeatedly, you abuse that child and teach mistrust. If children can't believe our pledges, can we expect them to attach much gravity to their own? They'll learn to say whatever they think we want to hear.

THOUGHT FOR TODAY: I won't make promises that I don't plan to keep, with my whole heart.

What poison is to food, self-pity is to life.
—Oliver G. Wilson

Poison changes food from a source of health to a source of illness. Self-pity, or "poor me," can similarly curdle life, changing it from an adventure to a prison sentence. Self-pity locks us into powerlessness, with no hope of widening our perspective.

"Poor me" is the attitude that everything in my life is someone else's fault—"I never get the good stuff," "You always make fun of me," "Mom always liked you best," and so forth. We must have learned "poor me" early, when we really were powerless. Parents can reinforce it by punishing children for initiative and independence and rewarding them for inaction, especially parents who feel swamped. They may feel good about their children only when they're quiet, and the children soon learn to blame any disturbance on outside forces.

Even the strongest of us has "poor me" moments, as even the most responsive parent has moments of feeling swamped. But by standing back and surrendering our self-pity, we can free ourselves from its narrow outlook and take a wider perspective in which our actions and passions fit into the greater pattern of human events. We're all actors and acted upon, independent and interdependent, pitiful, funny, compassionate, and strong.

THOUGHT FOR TODAY: Taken in moderation, self-pity won't sour my life, but I deserve better nourishment.

If the people have no center, they will perish.
—Black Elk

In the past, tribe or clan or family provided a center of certainty for most people, a point of reference for questions of right and wrong. As most of us have lost the sense of tribe and clan, and as the nuclear family exists in many various forms, today we lack this certainty, this reference point. We're painfully aware that for most of our pressing questions—for example, are children better off in the long run when unhappily married parents divorce, or when they stay together?—there are no simple answers.

The pressing questions that we need to ask as a species, like how to end war, or feed the world's hungry millions, also have no simple answers. Our ways of living have changed faster than our cultural wisdom; we work at jobs that didn't exist when our codes of ethics were forged. Our forms of relationship are new, but our emotions are ancient.

We have let ourselves lose touch with the center of all life—the wellspring of vitality and hope that powers all life on the planet. This center is within us, as accessible as our breath and steadfast against change. It's our connection to the spiritual source of all love and healing. If we will go within and tap this center, we will find all our questions can be answered.

THOUGHT FOR TODAY: When the outside world seems harsh to me, I can go within and renew myself from the center.

There are a lot of good things about Christmas. One of the best is Christmas talk. At Christmas you can say words you'd be embarrassed to utter on, say, Columbus Day.

Words like "snuggled." It's nice saying "snuggled."
—Russell Baker

Inside the toughest cop, the steeliest chief executive officer, the most brilliant engineer, are the same needs for touching and holding—for snuggling, in fact—that everyone feels. Touch warms us, opens us, soothes and alerts us, yet in the busyness of our lives we can forget to satisfy our need for it. People who live alone, especially old people, can suffer extreme snuggle deprivation. Even married couples can slip into relationships that may include love-making but leave out snuggling.

Some touch is inappropriate; sometimes family members trample over each other's boundaries, pinching cheeks or fondling teenage bodies. Fathers, brothers, uncles, mothers, can cross the boundary entirely and abuse children with their touch.

The young person who is abused by a family member suffers great confusion. On the one hand we all want and need touch; on the other, we must respect personal boundaries, even if this means limiting our own gratification. It's difficult to resolve the contradictory feelings aroused when someone in the family touches too much, too far. Help is always needed, both from professional helpers and from the source of spiritual help that's always available, night and day, for comfort and strength.

THOUGHT FOR TODAY: Prayer and meditation comfort my spirit, and human warmth blesses my body. Both are great gifts.

Life is what happens while you are making other plans.

—John Lennon

We live in the present tense, however much we may dream of the future or dwell upon the past. We can do nothing about past or future: the present is where our power lies.

In the present we can make plans; we can resolve to direct our energies in certain ways, toward certain outcomes. But in focusing on our plans we must never forget our lives. We may plan to succeed professionally, making money and distinguishing ourselves among our colleagues—but if these plans take us away from our families, then what is "success" for? Money and distinction may burnish one image of ourselves, but if we've had to endure years of overwork and estrangement from our loved ones, we've surely starved ourselves.

Life isn't what will happen when we retire or in twenty years, or next year, or even in next month's meeting. Life is now, today. Are we seeing enough of the people who share our lives—spouses, parents, children? Are we sharing intimacy with them, acceptance, creativity, emotional support? Without these, achievements are hollow; with them, life is a success.

THOUGHT FOR TODAY: Today is my own, to fill with love and satisfaction. If I can do this, my future is assured.

A thousand people drowned in floods are news; a solitary child drowned in a pond is tragedy.
—Josephine Tey

Great grief cuts deeply into our lives, unlike the vaguer sorrow we feel for the losses of others. We need time to heal from such pain, and when we treat ourselves with loving patience and prayer, mourning softens our spirits, making us compassionate even in detachment.

We can never feel the same grief for the unknown people killed in floods, famine, or volcanic eruption as we do for those we know, but they're more than news. They are sons, daughters, sisters, fathers, mothers, brothers, cousins, aunts, and uncles; other people feel their loss as keenly as we mourn ours.

Fully grieving our personal losses makes us understand how precious is the life of every individual. Compassion for others is different from personal agony, though the source of both is in the same wounded love. Accepting comfort from our spiritual source will strengthen us to face our next encounter, whatever it may be.

THOUGHT FOR TODAY: The gift of pain is compassion.

*The best way to cheer yourself up is to try to cheer
someone else up.*

—Mark Twain

When we feel swamped by our problems, paralyzed
by conflict, or struck down by misfortune, we can
be helped by concentrating on others. Sympathy ex-
ercises the imagination, which may have grown weak
with gloom and worry; when we return to our own
problems, often they've arranged themselves in mys-
teriously improved form.

   Committing ourselves to others doesn't mean neglecting our own needs. It does mean letting go of
egotistical preoccupation. Recentering ourselves is
the key. When we devote our energies to others'
welfare, we nourish our spirits along with theirs.
Encouraging our family members to grow and to
achieve their greatest potential is amazingly good for
us. When we spread this kind of cheer, we're apt to
find it's contagious.

THOUGHT FOR TODAY: Strange but true: Bitterness locks me into myself, but sweetness spreads.

An interior sense of self can also be nourished by impressive dreams, a chance poem, the habit of introspection.

—Penny Gill

Whatever our family income, there's one rich gift we can all share with our children: a strong and loving sense of self. We foster this in our family members when we pay attention to them, listen to their thoughts and questions, take them seriously as fellow travelers on life's journey. And we stifle it when we treat them like objects and reward them only for obedience and not for curiosity.

Without an awakened sense of self, adults—or children—lack firm grounding. They're unsure of their personal power and at risk for mistakes, from cults to addiction to empty consumerism. But once we discover how to nourish the self, through prayer and meditation, true freedom is ours: the freedom to choose to live well.

A sense of self lies kerneled within each of us, even the most emotionally abused, and it's within our power to awaken this loving core. Belief and trust in a source of spiritual guidance will feed that core, and the more we dwell peacefully with ourselves, accepting our past and surrendering our future, the stronger it will grow.

THOUGHT FOR TODAY: My inner strength includes a serious, joyous, loving spirit that knows how to make good choices.

Some things have to be believed to be seen.
—Ralph Hodgson

Reality is so rich, we can perceive only a fraction of it at any given time. We've been told that most of us use only ten or fifteen percent of our mental capacities. What would the other eighty-five percent be like? What could we see, hear, think, or imagine if we knew how to open ourselves to our fullest powers?

Perhaps a part of that power is spiritual. Perhaps *belief* is an intellectual function that we can cultivate in our children. If we encourage their spiritual development, perhaps they will become adults who are able to use some of their marvelous extra capacity for believing and seeing.

Thoughts are carried on electrochemical impulses; perhaps feelings are, too. Scientists may come to understand the chemistry of our brains, but love and faith are still mysteries. Where does courage come from? How do patience and generosity arise?

THOUGHT FOR TODAY: The more strongly I believe in goodness, the more of it I'll see.

The soul is healed by being with children.
—Fyodor Dostoyevsky

When we're with children, we're guided toward the child within us, our own magical, playful self. We can recall the terrors and wonders of childhood, the challenge of climbing a ridge of crusted snow or burying ourselves in leaves or sand. We can remember what it felt like to be small, agile, and vulnerable. Through being with children we can touch our younger selves, forgive them, and love them.

Though their company sends us deep within ourselves, children also take us out of ourselves. Their needs are immediate, and they haven't yet learned to stifle their urgent feelings for the sake of civilized behavior. They respond openly to the world, and we, who have learned to close ourselves to so much, are refreshed by their freshness. They have so much curiosity and so little information, to balance our oversupply of facts and our flagging enthusiasm.

THOUGHT FOR TODAY: The gift a child bestows is hope—the hope that fresh eyes and fresh energies will repair the world. Life leaves bruises; hope heals them.

*The older I grow, the more I distrust the familiar
doctrine that age brings wisdom.*

—H. L. Mencken

As we age, we watch our partners, our brothers and
sisters, and our friends grow frail or forgetful. Some
of them become chronic invalids. "They're all getting so old," we think ruefully, and then we realize
that we too are old, and getting older.

There's no help for it; but many of us find our
spirits struggling against the pull of our aging bodies, against the acceptance of these changes. We
contain within ourselves the seeds of everything we
can ever be: the potential for wisdom and goodness
as well as for narrow discontent. If we nurture our
spirits and allow them to grow with plenty of love,
faith, humility, and patience, we stand an excellent
chance of becoming wise and good as we grow old.
Nothing in life happens automatically, though; human beings can starve or bury their potential in many
ways.

For a well-nourished spirit, acceptance of change,
surrender to the process that we can't halt, is itself
great wisdom. To live in the moment, simply to be
where we are, is to be wise, for we are occupying the
space that was meant for us and fulfilling our part
of the grand design.

THOUGHT FOR TODAY: Surrender to the inevitable can call for as much courage as resistance to
injustice. I'll pray for both.

A child, like your stomach, doesn't need all you can afford to give it.

—Frank A. Clark

As soon as we start paying for our own groceries, we discover the limits of our appetites. Gradually we learn how to feed ourselves well, how to bring our eyes, our pocketbooks, and our stomachs into sync.

It's only natural for us to want our children to have everything. Especially if we feel we were deprived, we want them to have all the things we didn't have: games and pets and toys and lessons and clothes, all the outward signs of abundance and affection. But small children really don't need many possessions and distractions. Their world is full of wonder; a few sturdy toys, with love and encouragement from their caregivers, will do.

Perhaps it would be saner to think of giving our children the things we *did* have—honesty, humor, a strong faith. These intangibles are much more valuable than the latest computer game. Millions of advertising dollars are spent to turn children into eager consumers. As parents, our privilege is to show them intellectual and spiritual richness, gifts that benefit both recipient and giver.

THOUGHT FOR TODAY: I can teach my stomach to enjoy what is good for it, and my children, too.

Parents, however old they are and we may grow to be, serve among other things to shield us from a sense of our doom. As long as they are around, we can avoid the fact of our mortality; we can still be innocent children.

—Jane Howard

Some small part of us remains a child our whole life long—buried, sometimes, under layers of sophistication or pessimism or suffering—but the child is there. Our eternal child retains the freshness, the fears, and the capacity for astonishment that we had when we were young. We also retain our childish beliefs—in our own indestructibility, for example. Even when we're old and rather frail, a part of us belongs to youth and strength, and is sure we'll never die.

The death of our parents may be the first real blow to our conviction that we're immortal. For some of us, this comes tragically early. Some of us experience the death of siblings or of our own children, and we become aware in this terrible way of the closeness of death. We may feel rage and despair at the loss of those we love, but the fear and anger belong to us and not to death. Death is neutral and impartial, life's silent partner.

THOUGHT FOR TODAY: However it may come, the death of my loved ones is as natural as birth. I'll strive to accept it as a part of my own life.

O simple, precarious, eternal realm of snow! ...
You have created this indulgence—the duty to amuse
oneself.

—Colette

Hard workers sometimes have trouble with "the duty
to amuse oneself"; it feels immoral to have fun in a
world where so much sadness and suffering exist and
where so much needs to be done. But renewal of the
body and spirit are necessary to life's rhythms. A fresh
fall of snow or a beautiful sunny day invites us to
refresh our energies. Washing windows or getting to
the end of that phone list or cleaning off your desk
may have to take second place. Your spiritual well-
being just might depend on a cross-country skiing
jaunt—or a stroll through a favorite museum.

Many of us learn the pleasures of healthful amusements in our families, in outings or celebrations or just
daily observances, and we can carry on the tradition in
families of our own. People who don't learn that play
is as necessary as work may come to regard pleasure
as bad, and amusements as frivolous; they're in danger of abusing their physical and spiritual health.

Some of what we call pleasure may be destructive,
as everything is if carried to extremes. The surest
safeguard against unhealthy amusements is regular
indulgence in healthy ones. Pleasures of the body
and spirit are blessings to be thankful for, and to
share with those we love.

THOUGHT FOR TODAY: No one can breathe in
forever; I'll remember to exhale, and to renew myself in play.

Often . . . when the weeds are dead, so is the garden.
                                    —Erik Erikson

Weeds are merely flowers growing in the wrong place. Garbage is stuff in the wrong place. Poisons and pollutants are substances that are useful in one context but harmful in another. Similarly, the defects of character in those we love are usually exaggerations of their positive attributes: traits in the wrong place.

We discourage children from telling lies, yet reward them for creating colorful fantasies; we punish them for physical violence, yet praise them for athletic performance. Sometimes parents don't see the connections between the undesirable and the desirable traits, and they can discourage some behaviors so thoroughly that both kinds are stifled.

Perhaps this is how well-meaning parents keep on turning out men who can't express tenderness and women who can't feel anger. In their desire not to have sissy boys or shrewish girls, parents kill the weeds. Anger and affection are necessary human expressions. What parents need—and pray for!—is a sense of proportion, along with faith in the spiritual wholeness of their children.

THOUGHT FOR TODAY: My goal as a gardener will be to teach the garden to weed itself.

There is only one real deprivation, I decided this morning, and that is not being able to give one's gift to those one loves most.

—May Sarton

The true gifts we give to those we love most are seldom the obvious ones. Loyalty is within anyone's power to bestow, and what more valuable gift could there be than loyal support—to a child, a sister, a father, a spouse?

When we say we are not "able to give" such gifts, often it means that the gift is refused. Our loyalty, love, or support is turned away coldly. From some old bitterness, the recipient declines to accept our gift. This is deprivation indeed. One is powerless against it. All we can do is open ourselves, soften ourselves, and offer the gift again. It won't be lost. Though we may not be able to soften another's spirit, the act of offering deepens our own spiritual surrender.

THOUGHT FOR TODAY: Though it is blessed to give, I'll be sure I know how to receive, as well.

My heart is open wide tonight
For stranger, kith or kin.
I would not bar a single door
Where love might enter in.

—Kate Douglas Wiggin

Once I heard about a father who "found" a check in his stocking on Christmas morning. The check, made out in his own handwriting, was for a million dollars. As his children laughed in delight, he tore it into confetti, letting the pieces fall among the crumpled wrappings on the rug, and declared that the money meant nothing to him; he had everything he wanted.

His gesture seems both poignant and absolutely right, because he "gave" both gifts to himself—the bogus check, and the real gift of domestic happiness. In this winter holiday season some of us can be swept up in a frenzy of busyness on others' behalf, shopping, cleaning, wrapping, cooking, and baking. We risk emotional exhaustion from self-neglect. We owe ourselves, as well as our loved ones, the gifts of tenderness, time, and imagination.

THOUGHT FOR TODAY: While giving to others, I will not forget myself. I deserve the best I can give.

There are two ways of meeting difficulties: you alter the difficulties, or you alter yourself meeting them.
—Phyllis Bottome

We can't change other people. If the difficulties we experience are conflicts with our children, spouses, or parents, we can either ease the situation or change the way we deal with it.

If the difficulty centers around money, we can ask ourselves whether we've allowed money to take on other meanings for us—not just as a medium for getting what we want, a car or vacation, but as a symbol for love, power, or caring attention. If so, then we can teach ourselves to let go of the fantasies we've heaped on the dollar sign. Money is neutral. When we want love, money's not at stake. We may need to change the terms in which we think about love, and be sure we separate it from commodities.

If the difficulty has to do with trust, or ground rules, then we need to ask ourselves if we are genuinely present and negotiating, or sticking grimly to a position we chose long ago. If we're refusing to listen, we're part of the problem. When we can let go and enter the discussion respectfully, with real attention, we've changed both the way we meet the difficulty and the problem itself. We've also shown our family members that it's possible to change the way we think about conflicts, and that we can be part of the solution.

THOUGHT FOR TODAY: Our lifelong project of growth takes us through many changes. Some we seek, and some happen to us.

Maturity begins when we're content to feel right about something without feeling the necessity to prove someone else wrong.

—Sydney J. Harris

Once I heard two elderly sisters arguing about their childhood, about whether their father had been with them on a certain summer vacation or whether he'd had to stay in town. As they wrangled bitterly, it seemed to those of us listening—grandchildren, great-nieces and -nephews, and second cousins—that what was in dispute was not that summer memory, but which of them held title to their childhood. And what was more poignant, they believed that if one was right, the other had to be wrong.

Most questions have more than two sides, and few answers are uniquely right. Certainty and proof belong to mathematics, not to human behavior, and certainly not to memories. Every child in a family has a different set of parents from every other, and different sibling relationships. Our family constellations aren't fixed, like stars; they're mobile, alive.

Ambiguity and lack of clarity disturb many people, like the sisters I mentioned, who feel that another's rightness contradicts their own. When we're peaceful within ourselves, we're able to accept multiple rightnesses. There are as many different realities as there are different people, and about our own lives, we all are right.

THOUGHT FOR TODAY: Is my spirit large enough to accommodate different versions of reality? I'll practice humility and acceptance.

As a well-spent day brings happy sleep, so a life well used brings happy death.

—Leonardo da Vinci

Most children go through a period of anxiety about death, which seems mysterious and arbitrary, especially if they hear about such tragedies as crib deaths. They may be afraid to go to sleep, afraid they'll be translated without warning from life to death, from being to nonbeing. They need a lot of reassurance from loving adults that—after infancy, at least—random fatalities are so rare they don't merit much worry.

For an old person who has led a vigorous life filled with family, friends, and satisfying work, death seems much less dreadful. Spiritual connections come to seem more important than worldly ones. Death looks like a long rest.

One who has used life well deserves a happy death—a peaceful passage, with a reconciled heart. Death is such an important transition that it does merit thinking about—not worry, but planning. Do we want heroic efforts made to forestall death, if we're mortally ill? Whom can we trust to make decisions about our care? At least thinking about such important questions helps us organize our thoughts and feelings so that death, the inevitable completion of our lives, can be as happy as possible.

THOUGHT FOR TODAY: However old I live to be, I can make my existence radiant with faith.

No one can misunderstand a boy like his own mother.
—Norman Douglas

Parents think they know us, just because we grew up in their households. Understandably, they believe that years of intimate contact gives them the right to say what we're really like. Sometimes they claim to know us better than we know ourselves. Especially if our later choice of partners, work, or life-style is strange to them, our immediate family will try to understand—without enough knowledge.

Clearing up misunderstandings may seem like a risky, difficult endeavor, especially if early experiences made us reluctant to disclose our true selves to our families. But if we're happy in our lives and accept ourselves, self-disclosure can bond us warmly once again. The risk we run is that our families will be unwilling to accept our changes—but it helps to remember that they've gone through some changes as well. They may be less surprised than we think when we decide to tell them who we are.

THOUGHT FOR TODAY: I'm a lovable, valuable person. Disclosing myself to my family gifts them with my intimacy.

I think "someday" is now, if we will make it so.
—Arthur I. Waskow

Your dearest heart's desire can be achieved, if you'll achieve it. Most of us are so accustomed to separating what we have from what we want that we don't realize this. We put off happiness, thinking some day it will drop on us, like a piece of a meteorite.

If what we want is something material, that's easy: we have only to work and save for it. If it's spiritual, like family happiness, that's harder, yet still at hand. It must begin with us, therefore we must choose to be happy.

How do you become happy? First, you choose to be; then, you practice letting go of dissatisfactions and appreciating goodness. You pray for serenity to a power greater than yourself, to which you can turn over your cares and anxieties. And you meditate on the many wonders in your world.

The things we all desire—peace, equity, abundance, love—are within us, and we can achieve them, *if we will*. If we will surrender our cynicism, our resentment, and our despair, then our energies will be freed and we'll know how to become the just, loving, peaceful persons we desire to be. Why put off the good life? All we need do is find it within ourselves.

THOUGHT FOR TODAY: To be free, I must unbind myself. To be happy, I must choose happiness.

Don't cling to the old because it made you glad once; go on to the next, the next region, the next experience.

—Alfred North Whitehead

My daughter was a delightful baby. Would I want to keep her from growing into an obstreperous teenager? Perhaps some small part of me would; but holding her back (even if I could) would rob both her and me of the challenges of growth.

We're called on to respond to an ever-changing stream of events. Some will challenge us to our utmost. Living with children, we soon learn how rapidly they change, how their need for us changes. If we cling to a former pattern of relationship, we're depriving ourselves, stifling the response that our shimmering, changing child requires.

If we're always eager for growth, eager to "go on to the next," we'll meet whatever comes our way with grace and trust. Loving ourselves, staying in constant touch with our own need for spiritual nurture, prepares us to love others, and to welcome the experiences we share with them.

THOUGHT FOR TODAY: When I'm in touch with my spiritual source, all experience can make me glad.

SUBJECT INDEX

AUTHOR INDEX

About the Authors

MARTHA VANCEBURG grew up in Chicago and attended the University of Chicago, like her father and mother. In her family of parents, brother, grandparents, aunts, uncles, and cousins she—like most people—saw several extremes represented, from close and loving relationships to cold or cruel ones. She has worked as an actress, and advertising copywriter, a door-to-door interviewer, an editor, a college teacher, a waitress, and most recently a writer (*The Promise of a New Day* with Karen C. Elliott, Hazelden 1983). She makes her home in Minneapolis with her husband of thirty years and two cats. They have three grown children, two daughters and a son.

SYLVIA W. SILVERMAN, Martha Vanceburg's mother, is the eldest of five siblings. She and her brothers and sisters grew up in extended-family households on the North Side of Chicago. At the University of Chicago, she met the man who was her husband for nearly forty-five years, until his death in 1970. Holding a degree in social work, she was a caseworker for the Jewish Social Service Bureau during the 1930s, in which capacity she met and served many European refugee families. After the births of her son and daughter she returned to work as assistant director of Scholarship & Guidance Association, a Chicago agency serving adolescents and their families. She enjoys crossword puzzles, murder mysteries, and talking back to the Oprah Winfrey Show.

FAMILY FEELINGS represents a distillation of two long happy marriages, nine successful parent-child relationships, and one hundred thiry years of enthusiastic observation.